Destiny's
Tapestry

Destiny's Tapestry

I WALK THIS PATH

Betty June Gilliland

iUniverse LLC
Bloomington

DESTINY'S TAPESTRY
I Walk This Path

iUniverse books may be ordered through booksellers or by contacting:

iUniverse LLC
1663 Liberty Drive
Bloomington, IN 47403
www.iuniverse.com
1-800-Authors (1-800-288-4677)

ISBN: 978-1-4917-2850-5 (sc)
ISBN: 978-1-4917-2852-9 (hc)
ISBN: 978-1-4917-2851-2 (e)

Library of Congress Control Number: 2014905637

Printed in the United States of America.

iUniverse rev. date: 04/09/2014

Dedication

In memory of Cicero 'Bed' Kelly.
And all who walked the path of destiny before me!

CONTENTS

FOREWORD

The first time I spoke with Betty Lowery, I knew we were going to have a lot of adventures together, and I was so excited. She was searching for a man that I had searched for before, and was not able to find out anything about him after the year 1902.

My daddy (Ambers Kelley) was a story teller, and a farmer. He was the one to tell me of Cicero Kelley.

Betty and I became very good friends and I love her as my sister. We shared a lot about our lives, and about family, but the most important was about Cicero. When Daddy told the story, he always said for me to never forget the name Cicero Kelley, and too remember that he was one of our own.

While reading Betty's stories, I feel that Daddy is smiling down on me, and I was that little girl again. Like most people, I read to be entertained as well as informed. I found all one could want between the pages of Destiny's Tapestry. Thank you Betty, and I love you for helping us to never forget this man's name and that he was one of our own.

Dianna Kelley Patterson
Guntersville, Alabama
Genealogist

ACKNOWLEDGEMENTS

I give a heartfelt thank you to all iUniverse staff for making a dream become reality. Without them, my book would have remained a manuscript.

A personal thank you to the sisters of my heart. Nancy Chaney, Orene Finnell, Rita Jackson, Dianna Patterson, Virginia Dixon, Jenny Lampe, and my daughter Sandra Carroll. Your faith in me lifted me up. It held me there to look upon that faraway place from whence I fled so long ago. Without you, I would never have found the courage to go back and my story would never be told. My brother Bo (Jim Gentry) thank you. A special thank you to Allen Funderburk, my Wilmer Hall brother, for creating my beautiful book cover and all the research you did for me. Thank you Amy Pursley for your time and patients while correcting my many mistakes and typos.

INTRODUCTION

In any fine tapestry, we will find many pictures of rich colors and textures woven to depict more than one story. Yet through it all, there is one essential thread connecting them to make a whole. So it is with Destiny's Tapestry. There are many stories to be found between the pages. Yet, there is a common thread from beginning to end to make them one. There are stories of sadness, strife, and laughter, as you journey along the path and follow the life of one woman from childhood to the golden years. If I have done my job well, you will laugh and you will cry. You will find yourself there. It was first wrote as a legacy to my family. For there are stories passed down from ancestors of long ago. Then later published with the hope that there might be some enjoyment and enlightenment to be found there that might help others as they travel their life's pathways.

PROLOGUE

The Painter and the Poet

Once upon a silent tear, a wish was crystallized.
It fell like stone upon my heart and wrung an anguished cry.
If only I could paint, all the things I see.
The golden glow of moonlight, the mist upon the sea.
To bring life upon a canvass, with daring strokes of skill.
Would fill my soul with gladness would give me such a thrill.
Then from that inner well, where springs all life and hope.
An inner voice took over, and to my conscious self it spoke.
Why covet you the painter's skill? On envy you'll be stricken.
Leave the artists to their gift and read what you have written.
The painter captures beauty of bird upon the wing,
While the pen records the rapture of the lovely song it sings.

Destinies Tapestry is a history and stories of myself and family. It is
a gift of love to those who are still to walk this path. It is wrote with
the hope they will know and not forget those who have gone before.
Think of our tapestry as a picture in the mind, woven with words.
The warp of the tapestry will not follow a straight line from one
point to another. It weaves backwards and forwards, touching down
here and there to connect the past and present. While weaving,
the spinning wheel turns and the shuttle moves back and forth to
spin the warp between the wefts, much as my words will take you
back to my beginnings and forward again to my present. Then back
again from time to time. The picture may fast forward suddenly
from a time in the distant past to a place and time closer to now
where a connected event took place. It will reach back even beyond

my beginnings to a distant time and place, as I strive to bring forth those ancient ones from the mist of time. The names have not been changed to protect the innocent. They should be remembered. The names of those outside the family have been altered due to necessity. Come join me on the walk along Destiny's Tapestry.

Summerlin's Melody

As Gods smallest thought;
I slumbered beneath sun baked autumn leaves,
Was whiffed by lamb winds through the snows of winter.
There to gently nestle on spring's first bouquet.
Like a shooting star, I roared through the galaxy.
Investigating every shine, glow, and glimmer
in every nook and cranny.
On the threshold of knowledge I shed my wings.
I stretched fourth my arms to embrace that
which I am laughing, loving, and giving.
I am the melody to the song of man.
I am the reason he sings, I am a link in a chain.
Through my veins flow the tributaries from the rivers of yesterday,
To the seas of tomorrow, I am woman.

Betty Gilliland

Chapter 1

IN THE BEGINNING

When someone yells at me. "Shut the door, were you born in a barn?" I will invariably turn to them a bit startled and answer. "Well yes, as a matter of fact, I was and that ain't all of it.

I was also wrapped up and laid in a manger." It's the truth, and this is how it all began.

1940 through 1950 was noted as a decade when hurricane activity grew in frequency and intensity. During this period, they were not named. Hurricanes one and two struck the gulf coast in the year of nineteen forty. Right or wrong, I blame all the trouble on hurricane three. She beat her way up the Atlantic coast that came ashore in Charleston, South Carolina on the twelfth of September. I say she was at least the forerunning event, responsible for setting up the weather patterns that rained on my birthday party. The storm howled across Georgia, went north, then east and then dipped south again, before it took its worrisome self-back into the Atlantic. Finally, she went north to meet her applauded doom in the cold Atlantic water. The weather disturbance it left behind zeroed in on a little spot of trees and boulders at the foot of Sand Mountain called Snead's Crossroads. The storm created much havoc on what should have been a bright day in my daddy's life. September twenty six, nineteen forty was my birthday. I am yours truly, Betty June Gilliland. I was the first living child born of Thomas and Elizabeth Gilliland.

My father housed his family, my mother and four of her younger siblings; in a barn. My maternal grandmother Dovie Walden, whom

I will be referring to all through this book as Mama, was hiding out on the mountain somewhere. Mama and Grandpa John Walden had separated. The younger children were staying with my mother and father till things could be settled. They were sitting in the rafters of that old barn the night I was born. Aunt Lillie, one of my mother's sisters had left home to ride the rails. She was looking for a lost love and a better way of life. She was fishing down on the Mississippi that night. Uncle Tommy, the eldest Walden boy, was married to Aunt Ethel Posey Walden and lived in Gadsden, Alabama. Aunt Merty was married to Lewis Smith and lived in Albertville, Alabama.

Though it was late in the evening, the storm was moving in fast, Daddy could see Mother was laboring hard. He hitched the horse to the buggy and went to fetch the midwife while he could. I am told this was no ordinary storm. It consisted of screaming, tree ripping, debris packing wind with lighting and rain straight from the devil's nightmares. Daddy fought to hold the buggy in the middle of the road. The midwife fought to hold the top on the buggy. She lost that battle. The wind blew the top and the midwife into a tree, then was kind enough to blow down the tree so Daddy could drag the midwife back to the buggy. She came to Mother's side bruised and battered. Not a dry thread on her body, minus her shawl and bonnet with her topknot down in her face. All of her hairpins, according to her, were blown to a place she referred to as hell and gone. I entered this world sometime between ten and eleven p.m. on a homemade bed with a corn shuck mattress. The midwife cleaned, wrapped me, and laid me in a cow manger. My daddy while wiping his face was heard to say, "Lord, what is it coming to? You give me this pretty pat and break all hell loose over my head." Regardless of my given name, for many years I was called Pat by most of my relatives.

At some point during the first two years of my life, Daddy moved us out of the barn and into a cabin. My mother's siblings had gone home to their daddy and his new woman Kate. My daddy had bought me a pretty new dress and asked Mother to dress me up, so he could take me into town and show me off to his buddies. I was dressed and sitting on the floor when he reached for his tobacco.

I said, "ont bite, Dadie." "Dammit Jane," my father said. Everyone called Mother Jane. "I can't lay my tobacco down cuz she'll swoop down like a duck on a June bug. I gotta find a way to break her from my tobacco, now!" Then he gave me a bite. I chewed and swallowed. "Ont nutter bite, Dadie." He gave me another bite. I chewed and again swallowed, only to ask a third time. Daddy gave me another bite. "Stop Thomas, you will make her sick." Mothers warning came too late. My face turned green and I upchucked in my lap. My eyes rolled back in my head and as I passed out I said, "Ont nutter bite, Dadie."

Needless to say, Daddy went to town without me. Mother had been craving peanut brittle and he had promised her a box. Daddy came home late. He told her the store did not have any peanut brittle, so he bought popcorn instead. I do not believe you should offer a craving pregnant lady something salty for something sweet. Especially, since said popcorn box has the name of the local movie theater advertised on it. She threw the popcorn at his head, then a stick of stove wood. Daddy left and never returned. I suppose he did not like the idea of sharing his tobacco, or maybe it was the stove wood. I imagine Mother could pack a pretty good wallop. She was tall, and daddy was short. He could stand beneath her outstretched arm.

Of course, I have no memory of any of this. I can only relate what Mother has told to me. Some recall back then as the good old days, others say times were hard. Good men became hobos. It was called riding the rails. They jumped aboard train cars. Where they would hide from railroad employees. They would be pulled off the train, sometimes none to gently if they were caught. These men wandered from coast to coast, north to south, searching for jobs. It was a way to earn a little money to send home to destitute families. Sympathetic citizens provided food for the hobos whenever possible. "If tha latch was up on tha door, it meant you were welcome in," Mother said. There would be soup or beans on the back of the stove and hopefully a piece of fry bread, if you were lucky. The weary traveler would eat his fill and rest a spell. He would then look for any chore to be found to help his benefactor and salve his pride. Whether it would be chop fire wood, draw water from the well, or mend a broken chair, he would gladly do and be on his way. Those days of trust and human kindness are gone, but it is good to remember there was once such a time.

America was at war with Japan, and Daddy was drafted into the army. What can I say for him? He deserted the army and doing so, he deserted his family for he must forever hide. It is said that you can never miss what you never had, and I suppose that is true. He was not in my life long enough for me to miss him. For me, he was just a picture of a man in a uniform. All of the soldiers were daddy to me. If I was in the store with Mother and spotted a uniform, I would latch on to his leg and hang on. Tenaciously screaming, "Daddy, I want." Mother would try to disengage me but the solder, usually red faced with embarrassment would insist on buying me what I wanted. I knew better than to pull this trick with Mama around. She would pinch the devil out of me. I am a senior citizen now, but I still adore and admire any man or lady in a uniform, anywhere from police to military.

I saw my daddy three times in my life and only when I ask about him. He came to see me shortly after Mother remarried. He visited me twice when I lived in an orphanage home. He tried to get me to agree to run away and go with him on that last visit. I declined and never heard from him again, till the day I received news of his death. While at the Pascagoula ship yard working, he was in the hold of a barge when it exploded. It is my belief that Mama knew where he was at all times, and made sure he knew where I was, and what was happening where I was concerned. If this is true, it may explain some of the problems between Mama and Mother in the time to come.

In the early 1940s, everyone had yet recovered from WWI, the great depression, and now into WWII. The Americans had fought against Germany voluntarily to support our allies on many fronts, long before President Woodrow Wilson was granted his request to join WWI, on April 4, 1917. America declared war against Japan on December 8, 1941 after the Japanese bombed Pearl Harbor. Only days later, Hitler declared war on America and we fought Germany for the second time in WWII. I wish all would research and study this period in our history, that you might better understand, we, the Americans, owe no country apologies for what we did to end the wars brought to us by Germany and Japan.

I have taken this side trip into history for the benefit of those young ones who has cared enough to ask for the whys and wherefores of mine and Mothers circumstances in those first years of my life. I appreciate your interest and inclination to understand clearly. Many people suffered grave hardship at this time. October 29, 1929 went into the history of America as black Tuesday. The stock markets crashed. Men who had been rich and powerful lost everything. The enormity of financial ruin was so abhorrent to them that many committed suicide. The doors to all factories, mines, and mills were closed. There was no money, and jobs. Read my children. Learn, remember, and teach the next generation. Enlightenment can give the leaders we need in the future legislative body to govern our nation. It will send our people to the polls to vote with a better understanding of what our leaders should stand for. Else, we become as Diogenes with his lamp searching the dark for one honest man.

These were mighty lean days for all people. So much of the usual commodities we take for granted today were rationed. Bartering was a way of life, if you were fortunate enough to have hens that would lay eggs for trade, or a milking cow. Sugar and gasoline were rationed. Nipples for baby bottles were made of a low grade black rubber that would fit on the end of a God Rock Cola bottle.

No wonder my father-in-law whipped his sister's A double S with a picket fence board over a misunderstanding, incurred while trading sugar, and gasoline stamps. They went many years without speaking before patching their differences. Do not even dream of a pair of nylon stockings unless you knew someone who dealt in the black market. Nylon was used to make parachutes. Rubber was used to make tires to transport war materials and solders. Even a simple piece of chewing gum was almost nonexistent. One might grow a garden, if they could find seed and fertilizer. If so, you could have fresh vegetables for a while in the summer time, if you had land but there were usually no jars to can them for winter. If there were any

5

to be found they must be sealed with wax. There were no rubber sealed lids. People starved and suffered from illness caused by lack of proper nutrition. The disease of Pellagra and Rickets were the main killers of the time. Mother and I were sick with both. I also had whooping cough and chicken pox. I learned to walk then grew so weak I forgot how and had to learn all over again, several times. My tongue was grown to the bottom of my mouth. Mother managed to get an old country doctor to come to the cabin which consisted of one room. He shook his head and said to her. "The child is too frail and undernourished to survive the cough and fever." He told her of a few things she might try to make me more comfortable but warned her to be prepared for the worst. What food she could find, she cooked as soft as possible. She then chewed and poked it down my throat with her finger. She gave me Rock Cola laced with Paregoric.

Paregoric was legal to buy in any store at this time but became outlawed in the early 1960s, when it was recognized as an abused habit forming drug. It came to the attention of law enforcement and the courts that mothers were drugging their babies to make them sleep while they were being left alone. Paregoric was used in my case with the doctor's approval to control diarrhea and ease the pain in my aching joints. It was also a good expectorant. The doctor provided it for me from the goodness of his heart. Mother was so sick herself at times, she would have to crawl to the outhouse then back into the cabin to me. She dipped water from a spring for our needs. How she had the strength to bring it to the cabin, I don't know. She carried small rocks and a stick to knock down and kill any small game she could find for meat. She gathered herbs from the forest of Mother Earth, to cool my fever and feed us. She made a liniment of comfrey leaves and bird eggs to sooth the swelling and aches of our tormented bodies. Wild greens, nuts, roots, berries, and a special kind of white clay found on the mountain were our diet. These were home remedies learned at her mother's knee. They were taught to Mama by her father, Cicero Kelly. He was half Cherokee and known as Bed Kelly, for he had no bed to sleep in. To add to her miseries and humiliation, a male member of Daddy's family caught her at the spring. He physically abused and threatened her with worse if she didn't leave me with my father's mother, name unknown to me, and get her red skinned ass off the mountain.

Can you imagine the willpower and raw stamina of this young mother, who stared death and mean circumstance in the face and defied it to the last ditch? I can only look with awe and gratitude at the determination with which she faced her adversity. She held me, her first living born on her lap and desperately sought to force food down my throat. She brought me back with steel will as she rocked me and demanded. "You will not die. I won't let you." Her first child had died within a few hours of its birth and she was pregnant with her third, who was to be my Brother Jimmy Ray Gilliland.

There is a bit of mystery about my daddy and the oddity of his paternal name. His father's name was Tom Willet. Daddy's last name was Gilliland and he was very proud of it. In fact, when he came to see me after Mother divorced him and remarried, he taught me how to spell Gilliland and said to me. "Never forget who you are. If you ever need me, I will know and I'll be there." I never knew his mother's name. Mother would not as much as whisper it, let alone say it out loud. Mother seemed to fear this woman and Mother was not one to fear much of anything. Neither did she tell me why my daddy was a Gilliland when his daddy was a Willet. I do not believe she knew the answer to that one herself.

When my health began to show improvement, Mother knew I needed more than she could provide. She believed another reverse in my health would be more than my weak constitution could withstand. Against her better judgment, she decided to appeal to my daddy's mother. She wanted to ask her to keep me till she could make a way for the coming baby and me. Though when all was said and done, her resolve crumbled. When it came down to the final decision, she let me choose my way.

Let me attempt to clarify once again, who was who in my life. Elizabeth Walden is my mother. She married my birth father, Thomas Gilliland. His mother, I can only call my paternal grandmother because I was never told her name. My maternal grandmother was Dovie Kelly, who married John Walden. She retained the surname Walden the rest of her days. She never remarried. These were my mother, grandmother whom I call Mama, aunts and uncles, the dear ones who were with me on the first miles of my life's journey. Mother divorced Thomas Gilliland and married my stepdad, Louie Odell Gentry. I learned to call him daddy. His mother, Missouri Kauffman became my step grandma.

So starts the threads of Destiny's Tapestry. Which will go back three known life spans and then to those ancient people beyond yours and my time and place in our tapestry.

Fox Fire

Hear a story from the mountain, passed down from long ago,
Sitting warm before the hearth my Granny told it so.
In the forest tangled beauty, there are places dark and dread.
Where the sunlight never reaches, even strong men fear to tread.
Creatures lurk in sink holes deep, to drag a victim down.
In waters cold skimmed with mold, to be lost and never found.
Wandering in this wilderness, traversed one lost boy.
Searching for the path that would free him from this void.
Tired and sleepy he lay down beneath a willow tree,
Tussled curls there came to rest upon a bed of leaves.
In the gathering edge of glooming, a silent form took shape.
Large and white with fiery eyes, not a sound did the specter make.
It moved with quiet stealth, to settle beside the child.
No creature dared to challenge, this guardian of the wild.
He led the searchers to the boy, with a long and mournful bay.
Just an old white dog the young men say,
we scared him and he ran away.
The old ones held their peace, not a word would they insist.
They know this one called Fox Fire who dwells within the mist.
He comes where ere he's needed, in whatever shape or form.
A large white dog, a horse, a panther; but upon the day I was born,
He came as a snow white turtle dove and sang so long and sweet.
He called me gently to this world, and sang my Ma'am to sleep.

Betty Gilliland

Merty Walden Smith

Chapter 2

SAND MOUNTAIN

My paternal grandmother lived on Sand Mountain. Mother at last told me why she disliked and feared her. According to Mother, my Grandmother was literally, a black magic witch. She could cast spells on people and make them do what she wanted them to. She had boxes under a big table hidden by a large tablecloth. She told Mother to never touch those boxes. Mother told me this one day during the time we lived in Jemison. I was bored and begging for a story.

While her mother-in-law was away, Mother saw her chance to investigate the boxes. There she found books on magic, instructing how to make potions and cast spells. She found vials of powders, potions, and unidentifiable strange things in sealed jars. Mother said she was so frightened. She put the tablecloth back like she found it, then went and sat in the kitchen until her mother-in-law returned. When she came in she said to mother. "I told you to stay away from my boxes." In a rage, she pointed a finger at her and screeched, "Don't lie, won't do you no good. Do you think I am a fool? The key tells on you."

Mother then told me of this brass key on a black silk cord. Her mother-in-law would lay the key on a crack in the floor, then ask it a question. If the answer was yes, it would swing to the right of the crack or to the left for no. "Once the old woman calmed from her angry tirade, she took two packages of powders from one of the boxes and gave them to me," said Mother. "Instructing, I should put one in my bath water and Thomas should bath in the other one. She said it would bind us together. Then she raved at me to keep my nose

11

out of other people's business and never ever lie to her." Hanging on to every word with my eyes wide, I asked her. "What did you do with the powders, Mother?" "I put them away," she answered. "Then one day, Thomas asked what they were and when I told him, he took a bath in one. I threw the other one away. I was pregnant with you when she gave them to me. I was not about to use something she had conjured up. She cast a spell with them that made Thomas leave me and never come back." With tongue in cheek I asked her. "You don't think the popcorn and the stick of stove wood had anything to do with it?" Her mouth tightened. "Well it didn't help. It was bad enough before he left but afterwards, we both nearly starved to death. The kind of food you should have had was not to be found. Fresh fruit or anything like baby food was impossible to come by, plus you were too weak to swallow much less stand on your own two feet. Now miss smarty pants. Go peddle your little green apples someplace else and let me finish my chores." After she said this, she reached for the old flatiron and banged it down on the back of the wood stove so I knew then, it was time to beat feet for the great outdoors.

The first true memory of my own that was not told to me by someone else, was being taken to see my paternal grandmother after I began to recuperate from my long illness. Though it is more like a dream and somewhat confused as to who was who, I know it happened. I remember it.

Mother carried me to a place where there was a bridge. It was not a long bridge but it looked so to me. She stood me at the foot of the bridge and stayed behind me with her hands on my shoulders. There was a woman standing on the other side. The bridge crossed over a chasm, a gully Mother called it. The woman on the other side motioned with her hand for me to come to her. Mother removed her hands and stepped away from me. She said to me. "Go if you want to." I looked back at her. She was a tall slim figure that seemed to recede from me. It was much like looking down a long dim tunnel. She raised her hand as if to wave bye. Then she placed it over her mouth. I looked across the bridge once more. Again, the woman waved me forward. She taunted Mother. "Give her to me for a year and she will be mine." I turned to Mother. I wanted to run to her but my legs were too weak. I wanted to beg, do not leave me. But my throat closed up, which caused it to hurt. I did the only thing I could do. I raised my arms and beseeched with my eyes. Mother came swiftly and scooped me up. She answered the woman across the bridge. "She has chosen her way. You can't have her." Holding me against her shoulder, she whispered to me. "Close your eyes, baby. Don't look back." I think I went to sleep because I do not remember making the trip or how I got there. I only remembered arriving to a different place. I thought, this must be my grandmother's house.

I sat in Mother's lap at a table covered with a red and white checkered oil cloth, while the lady and Mother talked to each other. As they talked, the women took a large wooden spoon and drew on it with something she kept dipping into small jars of colors. I watched for a time till I became restless and Mother sat me on the floor. Even at that young age, I noticed how nice the wood floor was. There was no dirt on it and it smelled so pleasant. It had a bleached appearance to it. I later learned that the floor was scrubbed weekly with homemade lye soap and a scrub broom made of corn shucks.

The women gave me the spoon which she had painted a face on. What a wonderful thing! She gave me some pretty colored scraps of material to dress the spoon doll with. The doll and scraps occupied me for some time. When I looked up, Mother was gone. I wanted to go look for her but the lady began to talk to me. She had a sweet voice. She was doing some interesting things and I really wanted to see what was going too happened next. She placed two buckets on the table. One had water in it. The other was empty.

She plopped a white cloth in the one with water. I looked around to see what she was going to wash. Everything was spotless. There were no dirty dishes anywhere. I hoped she was not going to wash me. I wanted to go find my Mother. She reached into a cupboard and took down a small tin cup. Giving me the cup she said, "This is yours, don't lose it now." She picked up the buckets and I followed her out the back door, down a path to a barn.

In the barn were more wonderful things. Sweet smelling hay, a warm smelling cow, chickens, and oh my, soft fluffy kittens! She said to me, "Ye kin play with tha kittens but leave my hens and biddies alone and stay outten behind the cow. She will kick if tha flies git after her." The lady poured some feed in the trough. When the cow began to eat, the lady pulled up a stool and sat on it. She then shoved her shoulder against the cow and said, "Saa Flossie." The cow backed her leg and the women placed the bucket of water under the cow, then proceeded to wash her underneath. She removed the bucket of water and placed the empty one beneath Flossie. Ping! Ping! I looked under the cow as the kittens all gathered around. The lady turned her hand sideways. I could not believe my eyes when she squirted the milk at the kittens. They opened their little mouths and the milk went right in. I clapped my hands and laughed with glee at the wonder of it all. This seemed to please her greatly, for she reached with her other arm and gathered me close for a warm hug and kissed me on the cheek. "There now, ever things goanna be awright, Bedjune," she declared. "Now hand me yer cup." She filled my cup with warm frothy milk and handed it to me while she said, "Drink it all down. It will make you good and strong." This is something we did twice a day, morning and late afternoon.

It was not long before I could chew and swallow my own food. My legs grew stronger. I still remained silent for most of the time. I could pantomime with my hands and using very few words, I could make myself understand. Words were not necessary.

I do not know how long I stayed there. I do not remember any winter. Just dusty sun kissed idle days. Wild flowers were growing on the other side of the dirt road, covering the open fields between us and the mountain. It stood like a silent sentinel rising green and golden into the mysterious blue mist. My mother was there somewhere. It was nice here. I should have been happy but that mountain kept calling. Forever beaconed and bid me to come.

I stared at the mountain one day and listened to it whisper its secrets. Something or someone wanted and needed me with an unutterable sadness, so wrenching it shook me to my very soul. I made up my mind. My Mother was out there somewhere, so I planned on going out to find her. It did not look so far away. My legs were stronger now. I could do it. I set off for the mountain. I trudged my way across the uneven fields till I grew thirsty, hot, and oh so tired. It did not look like fields of flowers now. It just looked like weeds and brambles. The mountain did not look any closer either. It looked the same distance away. I turned and looked at the house. It was a tiny white dot in the distance. I sat down in the tall grass to think about this. If that mountain did not get closer and I lost sight of the house, I would be lost. My lady, I had begun to think of her that way now, mine. She might miss me and cry. She might get mad and send me to that place where the bridge crosses the gully. It might not be my mountain mother calling me. It might be the old women at the bridge. I got up and went back to the white house. My Lady was humming in the kitchen. If she missed me, she never said so. In all the years that have since passed, there would be times when I would feel a sad, haunting, and a restless urge. A certain sound, like the whistle of a train in the middle of the night, or a misty memory not quiet grasped. I will hear the wind sowing in the trees, smell sun baked red dust, wild flowers, and hear a soft whisper. "Come, way up on the mountain. I wait for you."

After I was grown and married with children of my own, Aunt Merty came to visit. She sat with me in Mother's home and we talked about times gone by. I told her of my memories of the women at the bridge. I spoke of the lady at the white house with the red checked table cloth, whom I gave much of the credit for restoring my health. I told her about the sadness, the lost abandoned feeling, and the calling of the mountain. She looked at me with a stricken expression on her face. "Oh honey, I don't know what to say." She then gave me this explanation. "I didn't realize you didn't know me Bedjune. That was me. I took you and kept you for your mother. She was pregnant with Jimmy Ray and your daddy had left. You were so sick. You and Jane both, would have starved to death if she had stayed with you on the mountain. The woman at the bridge was your grandmother. She was your daddy's mother. You refused to stay with her and Jane feared your daddy's people were going to take you away from her. She had to leave the mountain and have her baby. She needed time to do this. To find a job and a home for both of you. I took care of you, to give her that time. Don't you remember your

Uncle Lewis and my boys living there with us?" I answered her. "No, I don't remember anything except the white house and the lady and all she did for me." Aunt Merty shook her head in disbelief. "Have mercy," she exclaimed. "Well, you were such a strange little girl. You played so quietly. Most times you sat and stared at the mountain and seemed to be off in your own little world. I just left you alone. I didn't know how to help you. It was me, Bedjune." She reached and put her arms around me. "I loved you then, and I love you now, and I always will." I remembered the unusual way she spoke my name. I had found My Lady. The gap closed a little then and the call from the mountain was somewhat appeased for a time, but I know there are others I have lost. Maybe, I will find them on this journey as I travel back along Destiny's Tapestry.

When I have a story about long ago and far away, I go to Aunt Ethel for verification. This wonderful lady is ninety three years old and still sharp as a tack. She proves it regularly, by whipping on my cousins and myself in any card game we might choose to play. Aunt Ethel is a quite person, who is comfortable with her own thoughts and council. When she does speak, it behooves one to listen, for her words are pearls of true enlightenment from a murky past. She has lived long enough to personally know some of the people, of whom I write. I have found her information to be more correct then any U.S.A. census from that long ago time. This notion is due to the fact that those people resented the Federal Government sticking its intrusive nose into their personal space. So the pendulum swings as destiny weaves. Does it not?

Some of those families on Sand Mountain made and bootlegged moonshine in the days of prohibition. They were not about to tell the Federal Government the truth of the number, names, age or gender of their offspring. It is said, many revenue men went up that mountain but not all came back. Uncle Tommy told me the story of one such family. This story was told to him by Allace Virginia Coe Walden. She was Uncle Tommy's paternal grandmother.

At the young age of twelve, Marshal Baldwin helped dig the lifeless body of his father from a Tennessee coal mine. After the funeral, he went to the little shotgun house to gather his meager belongings. He went to the kitchen and put his arms around his mother. "Ma ken you pack me a few biscuits and some tatties?" She ducked her head and nodded yes. He poured a cup of coffee and sat while he waited on her to gather his food and pack it in his Da's old lunch bucket. "Wher ye be goin son," she asked. "Don't know ma." He heaved a deep sigh and shuttered. "Thet ol mine done took Granda with black lung. Now it's killed me Da outright. Well it ain't gonna get me. Wherever I be, it won't be in a black hole in the ground. I'll be back fur ye someday Ma." His mother stood on the porch as she watched her determined son trudge away from her toward yonder, she knew not where.

Marshal found his way to Sand Mountain. Here, he built himself a log cabin and put down his roots. At the age of fifteen, he returned to his mother, to whom he declared, "I come to fetch you iffin you want to go Ma, I got me a wife. I have built me a home and I got me self a right smart business going. Now alls I need is me some son's to help me run it." Marshal Baldwin married my great aunt, Mandy Kelly, my grandmother's sister. Aunt Mandy presented Marshal with thirteen daughters! Marshal taught twelve of those girls to run the whiskey stills and mind the trails to said stills. On the weekend, they would hitch up the mules to a wagon load of the smoothest shine that ever came off the mountain. One drove the mule team while two rode shot gun. Do not take shot gun for a local colloquialism. Those shotguns spoke long and loud. "The Baldwin girls weren't called the dirty dozen for their southern hospitality," declared Uncle Tommy. "They was mean as stripped legged mules."

The thirteenth child that was born to Marshall and Mandy, was also a girl. Her mother named her Amanda. It is said, she had corn flower blue eyes and silver hair. As dainty and pretty as any mountain flower that grew in the wild woods. Aunt Mandy put her foot down about this child. "Marshal, you have taken all my girls and turned them into men. Well Sir, this one stays with me. You just leave her be." Aunt Mandy had her way and little Mandy grew into a quite introspective young lady.

One day, she sat on the front porch of the cabin and along came a revenue man. He tied his horse to the porch rail and dismounted.

Removing his hat as he approached Amanda. He asked for the man of the house. "My guess, Da be up on the mountain," Amanda replied. The man smiled and asked her. "I wonder what he would be doing up there?" "Minding his business like you ought to be doing." she answered. He placed his well shod foot on the edge of the porch and braced his elbow on his knee. He looked around while he fiddled with his hat. While glancing up at her he said. "Sure is peaceful around here but I bet you get bored with it sometime." She just stared at him with no expression from those deep blue eyes. He cleared his throat as he sought to establish a common ground with this reticent young creature. "You ever go to the dance down in the valley?" He asked her. "Nope," she answered. "As pretty as you are? I find that a crying shame. I saw a blue dress at the trading store just yesterday. It would look real nice with those blue eyes of yours. With that dress and a pair of new shoes, why! You could go to the dance and find yourself a good husband." She replied with a smile, "May hap." Encouraged by that sunny smile, he thought he was gaining ground. "I tell you what, you show me the trail to go on to get to your Pa and I will give you five dollars to buy that blue dress and a pair of shoes to wear to the dance." She agreed and asked for the five dollars. "Oh no," he said. "I will try the trail you show me and if it's the right one, I will give you the money when I get back from talking to your Pa." She shook her head no and said, "I am going to show you the right path but you won't be coming back." He stared hard at her for a moment, and then slapped his hat back on his head. Biding her good day, he mounted his horse and went back down the mountain.

Chapter 3

NOAH'S ARK

Left to Right
Lilly Walden
Elizabeth Walden

left to right
Doyle, J.D, Tommy Walden

When Mother left me on the mountain, she went to Alabama City where she sought sanctuary with the Collins family, who had been friends of our family for a long time. They were able to reach Uncle Tommy, who knew how to find Uncle J.D. and Mama. Uncle J.D. somehow caught up with Aunt Lilly. He also went by Grandpa's and brought Uncle Doyle with him. They all gathered there at the Collins house. Where brothers and sisters reunited with their mama, they made plans for the future and vowed to stick together to help each other. They all made the decision to go to Birmingham,

Alabama. They were told that the Avondale Cotton Mill had opened and was in full operation. Uncle J.D., Mother, and Aunt Lilly went to work in the mill. They rented the upstairs portion of an apartment house called Noah's Ark in Avondale, which was a suburb of Birmingham. Mama cooked and kept house. Mother stopped work long enough to give birth to Jimmy Ray. Once she was strong enough, she came to fetch me from the mountain and brought me to Noah's Ark. Mama then took on the care of me and my little brother. I do not remember Mother coming for me. I only know, first I was there on the mountain and then I was living at Noah's Ark. It was Mama's loving arms and crooning chants that brought me from my quite gray world and made me feel alive again.

A call came from the mountain. It seemed that Grandpa had settled in nicely with his new wife Kate, but Aunt Burma Inez just was not getting alone with dear Kate to well. Poor Kate just could not deal with it. "Would someone please come and get Inez and take her to her mama," asked Kate. Most people called Burma Inez by her middle name. She told me she was my Aunt Burma, so that is what I called her. When someone was mad at her, they called her Burma Inez. She was called that a lot. Mother and Aunt Lilly went back to the mountain to bring her to Birmingham. Grandpa kept Uncle John L. with him. He was to sickly to cause any problems, so they kept him, the youngest of the family.

Kate's teenage daughter had cut and ran at the beginning. No one knew where she disappeared to or why she went. It could have been the disgrace she felt at her mother's actions, when she broke up a married man's family, or maybe, she just did not like Grandpa Walden. There was a lot of speculation but no one knew anything for sure. She was gone and was never found nor heard from since. I cannot find anyone who remembers the young girls name but the presence of her memory remains with us still.

There was a small business in Avondale that was called the ice cream shack. On payday, Aunt Lilly took us all downtown for a treat. We were served our orders through a window and we sat at little tables under umbrellas. Aunt Burma did not seem near as interested in ice cream as she was in a man she met there. I guess some would have said he was handsome. To me, he appeared to be slick. Smarmy, as if he made to much effort to be charming. His hair looked oiled and tied back with a black string at the nape of his neck. His features were sharp in appearance with thin lips and dark glittering eyes. His teeth flashed white in his face when he smiled. Aunt Burma leaned against his midnight blue vehicle as she laughed and flirted with him. He placed one hand on top of the car above her head and leaned in close as he talked to her. Mama, who had been watching the antics taking place, asked Aunt Lilly. "Who is the dark one?" Aunt Lilly handed her malted milk to Mama without an answer and walked over to the car. She caught Aunt Burma by the arm and pulled her away. The man backed away with a hands up, palms out gesture. "No problem," he said with a smile. "None, if you don't make any," replied Aunt Lilly as she drew Aunt Burma to her side and led her to the other side of the parking lot. She gave Aunt Burma a dressing down, while out of earshot before they returned to the table. I noticed the man was not smiling as he watched from across the parking lot. His face had a tight angry expression. Aunt Burma was sullen and refused her ice cream when she returned to the table. Mama made her eat it anyway. I could not imagine why anyone would have to be forced to eat ice cream.

I wanted to watch the road grader up close. It was the first time I had seen a piece of large machinery at work and I was curious. Aunt Burma took me down stairs to see this modern marvel. We had to be careful where we put our feet, for there were large clumps of red clay everywhere. As we watched beside the road, a big white car pulled up next to us. "Well lookit tha dollies!" A man with a beefy red face, sandy white hair and bushy white eyebrows exclaimed, as he stuck his head out of the car window. He waggled his eyebrows up and down and licked his thick red lips. I thought, ugh a white slug! Aunt Burma grabbed my hand and backed away from the man. "Aw, come on baby. Old Jack just wants to get acquainted." He put his arm out of the car window and reached for Aunt Burma. She drug me back another step or two. "You want to ride in my new car," he wheedled. "You can bring the little one with you. She sure is a pretty little thing. Come on and hop in. We will go to the ice cream shack and be back before any one knows we are gone. I know you like to go there. Carlos really would like to see you. He may be there." Before you could say scat, Mother and Aunt Lillie roiled out of the back stairwell like two spitting cats. Aunt Lilly ordered Aunt Burma to get upstairs and take me with her. Mother focused on the man. "What do you want?" She hissed at him. "Well now, you mean I get to take my pick?" He drew back with a big grin on his ugly face. "Here is what you get, you baby thieving bastard." Aunt Lilly snarled as she wound up and let fly a big red dirt clod. Whap! It smacked the car door and splattered. "Now, jest a damn minute." He fumbled with his door handle as if to get out of the car. "You don't have a minute. Git gone now," screeched Mother as she sailed another clod through his window, catching him on his forehead. Aunt Lilly sent another one right behind it. He sputtered and spat, while trying to wipe his face with his hands and shirt sleeves. "I'll be back," he hollered. "You bitches don't know who you messing with." Aunt Lillie laughed and I could see her gold tooth glitter in the sunlight. "We do know and you show yer mug around here again, I will have something to whittle you down to my size. J. D. Walden knows you to. I'll have him give you my regards, next time you meet." He drove away in a cloud of dust while the two furies gave chase with their clay dirt bombs and curses. Aunt Burma ran up the stairs and burst into the kitchen with me in tow. Mama stood there, arms akimbo like six feet of solid red oak. Her face looked like thunder and I could swear there was flame in her coal black eyes. Aunt Burma's face was the color of my play paste. Her eyes stretched wide, for all the world like the centers of Black Eyed Suzie's. Mama perused her youngest daughter with a shrewd eye. "Burma Inez, who is that man?" She asked sternly. Aunt Burma denied knowing the man. Mama pursed her lips and did that tuneless little shu-shu-shu sound, half whistle half hum, which she did when she was cogitating on something real hard. Aunt Burma had her skirt tail clutched in her fist and was fidgeting and wringing it. "I didn't do nuttin Mama. Swear, I ain't done nuttin I shouldn't. I never saw that man before." Mama squinted her eyes and answered. "Well if ye did no wrong then ye got nothing to worry about, now do ya?" "No Ma'am." Mama sent me toward the bedroom and ordered, "Close the door, Pat." I made to head in that direction then ducked behind the wood stove. I crawled into the little cave I had made by stacking the stove wood just so. Uncle Doyle showed me how. I had my own little privet wigwam back there. Mother and Aunt Lilly made it back into the kitchen with a full head of steam. "Now hold on Jane. Both you girls just slow down and cool yer tatters a minute," admonished Mama. "I ain't cooling nuthin," huffed Aunt Lilly. "I will beat the holy snot out of her for bringing that kind of garbage down on us." "I don't know him," screamed Aunt Burma. "That may be, but you damn well know his partner. I warned you about him last Sunday, when you were making goo-goo eyes at that yoyo down at the Ice Cream Shack. But do you listen? Nooo! Little miss boy crazy is all grown up now," Aunt Lilly responded. As she put her hand on her hip, she sashayed across the floor. She leaned into her sister's face and yelled. "He sent that white headed sum-bitch after you, little stupid." "That's enough Lilly, you ain't too old to get yer own mouth mashed," said Mama. "She done told you she don't know him." Aunt Lilly banged her fist on the table. "Well, ain't this some happy horse." "Hush Lilly, hush." Mother soothed her as she eased her into a chair at the table. Mother poured them both a cup of coffee and then turned to Mama and spoke in a softer tone. "I got a little girl and a baby to protect here. I brought her off that mountain to this place and we are trying to make a safe home for all of us. I know Noah's Ark ain't no fine home and all, but it was the best we could do, and I won't allow trashy men sniffing around our dress tails here. We can't put up with it, Mama." Aunt Lilly had quieted some but she was still agitated. "Tell her the truth, Jane." She blew on her coffee and waited. Mother chewed on her lip and took a deep breath. Mama's eyes went back and forth between the two. "We can't be sure." Mother looked uncomfortable. "You may not be but I am. Sure enough that, I know I am not gonna let it happen," Aunt Lilly said quietly. "What are ya'll talking about? I think you best tell me what's going on." Mama said as she crossed her arms and stared them down. Mother went to the table, where she sat down next to her baby sister. Aunt Lilly took a deep breath and wiped her hand across her face before she blew it out. "Look!" She said, "I didn't come out of those piney woods just yesterday. I have been up and down the tracks a few times. I didn't make it and come back in one piece by keeping my head in the sand. I have been watching and paying attention to what's going on in this town. You mark what I say. That hog pen slop that was out there today is the come on man for a ring of white slavers that are suspected to be operating in and around Alabama. It's been in all the news. It seems there are a lot of young women going missing. He is working with the guy Inez has been talking to. They are snatching up young women and girls to sell across the border to fill the whorehouses. Is that what you want to be little sister?" She snarled as she leaned across the table. "That's a lie. Carlos is not like that!" Aunt Burma cried as she jumped up and ran to her bedroom where she slammed the door behind her. "Who is Carlos," asked Mama. Aunt Lilly braced her arm on the table while she bowed and shook her head. "The one she was hanging around at the ice cream shack, I guess. You remember? You called him the dark one," she explained. The room was very quiet for a short time. Mother said, "We know what we know but with no real proof, we can't go to the law." Aunt Lilly opined at least one of them was the law. "York is protecting them and lining his pocket. Everybody knows he's dirty. He even tried to shake us down, when J.D. beat the hell out of Otis." Otis was an ex-boyfriend that did not want to be an ex to Mother. She had a new sweetheart now. His name was Louie Gentry. I had heard the family talk about him but Mother and Aunt Lilly did not bring their boyfriends to the apartment. It was one of the rules. "Since when have we depended on the law," asked Mama. "We are our own law. Go fetch Doyle and J.D." Mother protested at the notion of bringing Uncle Doyle into the picture. She said, "He is just a boy. Why bring him into this mess." Aunt Lilly put down Mother's objection "He may be but we need him. He can go unnoticed in places we can't. He can be our eyes and ears and believe it or not, he can and will scrap if he has to." They went down the back stairs. Aunt Burma had stopped crying and everything had gone quite. "Come out from behind that stove, Pat," Mama ordered. I crawled out with my head hung low and played with my fingers, as I tried to think of anything that might distract her attention away from me. "Look at you. You look like you been sucking a sow. I should tan your fanny.

You want Uncle J.D. to see you like that?" I shook my head no. "Well come on then. Let's get you cleaned up fore he gets here." How I loved my Uncle J.D.! He was tall and handsome, with hair as black as a raven's wing, and eyes like rich dark chocolate. Always teasing and laughing. He had all the girls on a string. He would tell them his name was Josephine. When he asked me, "Who am I." I threw my arms around his neck and said, "Uncle Josephine." This made him laugh out loud. From then on, he was my Uncle Josephine. He picked me up with a hug and a kiss, when he came in and put me to bed. "Now go to sleep, Patty Pat. See, I will put little brother in bed with you so you can be a big girl and help Mama watch over him till your mother gets back home. I will see you in the morning." He went back in the kitchen which joined both my mother's and my bedroom. I knew the trouble was just about to really start because I had caught a fast glimpse of Aunt Burma as she slipped down the front stairway, while Mama had Jim and me in the bathtub. I did not tell because that was the grown up's business and little ones were there to be seen and not heard. I did not want to be seen or heard this night. I just wanted to see and hear. I vacated the bed and went to the door, which I opened just a wee bit. I heard Uncle Josephine's footsteps as he went to the front of the house and heard him call, "Burma Inez, come out here." A door slammed and bedlam broke loose. "Mother Mary on a broomstick!" Uncle Josephine's voice boomed. "She's gone!" Then the sound of more running footsteps and the door slammed. "I can't believe the little twit is so stupid," said Mother. "I can. She ain't got the sense God gave a last year's bird nest," fumed Aunt Lilly. "Well doesn't that set the cat amongst the pidgins?" Uncle Doyle laughed as he sprawled in a chair and began to roll a Prince Albert. "We set to hunt em down and I bet ya little sister is out to warn the bastards." My mouth watered. Maybe Mama would forget to throw the left over butt out before she went to bed. I would squirrel it away just like my friend Marshal showed me and we could share it tomorrow out at the wood pile. Maybe then, he would not be so mean and tear my dolly head off again. Besides, I heard Mama say that tobacco killed worms. Teach Aunt Lilly to call me wormy butt. I was feeling a bit cranky and rebellious myself, by this time. I might not understand all that was taking place but I understood enough to know that we were all facing a family crises. Mama was in tears and begging them to find her girl. She said Aunt Burma was still wet behind the ears and did not realize the danger she was in. They promised to find her, and they all left together. I went back to bed and slept for a while. When they returned, poor Aunt Burma looked like she had been greased and drug up the back ally. I think Mother and Aunt Lilly had given her the whipping they had promised before they got her in Mama's presence. I had never saw Uncle Josephine look so stern. It gave me the shivers. "Talk to her Mama," he pleaded. "Make her give us names and tell us where to find them if she knows." "I don't know," Aunt Burma sobbed. Mother tried to get past Mama while reaching for Aunt Burma. "I'll snatch you baldheaded, if you don't quit yer lying." Mama got between them and ordered, "All of you calm down." "Sit, Burma Inez," she said as she leaned over and shook her finger in Aunt Burma's face. "You hear me and hear me well. When snakes stay in their place you live and let live but when they invade your life up close, you must fight back. These are not men. They are lower than a snake's belly. They are bad. We protect what is ours. Now you tell us what we need to know and I will make them leave you alone." Aunt Burma must have finally told them enough to satisfy them, for they sent her to bed and they all left. I went back to bed but I did not sleep this time. I laid awake and waited for them to come home. Upon their return, I laid in bed and listened. They told Mama of all that had taken place. This time there was a policeman with them. He was Aunt Lilly's friend. "Well, at least that white headed degenerate won't be around anymore," said Uncle Doyle. You could hear his neck crack a mile away when J.D. jacked his jaw. Mama questioned the policeman. "It was a fair fight, Dovie. I kept the boy well out of it. J.D. may have to serve a little time. As far as anyone knows, it was just another barroom disagreement. I am sorry I couldn't do better. I did what I could." "How about the other one, that Carlos," Mama asked. "He is gone, don't worry. No one saw but the denizens of Tin Pan Alley. He will never be heard from again. Even they were glad to see the last of him." "So be his epitaph," said Mama. She and Uncle Doyle went to bed. Mother left for a while. The house became quite once again. I heard Aunt Lilly and the policeman talking at the back stairway. I tiptoed to my bedroom door once more. They were in shadow, there at the head of the stairway but I could tell he was a large man with thick shoulders and muscular arms. His voice was deep but gentle. It was a comforting voice made for laughter. I could tell by the way it rumbled in that deep barrel chest. "Did you know someone else was with ya'll tonight, Lil?" He asked as he snuggled her in close. "No. Who?" "Don't know but York went down. Not that I be aggrieving. He was dirty. Nobody will miss him much, I recon. Know his wife won't. He beat the hell out of her and them young'uns regular. Maybe without his protection, we can round up a few more of the low lives. Steer clear of em, Lilly. We ain't broke em by a long shot. We just beat em up a little." They cuddled some more and Aunt Lillie asked. "Was it one of you got York?" "Naw, I saw him in the alley standing in the edge of a street light. Someone slipped up behind him. All I saw was the toes of a pair of shiny black Patent Leather shoes and the glint of the switch blade. They drug him back into the alley and that's all I saw." "Ahh so, I didn't think Louie would let Jane go into that kind of ruckus without him behind her. That was what she was up to when she disappeared there for a few minutes. She was making a phone call."

It was a good five years before I saw my Uncle Josephine again. I heard he served time on a manslaughter charge. I say it was a righteous extermination. When has it been wrong to kill snakes? While he was away, the bad men did manage to grab my Aunt Burma off the street one day. But she had come to realize what kind of people they were. She fought with all her might. She did not know if she got the car door opened and jumped or if the men fearing detection because of the commotion she was creating, opened the car door and threw her out, but she did get out. The Lights of Birmingham are mounted on green iron post. Aunt Burma's head connected with one of the posts. Help reached her in time. She lived the rest of her days with a steel plate in her head, but at least she lived a long and fruitful life.

Chapter 4

THE MAGIC SHILLELAGH

Birmingham, Alabama has been plagued with an overabundance of rats since time began, or Birmingham time anyway. Not cute soft little critters with pansy eyes and panda ears. I'm talking long nosed with buckteeth, beady eyes, and pointy eared, huge ugly buggers with long skinny tails. They are called gopher rats by the natives that lived there. "They mean and tough," said Mama. I would get a cat but I figure it would take a mountain lion to stand up to them. Even the junk yard dogs would not take them on. They smart too! I baited my traps and the varmints would drag a piece of newspaper across the trap to trip it and make off with my cheese. I be swiggeled, if I know what to do about the nasty vermin." "I killed one with a stick of stove wood," said Mother. She was referring to coming home one night and finding a large rat in Jim's bed. I woke up when I heard her say, "I'll teach you to bite my baby." I sat up and saw Mother with that inevitable stick of stove wood in her hand and a humongous rat with his back to the wall. He stood on his hind legs with his teeth barred and growled at her. Mother brought the piece of wood down on his head. Then picked him up by his tail and walked out of the room. In a few minutes, she came back in with a bag in her hand. "Look what Mother got her little girl," she said as she sat on the side of the bed and hugged me. "Oh." I breathed when she took a beautiful doll from the bag. The doll had long black curls and big brown eyes that opened when she sat up and closed when she lay down. "Huh, ook Ike Aunt Yiddie?" I asked as I circled my finger around her face. "I name Yill." Mother Laughed. "It should look like Lilly. She went shopping with me. That stinker searched every store until she found a doll she thought favored her, before she would let me buy it. I thought I would never finish my shopping. She will be proud of her new namesake. Mama sewed the head back on your other baby. Why don't you take her with you when you play down stairs? Lill can stay up stairs. That way she will be safe. Keep Marshall from tearing her head off." "I keep safe, I not let em." "He's too big for you to be fighting sugar. You can protect your baby best by keeping her away from him." Marshall was mean only when he was around the other boys. They wanted to tear my dolly heads off so they could rip their hearts out and use them to signal each other, when they were playing cowboys and Indians. When tipped back and forth the heart makes a crying sound. Mama said that they were too dumb to learn the owl hoot. Mother pulled me into her arms and asked me. "Do you like your new baby?" "Wove huh," I answered as I threw my arms around Mother and gave her a big kiss. "Well, I want to ask you to do something for me. Do you remember the nice doctor you went to when Marshall poked the rock in your ear?" Oh-boy, did I ever! It hurt so badly. Mother carried me to several doctors before she found one who found the problem and took that rock out of my ear. The relief was so great that I will never forget. "Well, this nice doctor says we need to fix your mouth so you can talk. Your tongue is grown to the bottom of your mouth. He can fix that. Would you like for him to do this for us?" I nodded my head in consent. Mother tucked me in and whispered, "Goodnight, go to sleep. We will see the doctor tomorrow." I reached for Lil and snuggled in. "I take care of you, Yill," I promised as I drifted off to sleep. When I can talk, I will be a big girl.

"Pat, put brother down fore you drop him. You can't wag him everywhere you go," Mama scolded me. "Bo hunggie," I whispered. Brother was too big a word for me, so little brother had become Bo. My mouth was still too sore from surgery to say much even if I had wanted to. The doctor had cut a lot of meat from under my tongue. He advised mother to let him cut my tongue free from the bottom of my mouth with the hope my speech would improve. That way, I would want to talk more. If I could communicate, he reasoned it would relieve some of the stress and I would hopefully be more even tempered. He could not find any other reason for the horrible head banging rages that I could fly into. Bo turned his head and smiled a big one toothed grin at me. I had him under his arms while I walked backwards dragging him as I went, his fat little feet bumping along the floor. He waggled his head and burbled a little tune for me as I determinedly drug him into the kitchen and deposited him on the floor. I went to the ice box and slapped it openhanded. Then one palm up and one down, I clapped my hands together to sign sandwich. I pointed at the buttered grits sitting on the warmer of the stove. Bo would choke on peanut butter and jelly. Mama sighed as she dried her hands on her apron. "Just hold your horses, Miss Ramrod. I will make you a sandwich as soon as Uncle Doyle gets back with a loaf of bread." I sat in the floor in front of Bo and played patty cake while we waited for the bread to come. We heard a voice float up through the window from the alley. "Seven come eleven. Baby needs new shoes." It was without a doubt Uncle Doyle's voice. I ran to the window and looked down. For sure, it was Uncle Doyle and some of his buddies. They were down on their knees in the alley. Another voice rang out. "Snake eyes, give over Walden you crapped out!" "Like hell I will, you bastard. You brung them loaded dice in," Uncle Doyle accused. In a matter of seconds, the alley was a melee of arms and legs with swinging fist and curses. Mama pulled me back from the window and leaned out. "Doyle Walden, you bring me my money and my bread up here. All of it, right now," she bellowed. Then she began to throw sticks of wood out the window hard and fast. I heard loud squawks, grunts, and curses. I got my head out the window just in time to see shirttails and heels doing double time around the corners at both ends of the alley. Some were running and some crawling. They were all scrambling for dear life. Very calmly, Mama went back to her dish washing while she shu-shu-shued through her teeth. We did not have to wait long. Uncle Doyle appeared at the top of the kitchen stairs with a loaf of bread. He laid it on the table and dug in his jean pocket and pulled out a fist full of dollar bills and change, which he also laid on the table. "That all of it boy?" "Yes—um," he replied. He was bleeding from a cut over one eye. His shirt collar was ripped loose and most of his shirt buttons were gone. I trotted behind him as he headed for the bath room. Standing in the door way, I watched as he washed his face and placed a cold rag on the knot on his noggin. One eye was already beginning to swell shut. He turned and winked at me out of the other one. "You Walden wimmen is hell on a man with that stick of stove wood, ain't cha Pattie cake?" While Mama fed Bo his grits, I sat at the table and ate my sandwich. I hummed shu-shu-shu through my puckered lips. I could almost do it with a mouth full of peanut butter. I had a lot of important things running through my mind. Things like my new dolly to protect, stove wood, Walden wimmen, and last but not least, oh yea, Marshall.

I put my thoughts of Marshal, broken dolls, and revenge out of my mind for today. Aunt Ethel and Uncle Tommy with their children, Bonnie and Billy and baby Virginia had come to visit. Everyone was gathering to help Aunt Merty and her family move to Birmingham. They were moving one street over from us. One would think I would have recognized Aunt Merty as the lady I had lived with on Sand Mountain. I did not. I can only suppose my being so traumatized by the long illness and being suddenly separated from my mother had sent me into a mental vacuum. Upon leaving that silent world, I distanced myself so far from it, I did not connect it to the happy time and place here at Noah's Ark. Therefore, I did not recognize Aunt Merty as my lady of the white house.

We children played all day while the adults worked to unpack and set up furniture in Aunt Merty's new house. I had a beautiful Bo Hunk marble. Uncle Doyle had taught me how to knuckle under and shoot a Bo Hunk. The boys on my street thought they had found an easy mark when I asked to shoot marbles with them. They were all for it till; surprise, surprise! I won all of their marbles. They refused to pay up. There was a big squabble and Uncle Doyle turned them upside down and shook them until their marbles rolled out. I picked up my winnings and went home. They would not play with me anymore and put Marshall up to rip my doll's heads off any time they found me alone and unprotected. When I cried and tried to fight back, he tried to twist my head off too. Billy greatly admired and coveted that Bo Hunk. I made sure I kept it in his eyesight as much as possible that day, just to tease him. After supper, Aunt

Lilly gave us all a large chunk of bubble gum. We chewed and blew bubbles till bed time. The elders took the beds and we children were to sleep on quilt pallets on the floor. As we headed for our pallets, Aunt Ethel yelled at us to spit out the gum. "If you go to bed with it in your mouth, it will end up in your hair. If it does, I am going to cut it out and give you a licking you will remember." Everybody dutifully spit out their gum but me. Billy lay down beside me and gave me a mean glare. "You didn't spit out your gum," he said balefully. I blew a bubble in his face. "Your butt, your hair," he grunted. He turned his back and went to sleep. I chewed for a while longer. As I grew sleepy, I took the gum out of my mouth. Now, what to do? I did not want to get up and walk in the dark to the bathroom. It was farther away from the pallet then it was from my bed. Not my fault. They should not have taken my bed. I stuck my gum on top of Billy's head. He kept on sleeping. Morning came as it surely must and Aunt Ethel kept her word. She boxed poor Billy's ears soundly and verbally reprimanded while she relieved him of my gum and a large amount of his hair.

All the women gathered in the kitchen and cooked a large dinner. I could hardly wait. We could smell all of the good aromas, long before dinner time. Especially, Aunt Ethel's chicken and dumplings. They finally called us to the table. This was a very long table with a bench down each side. With a big smile, Aunt Ethel set a heavenly bowl of dumplings in the middle of the table. Oh my! They looked as light and fluffy as little angel wings bobbing around in a sea of buttered broth, with a light sprinkle of black pepper floating on top. After the blessing was said, Aunt Ethel smiled at me and said. "Here Honey, you have been such a good girl." She then filled my plate with dumplings. I dug in but with my first spoonful, I glanced up. Billy was sitting directly across the table from me and I choked. That dumpling turned to rubber in my mouth. There he sat with sad eyes. For all the world, like a monk in morning with a bald tonsure atop his head. I could not eat a bite if my life depended on it. I played with my food and whined. "Poor baby; she has played so hard, she is plumb tuckered out." After that was said, Mama put me to bed with no dinner. When I was allowed to get up to play again, I went to Billy. I took his hand in mine and placed my much loved Bo Hunk in his hand. "Yours," I said as I closed his fingers around the marble. My little cousin played the rest of the day with me peacefully. He sat beside me that night at the supper table and spooned his dumplings on to my plate after I ate all of mine.

I had a big day planed today. The wood man delivered once a month and today was the day. I had gone through the wood pile a few times but just could not find what I wanted. Maybe there would be something to suit me in the new batch that was coming in. Mr. Mac Gother was my friend. He would help me find what I needed. I watched through the side window until I saw him pull in, back his old truck to the woodpile and began to unload. Impatiently, I yanked on Mama's apron and pointed at the latched door to the back stairs. "What kind of bee you got in yer bonnet now, I wonder," she said as she withdrew the door latch. I pushed past her and went careening down the stairs. "Slow down Pat. You gonna come a cropper and break yer neck." I raced on, paying no mind. I meant to be at that wood pile for first choice. I scrambled around the outer edges searching frantically for just the right piece. I would pick up one, heft it, swing it, and throw it down. Mr. Mac scrunched his face sideways and eyed me dubiously with one eye while he lifted his cap and scratched his gray head. Mama looked as though she suspected I had taken leave of my senses and said as much. I went about my search with nary a word but alas, it seemed fruitless. I felt angry and frustrated. I did not know exactly what I was searching for but knew I would recognize it when I found it. I began to throw the wood down hard and stomp and snort around the pile with my bottom lip stuck out. I knew one of those screeching fits was about to start but I just did not know how to stop it. Usually when it started, one of the adults would tease me and egg it on. I do not think they understood how bad the temper seizure hurt me. I fought the red haze to keep it from consuming me. "I want!" I growled deep in my throat. "Now, I want." "Shush lass. Come to ole Mac. Come now. Go Dovie, bring a glass of cold water and a wet cloth. Tha lass is having a bit of a temper. She just needs ta cool down." He cradled me in his arms as he perched on the tail gate of his truck. His voice had a cheerful lilt and charm made to turn storm clouds to sunshine. I know Mac Gother is a Scottish Name, so I suppose there was a Scottish ancestor somewhere in his past genealogy but my Mac was Irish to the bone. With my head snuggled against his chest, I could hear and feel his beautiful brogue rumble there. It had a soothing effect. "Ta be such a wee one, tis a mighty powerful hag ye got leashed lass. Now, there comes to me mind," he mused. "There just may be a thing ole Mac has that would fit uer hand better een tha clumsy bits cut fur stove burning. Ahh, here comes ye cool drink." He wiped my face and hands and gave me the glass of water. "Now," he said. "Sip a bit and rest while I see what can be done." He sat me down on the tail gate and went to the front of the truck. Mama began to stack her wood aside to be carried upstairs, while Mr. Mac rummaged under the seat of his truck. He returned to me with a piece of wood in his hand. "Try this one lass. Tis a right nice little shillelagh, made just the right fit. I would say the one made it, had you in mind." My hands shook as I reached for it. It glowed with a soft red brown patina and felt like satin to the touch. Mr. Mac informed me that it was treated with oxblood and bee's wax. It was carved to fit the hand with a knot at the end of the hand hold. The handle felt rough and there were marks carved down one side. Mr. Mac took my finger and traced it down the markings. "Runes," he whispered, "They are blessings of the Danu and here on the handle, is sand taken from the shores of Ireland mixed with the resin of the Rowan tree. Tis a wondrous tree, the Rowan. Why, the ladies say." He cocked one quizzical eyebrow at Mama. "Never mind what the ladies say," he mumbled and cleared his throat. I looked up with the question in my eyes." The auld ones lass, those who came first to Ireland and set the stone on Tara that called the great warrior kings to serve her people. De ye not know of the Tuatha De Danann and those who came after, the children of the Danu?" Mama spoke with a stern voice, "Mac, we got troubles enough with her and these worrisome spells she has. Don't start with all this fairy tale junk and she don't need a battle stick for sure. She is hard enough to deal with without putting a weapon in her hand. Jane won't appreciate yer meddling. She already carried her to the doctor. He fixed her mouth so she

could talk, if she would do it. He seemed to think it would help."
"Well, has it?" He asked testily. "No, can't say it has. In fact, it seems
worse. It's so bad when she turns her wolf loose, we have to hold
her down to keep her from hurting herself. She beats herself against
the floor and the walls. God help us if she is this way when she
gets big enough to turn it on others." Mr. Mac made a rude sound
with his mouth. "If tha wee paddy feels tha need of protection, she
should have it. I will teach her how to respect it, meself. Mayhap, it
will help this problem. Dovie, I ken ye have tended the Cherokee
verra well. But ye be trying to strangle the other side. Tha lass
has no understanding of the blude that runs in her veins. To have
control, she needs to understand her heritage and the passions that
come with it. The Kelly's are honorable Irish, and the Smiths are
not to be discounted. They were artist all." He declared. "They took
their names from the first four. Gold Smiths, Silver Smiths, Iron
Smiths, and the bards were the Smiths of the history and poetry
of Ire. Tis proud of our bards we be, for there is no written word
of our history but the telling of it by them. Their place in life was
to remember true. They must be accurate as they carried the news
and messages from one village or castle holding to the next. How
do ye know where this wee one may go if ye will but teach her of the
proud people from whence she came. Ye on dear mother, God rest
her, gave ye a fine example wit ye verra own name. Dovie means a
quite peaceful place. Tha Welsh had a way of taken a whole thought
into one word. Ye must tend tha bairn's nature that's all I'm saying."
Mama looked at the ground for a time then slowly raised her head
to look Mr. Mac in the face "I don't know how, Mac. Nobody ever
tended mine." He stood up from the tailgate and reached for her.
"Aw hell, Dovie," he said as he drew her close. She leaned into him
for a time while he talked softly into her ear. I did not know what
he said but she seemed to take heart from his words. She gathered •
herself up and stood tall with her shoulders back and that proud
look on her face that only Mama could hold one spellbound with.
So much hurt and lose could be seen in her eyes and so much hope
for the future. "Okay Mac, we will try it your way for now, but you
mind my word. You make sure she knows the difference between

history and fairy tales, and while you are at it take that wart off you promised to get rid of the last time you were here." She held out her arms and said, "Here man, make yerself useful as well as so ornamental." As he stacked wood in her outstretched arms he said. "Now, Dovie lovey be easy. I willna turn the lass over to the dark side of Morrigan. She is a smart paddy who well knows the difference tween a wee imaginary critter with wings hiding under a toadstool and a being fighting for right to life and all he holds dear and sacred. With a wink of his roguish eye and a grin at me, he sent her upstairs with a smart slap on her backside. He watched her depart with a pleased look upon his face.

"Uhmm, now what was we about," he asked as he turned back to me. I stuck my wrist in his face and waggled it "Wart," I said. He began to pat his pockets then reached behind my ear and withdrew a shiny nickel. "Now, there be jist what I need to purchase meself, a fine wart. I do find meself in need of one today." He put his eye close to the wart and rubbed it with his thumb while he mumbled to himself. Then he offered me the nickel and asked, "Would ye be willing to sell it to me lass." A nickel would buy me a Popsicle when the ice cream truck come by. I nodded my head yes. "Na na, ye must say it aloud now." I took a deep breath, swelled out my chest and answered, "Yes, I sell." "Tis done," he said. I looked at my wrist and shook my head no. Holding up my arm, I pointed at the wart which was still very much in evidence. "Weell now, do ye expect good things to come in a flash? They dinna ye know. Ye must wait for good things with patience and a grace that is pleasing to those ye be asking tha boon of. Tha auld wise ones dinna do things willie nillie ye kin. They think first." I might add I did not know when it disappeared. Mr. Mac had begun to come by a lot more regular then once a month but the next time he came, he asked about the wart.
· I looked down at my wrist and to my surprise, it was gone. Thus, I learned my first lesson in patience and graciousness.

Regardless of Mama's warning Mr. Mac did sprinkle my education with many tails of the wee people of Ireland. He told me of Banshees. Those dread creatures that warned of death and devastation with their wailing. He told me of the beautiful Selkies.

They were seals of the Hebrides that could shed their skin and come ashore as humans for a time. If one could find and steal the skin of the Selkie and hide it, the Selkie could not return to the sea. "Oh! That would be so cruel. I would never hold anything against its will." Mac agreed. Many afternoons were spent sitting on the tailgate of the old wood truck while he carried me to a magical place far and away, east of the sun and west of the moon across The Bridge of Twilight. If I had the courage and wisdom to outwit the ugly troll who lived beneath the bridge, I could cross to the far side where all manner of wonderful things could and did happen. Be brave enough to look upon ugliness and smart enough to conquer it with goodness. Mac taught me to see the magic and beauty in a spider web that glistened with dew. Instead of cringing with fear of the tiny weaver, I looked with wonder at a fragile crossing sprinkled with glittering diamond chips reflecting rainbow colors. If I looked long enough, I might glimpse a wee winged creature skip across from one blossom to another. I loved my teacher, who has earned his place in my tapestry.

This day, I had a special task to do. It was a little early in the morning yet for Marshal to be out and about, so I would bide my time a little longer. I carried Bo into the front room and sat him where the sunlight beamed through the window. Poor little feller, he had just spent a bad night. He was cutting a tooth that was being stubborn about presenting itself. Mama rubbed his gums with her thimble. I remembered what torture that was. I talked to him as I pulled a chair under the colored wind chimes that hung from the ceiling. "We are going to make magic, Bo. You will feel much better when we are done." Yes, by standing on the chair, I could just tip the chimes with my Shillelagh enough to make them dance and sing. They tinkled and gave voice like the sound of fairies. Rainbow colors danced around the room. My Bo bounced and cooed with delight. He reached out his hands and tried to grasp the colors that swirled around him. I looked down at his smile and saw a new tooth. I felt pleased with my magic. With my shillelagh, the world was mine. I named her Fair Fey.

I went to the bedroom and fetched Bo's quilt and bottle. Mama had made the quilt so heavy, I could scarce drag it behind me. Spreading it on the floor and setting the bottle on it, did the trick. Bo crawled onto the quilt and grabbed the bottle, he flipped onto his back. I curled up beside him. He placed one hand on my face and patted while he went to sleep. I slipped away and left him there. I knew Mama would take him to his crib when she came back upstairs. I went to my room and picked up Lill and Sarrie, the broken one. With my dolls under my arm and Fair Fey in my hand, I reattached the barrier across the door, in case Bo awoke and crawled off the pallet before Mama came back. I went down the front stairs. As I slipped across the little strip of yard, I came to the wood fence that separated the two properties. I leaned my ear to the board Marshall and I had loosened. I could hear him. "Vroom, vroom." He was playing with his beloved trucks. Those he would never let me touch, I thought resentfully. I sat down and leaned against the fence. Laying Sarrie beside me, I placed the shillelagh across my lap. I picked up Lill and tilted her forward. Whaaa, she wailed. It got very quiet on the other side of the fence. I tilted her back. Whaaa, she cried again. Then I laid her down beside her sister. I picked up Fair Fey and kept my eye on the loose board. It moved sideways and Marshall's head came poking through. I waited till I saw his shoulders began to appear. I had laid my plan well. I brought the shillelagh down and gave him a right smart rap. I had every intention of leaving a whistling knot on that hard head and daring it to whistle. Marshall flattened out and lay very still. I drug him farther through the fence and turned him on his back. I was glad he was such a skinny boy. I really did want to see his face. I watched till his eyes began to flutter and he moaned. Then I slapped poor Sarrie down on his chest. I picked up Lill and Fair Fey and went back upstairs as fast as I could scurry. I had heard the bag pipes calling blocks away. The soldiers were marching. I must hurry.

I pushed my feet into my boots and slapped my black and red plaid tam-o-chanter on my head. Putting Fair Fey over my shoulder, I raced back down the stairs where I stood in the crowd of cheering people, but not for long. I picked a likely looking compatriot who stood head and shoulders above the other men with a crop of carrot colored hair on his head. He smiled at me when he marched by. His eyes were as blue and bright as the sky above. I could have sworn I heard harps and angles singing. I fell into step beside him and marched cadence for at least a block before the sergeant called a halt. He came back to where I stood beside my soldier. With his hands on his hips, he stared down at me. I put my hand on my hip and stared silently back. He looked up at the soldier and asked. "Where did she come from?" The soldier stood straight and replied. "Back there a ways, Sir." The sergeant picked me up and kissed me on the head. "Well take her back to her ma, son. She's too little to keep." The soldier took me from the Sargent. Placing me on his shoulders, he trotted back down the street. I pointed out Mama. She was there with her hands over her face. Miss Maude was laughing. "Lud Dovie, where do the bairn get her notions." "From yer brother most like." With a good natured grin, Maude teased. "Aye, Mac do have a way with the ladies, no mind the age." My soldier lifted me from his shoulders and I wrapped my arms around his neck. I leaned in close to his ear and spoke clearly. "Blessings of the Danu be to ye. May the strength of Lugh fill ye hand and a strong horse carry ye. God and angles keep you from harm." Then I kissed him. A startled expression was upon his face as he handed me to Mama. "It's a Kelly," she laughed as she took me from him. His blue eyes twinkled as he leaned towards me. "And it's a McKnight wishing ye safe journey on the high road. The sun to ye face and fair wind to ye back." With one last farewell hug and kiss, he was gone. "So many leaving," sighed Mama. "And so many will not return." As I put my hands on each side of Mama's face, I turned her head to me and said, "He will come back." Hefting me to her hip, she murmured as she carried me up the stairs. "I do believe he will. Yes I surely do."

The next morning, Mama found my doll, Sarrie, lying at the top of the stairs. A silk red and black plaid scarf tied around her stitched neck. Marshall's favorite buck eye tied in one corner of the scarf. "Now, what is this about," she wondered. I never answered her. After that, Marshall and I became the best of friends. We were always together and always in accord. He asked me if I would marry him when we grew up. I said I would and we slipped away to downtown Avondale. We window shopped for the furniture we would have someday. Then we went to a movie. I was enjoying my favorite cartoon of Tweety Bird, when I was unceremoniously plucked from my seat. Aunt Lilly held me by the scruff of my neck while she frowned down at me. "We have searched for you half the day. Your mother and I have missed work because of you." She dragged me outside with Marshall tagging woefully behind. "Do you remember the man who tried to snatch you and Inez? Well there are others out there, just like him. They will do bad things to you, if they catch you. I should take a switch to your behind." I felt my face crumple and my lips began to tremble. "I sorry, Aunt Lilly. I won't do it ever again." With her hands on her hips, she asked sternly. "Why did you do it this time?" I twisted my fingers together and gulped. "Me and Marshall got gaged and we was picking furniture for when we get our house." Her mouth fell open and she leaned way back and stared at the sky. "God help us all," she muttered. Squatting down, she took my hands in hers then looked up at Marshall. "I don't see a ring, young man." He shrugged his shoulders. "I bought her popcorn," he stammered. She chewed her lip and studied for a bit. "Well Mr. Big Spender, if you love her so much, you will take her home and make sure she stays safe. Don't you ever take her off where we can't find her! If you do, I will strip the hide off you. Do you understand me?" He answered with a heartfelt nod of his head, for he seemed too scared to speak. "Now you," she said shaking me gently. "Go home. I will get Jane and we will go on to work. I will tell her I have found and dealt with you if you promise to never slip off again." Marshall and I made that promise, then ran all the way home. "Go get your doll babies," he said. "We can ride them on my truck and nobody will bother you behind my fence. My mum will help me take care of you."

I went to bed at night with visions of a bright shining people, who were gentle in their love and fierce in their defense of what they loved. My dreams were of Lugh the long arm, with his sword aloft as he rode in battle on his magnificent war horse. One trained to fight as valiant as the warrior who rode him. I could hear the ringing clash of sword against shield. I could hear the wild sweet song of the harps where the wily Bard, Fergus placed them in the hills and called the winds to blow through so he could be free to pick up his sword and join Cuculian in battle. The drum of hundreds of horse's hooves wove through my dreams with the choking smell of dust swirling on the wind where it carried the battle cries of brave men. My imagination fired and nourished my determination to stand for all that was fair and just. I had found my way. To my vow, I must remain true. Defend and never harm those which are weaker than myself. Be truthful and deal with honor in word and deed so as not to bring dishonor to those who have gone before me, or those who are destined to follow me. Be mindful of the power of my magic shillelagh. Use it only to protect or defend but never to harm an innocent. So the gifted seed of the bard was conceived and born anew. Not by choice but passed to me to cherish. That I might weave the words of our joys and struggles in the tapestry to mark our passing, that we be not forgotten.

It was such a beautiful day, with no inkling of the troubles and heartbreak that was to transpire before its closing. Mama washed our laundry in the bathtub and hung the wet clothes on the line that ran around the top of the balcony at the front of our apartment. Mac was downstairs with Miss Maude. Mama with Bo on her hip was on her way down to visit. I called to her. "Where's my red sock?" I loved those socks and thought the world was coming to an end if I did not have them for every occasion. Mama kept going down the stairs but called back to me. She told me later that she had answered, "They are wet. Let them dry. Then I will get them down for you." I did not understand all she said but I heard wet. Well, wet or not, miss stubborn intended to have those socks. As I grumbled under my breath, I marched out to the balcony. I looked up to the line. There hung the socks just a bit out of reach. Did I let that fact stop me? No sir, I did not. As I looked the situation over, I spied a large bag of quilting cotton leaning against the balcony rail, just below where the socks hung. I climbed the bag and stepped onto the balcony banister. I reached up for the socks. I had them in my hand and tipped over. I had landed in a sit down position, in a cinder bed within inches of the cement sidewalk. I was unconscious till the ambulance came. I roused long enough to hear a stranger who said, "Move her easy. Careful with her neck and spine." I felt gentle hands wrapping me tightly in something. A scattered thought flashed in an instant through my mind. They are taking me way up on the mountain, where they bury dead people. Someone waits for me. I could smell wildflowers. I heard Marshall crying for his Patty. His sweetheart was hurt. I heard Mama crying and Miss Maud said, "Dovie don't. We all know you take good care of the child." For an instant, I saw Mac's gentle blue eyes as he leaned in to kiss me and place his hand on my neck. Then I was out again. I woke once more in the ambulance. Mama was beside me. She was praying for forgiveness. "Lord, please don't take Jane's baby because of my sin," She wept softly. I had a small moment to wonder, what sin? Mama was good. I was the bad one who disobeyed. Before I could finish forming my thoughts or comfort her, I was lost in the darkness again. I was only dimly aware of hands turning me and a light in my eyes at times. At last, I awoke in a little bed with rails on the sides. I was told to try to be very still. I could not be much else. I was braced and padded to a fair thee well. Mother stepped to the side of the bed. "You will stay here for now. I will be back tomorrow." Her eyes were cold and her lips had a tight pinched look. I knew she was furious. I wished she would hold me a minute but she left without another word. I cried myself to sleep with only Jesus to love me and forgive my foolish transgressions. Mother came back the next day. The doctors had made more x-rays before she came in and met her with good news. The neck and spine were not fractured. Only drove up and the coccyx bone had been broken. Mother began to cry. "They told me that my baby had fallen," she tried to explain to the doctor. "I was so scared, I left all of the dishpans I had shopped for, at the bus stop. I thought it was my baby." As I watched her dry her tears, I thought with dismay. She thought it was Bo. Was she glad it was me, instead of him? I felt very sad, unloved and unlovable, for the first time in my short life.

We left the hospital and returned home on the bus. I was sore and ached all over but I did not complain. I just wanted things to get back to normal as soon as possible. Mama seemed to be a shadow of her old self. She walked with her head down and her eyes swollen and red. Mother and she seldom spoke. I asked for Mac and was told Mac was not coming back. Mother had sent him away and Mama had stayed with us instead of going with him. I protested and tried to tell Mother it was not Mama or Mac's fault. I had disobeyed Mama. It was my fault I had fallen. It was my fault I had slipped away and gone downtown. Mother told me to shut my mouth and stay out of grown folks business. Aunt Burma said, "Jane ain't ever took to the notion of Mama taking up with Mac. Now she thinks she is justified." She made sure Mother was not around when she stated that opinion but I believe it was true. She nipped that romance in the bud. I gave her the tool with which to accomplish the doing. It took a very long time for the healing to begin. There was to be half a lifetime of mistakes, injustice and straying pathways before things came right between mothers and daughters.

Mother soon married Louie Gentry and moved Bo and I to another apartment across town. I did not see much of Mama after that. She only came by once in a great while it seemed. The last time she come to visit, Mother stopped her at the top of the stairs. She said, "Mama, I don't want you to come here anymore." Mama clutched the banister railing till her knuckles turned white. "I have done all in my power to make things right Jane. All that you have asked of me, I have done. What more can I do? You are punishing me for things that have happened that were beyond my control." I put my arms around her legs and buried my face against her. I could feel her trembling. Mother pulled me away from her. "You go play." I moved a few stairs down and sat. Mother turned back to Mama and I heard her say. "Louie doesn't want you here. He feels you are a disruptive influence and it makes problems for us when you come around. He is my husband now and I have to do like he asks if we are to be a family and get along." I knew he and Mother had quarreled after Mama left the last time she was here. He referred to her as that damned old squaw women. There were more words exchanged between them there on the stairs but I did not understand what I was hearing. It was something about having a better life then mama's children. Mother wanted her children to grow up respectable and looked up to instead of down on. She wanted them to grow without the stigma of the past hanging over their heads. I did not understand the word stigma then. Now I do but I still asked myself. "What stigma?" Mama was the daughter of a born on the wrong side of the blanket half breed. For long years, our family was lied to about how our Indian blood came to run in our veins. We were poor and Mama had been through a bad divorce. Which of these had Mother's new family convinced her were so disgraceful that she should disown her own mother? My Mother went back inside the apartment and firmly closed the door. Mama came slowly down the stairs. She appeared majestic to me with her shoulders back and head held high. She walked past me without a word. I do not believe she even knew I was there. There was nothing I could say. Mother had been awfully quick tempered here lately. I had never been hit before but now it seemed I was always getting smacked for first one infraction or the other. I had begun to pretend I was a little ghost that no one could see or hear. Maybe then, I would not offend so often. Step Grandma Missouri advised Mother that Mama had let me go undisciplined too long. Mother said all that had to change. I had a new daddy and I must learn to be a little lady. Missouri Coffman turned out to be a fly in my mother's and my ointment till the day she died. If she had any redeeming qualities I never found them. Bless her little heart.

All I knew, right now, everything was askew. Everybody was sad and I was not allowed to protest because grownups knew best. Mother had even ruined my teddy bear. She slipped around while I was asleep and washed him. Now his eyes were all cockeyed and his smile was gone. I took my forlorn little self to the coal bin and crawled inside so I could be alone to think. Surely, there was something I could do to make it all better. I sure did miss my wigwam behind the old wood stove but the coal bin would have to do. I huddled there beside the door inside the smutty little hole and kept a sharp ear out for the coal truck. I had been warned to never go in there. If that truck pulled up and dumped down the chute, I might not be able to get out in time and I would be buried alive. I did not like the thought of that but I needed to be alone and this apartment house was so noisy and busy, the bin was the only solitary place I could find. We did not even have a private bathroom. It was shared with the rest of the borders. I had found a dead man in there one day. He had a heart attack in the bathtub. Now I was uneasy about going in there alone. Sometimes, I wet my pants if there was no one to go with me. I needed a quiet place where Jesus could hear me. He was the only one I had left who might listen to me. When I finally crawled out and went back upstairs, Mother took one look and shrieked. She made a wild eyed lunge at me but Louie laughed and caught her around the waist with both arms. "Come on Jane, don't get all worked up. She's just been playing in the coal bin but thankfully that won't be a problem much longer." He seemed in a cheerful mood. "Don't be fussing tonight. I have something to talk to you about. We need some peace and quiet. Why don't you take her and clean her up while I fix supper. Then I will tell you all about it." He made something he called slum gullion. Ground beef with onions and a red sauce served over hamburger buns. It was very spicy and delicious. He watched me take my first bite. When my eyes grew round and watered, he grinned at me and asked, "To hot for you girl? Try this." He poured some of his beer into a glass and slid it across the table. I was astonished, he usually paid me no mind one way or the other. I drank my beer and ate my sandwich while he talked to Mother. He was very excited about this farm he had found in a town called Jemison. The man who owned the farm promised a mule, a plow and a truck to haul the produce to market. A house and all the food he and Mother could grow. They would have a cow for milk and butter, chickens and eggs. There would be pigs to butcher. He and Mother were so happy that night. I heard them laughing and talking way into the night. It seemed we were moving to Jemison, Alabama. Maybe things would be all right. Oh, how I was going to miss, Mama and Mac. Maybe if I was real good and prayed hard, God would fix the rest of the things that were wrong. He seemed to be doing pretty good so far. Maybe he did hear me in the coal bin today. Maybe, there were some things I was just too little to fix myself. But I would grow up some day.

Mama did come back to us eventually. After Mother's second marriage ended in divorce and right before I went to live in the orphanage home, Mama moved to Mobile, Alabama. Other members of the family moved down there later. Grandpa John Walden came to visit those of his children who now lived here. He brought Kate, the women he had left Mama for. For reasons I could not phantom, he went by Mama's house to say hello. He walked in without even a polite knock with Kate trailing behind him. Kate did not sit down. Truth to tell, nobody ask her to. She stood by the front door with her arms akimbo. Grandpa went where Mama sat and put his arm around her neck. "How you doing, Dovie," he asked. "I am very well John." Mama sat looking down at her lap while pleating her apron with busy fingers. She not once looked up. He stood beside Mama and awkwardly patted her back while he made some insane remark about wanting to say hello on his way out of town. I ground my teeth and my hand itched to slap Kate's face. I fumed all the way back to Mother's house. I slammed the door as I went in. Mother took one look at my face and laid her quilting in her lap. "What ails you," she asks. "You're in a rage fit to commit murder." I flopped back into a chair. "No, em not." She smoothed her hand over her sewing. "The back of your neck is swelled out like a Spreading Adder, Thomas Gilliland. You can't tell me. I know you to well." I got up and went into the kitchen to pour me a glass of iced tea just to try to cool off and buy myself a little time to collect my wits. Am I being unreasonable? I asked myself. Hell no. I took my tea and stomped back into the living room. Sinking down to the chair, I asked Mother. "Did you know Grandpa and Kate were going to Mama's today?" "I heard," she said. I opened my mouth but before I could spit out the expletive I was conjuring she raised her hand. "It's been years, Betty June. Don't you think it's time to bury the hatchet?" "Somebody should have done that the first time that whey faced snake come crawling through the cornfield sniffing after Grandpa." With a deep sigh, Mother said. "I am surprised at your narrow-mindedness. It takes two you know." "Yea," I exploded. "Give me a sack, a rock, and a river and I will take care of both of em. If you think just because years have gone by that pie faced bitch can worm her way into acceptance in this family think again. I will never accept her and if the rest of the family does that's up to them. I don't care what they do. Just so Mama doesn't have to feel forced to accept her because she thinks everyone else wants her to. That dear lady has spent her life alone with no one special while Kate has had a full life and bragged in our faces about how virile John Walden is. She had this full life at Mama's expense. I find her odious and disgusting." Mother went back to quilting. She did not look at me as she quietly said. "Mama met someone once. I guess she could have loved him and I believe he loved her but I just couldn't accept it. I don't know why. I just couldn't see another man with my Mama in my Daddy's place. What I did was wrong. I made her send him away. I have regretted it a lot of times." I had no absolution for her. I turned my back and walked out the door. I wandered out in the woods behind Mother's house and felt bitterness when I thought of all the wrongs she had done and the hurt she had caused others. It was her fault, I had lost Mama and Mac all those years ago. I sat on the ground and hugged myself letting the peace of my surroundings sooth my anger. The warmth of the sun, dappled through the needles of the pine trees lay soft across my back. A squirrel scolded a pesky blue jay and dropped an acorn nearby before scampering away to finish his irate quarrel with his neighbor at a farther distance. I shivered as I thought of my own careless sins and wrong decisions. Who was I to judge? At least, there was some excuse for Mother. At times, she was not of sound mind. Mother had begun to suffer from early dementia years ago. At times like today, she seemed so reasonable, normal, and gentle. At others, well let's just say, she would be totally opposite. She could become a different person all together. I took a deep cleansing breath. She was right about one thing. It was time to heal and forgive. If I could find a measure of forgiveness for her, maybe I could manage to forgive myself for some of the terrible decisions and wrongs I had done in the past. As for Kate, let a power higher then I deal with her. I would not let myself hate. Neither would I let her touch Mama's life again. Mama had suffered enough at Kate's hands. I went back in the house and put my arms around Mother. For the first time in years, I told her how much I loved her, and meant every word of it. It did not happen quickly but the healing process began at that moment.

Louie Gentry and
Elizabeth Gentry

Chapter 5

BARNYARDS AND FIREFLIES

Mother's new husband went ahead of us to get the farm and house ready. Within three months, we moved with our few belongings to Jemison, Alabama. On the trip down, he explained to mother. "I spent most of my money on livestock and feed. Mr. Deel paid for all the seed and fertilizer. I will pay him his share and the land rent when I take the produce to market. We will share the meat and vegetables between us to feed our families. But the extra hogs and cattle I raise, will be ours. The chickens are all ours. I have my check once a month, so we should do fine till I can get our first crop to market."

While in the Army, he lost the sight in his right eye. This was due to a blow on the back of his head. Though the incident was a personal attack, it did not happen in combat, he received a medical discharge with all G. I. benefits.

Mother bounced on the seat. "Oh darling, I can hardly wait to see it. I am so excited." Her face glowed with her delight. "How long fore us gets Dare Dalin," I asked. They both chuckled. I felt embarrassed but no one had ever told me what to call him. I knew I was not supposed to call grownups by their first name. Up till now, I had avoided calling him anything by ignoring him. I reckoned I should have kept my big mouth shut this time too. "I call him darling. You call him Daddy," Mother informed me. I felt confused and did not know how to reply to her statement. This man, whom I had just been told to call Daddy looked down at me and smiled. "I am going to adopt you soon," he declared in a jovial voice. "What do you think about that girl?" I felt my face burn and I stammered, "But I, ah, ah alweady gots a Daddy. See?" "Louie will be your Daddy from now on. He is going to adopt you and give you his name. You will be Betty June Gentry when you start to school," declared Mother. Distressed and unsure of myself, I blurted out, "Why." Mother answered me. "My name is Gentry because Louie and I have married. Yours and Jim's last name should be the same as mine." The man cautioned her gently. "Why don't you ease off for now Jane? Let it rest awhile. Okay?" We all grew quite except Bo. We had woke him from his nap and he began to fret. I reached and took his hand, while I hummed one of Mama's sleeping chants to him. "You couldn't carry a tune in a water bucket. Stop that racket before you really make him cry," snapped Mother. Bo put his thumb in his mouth, snuggled against her breast and went back to sleep. "Jane honey, it doesn't bother me if the girl wants to sing. It's not that bad." He nudged me with his elbow and winked at me. Maybe, I would call him Daddy after all. No matter what they named me, I was a Gilliland. I would not forget, I vowed to myself. I dozed off and slept to the song of the truck wheels. It seemed the smartest thing to do at the time.

It was impossible to count the little piglets as they squealed and trotted in dizzying circles. They did not seem to know which mother they belonged to. I heard Daddy say, he was broke as a she haint in hell, but not to worry. It would all pay off at hog killing time. The little piglets were to be killed? Oh no! I ran away from the pig pen and went to the pasture. Mother and Daddy ambled along behind me. Daddy carried Bo in one arm and kept the other one around Mother's waist. He was all excited and full of plans. Mother listened and smiled up at him while she hung on to his every word. I was glad he changed the subject. I didn't want to hear about killing little pigs. I would just stay away from the pig pen. They stank any way.

"I bought two milk cows. Would you believe the little Guernsey birthed twins?" He pointed at the small gold colored cow. "I saved a pretty penny buying them before they calved. I think old man Burns suspected something wasn't quite right with the Guernsey. He wanted to unload her before her time was due. I would have lost her and at least the second calf, maybe all three if not for the help of my teacher. Did I tell you I had signed up for Agriculture and Animal Husbandry? I take night classes at the school house twice a week." Mother threw her arms around his neck. She kissed him on his cheek and cooed. "Why Louie, I think that is wonderful." He puffed with pride as he held Bo on the gate rail. "There is Egore the bull, and two mules, Aider and Flimflam, the one named Flimflam because he would do all kinds of tricks to get out of pulling the plow."

The pasture was huge and lush with grass. Daddy said it took him a solid week to go over it and pull out the stink weeds. He and Mother agreed this would be a good job for me. I could walk the pasture every few days and pull the weeds so the cow's milk would not taste bitter. I thought this would be fun. At the time, I did not know about the big black and white bull grazing on the back side of the pasture. At a later date, I came to know him very well. He chased me up the persimmon tree that grew in the middle of the pasture. The ornery critter stayed close by all afternoon. Every so often; he would paw, snort, and sometimes attack the tree. The tree wasn't that sturdy. I clung to the limb I was perched on, and I prayed it would hold. I alternated my prayers with curses on the bull and all his ancestors. Come suppertime, Mother sent Daddy on a search and rescue mission. That damn bull acted totally innocent while Daddy fished me out of the tree and carried me across the pasture. "Aw, she was just scared of old Egore," he told mother. "But he's as gentle as a lamb." I had issues with that bull from then on. He hated my guts. Actually yearned to see what they looked like, and I believed the feeling was mutual. Daddy sawed his horns off and gave one of them to me. Egore the bull was certain I had single handedly engineered this coup d'état. Not true. If it had been me, I would have gone after his balls. Too this day, I still will not eat a persimmon, but I get a real charge when I eat steak. Daddy led us to the barnyard next. The first thing to catch the eye was a gaggle of geese. There were lots of hens and four roosters. Adorable little biddies ran to their mothers when they scratched the ground and clucked to them. "There is your Dominecker, you wanted."

He whispered to Mother as he pointed to a large white and black speckled hen surrounded by her chicks. "I wanted them to hatch before you got here. I got my wish last week." Mother turned in slow circles while she admired all she surveyed, but most of all the man who stood before her. Happy brown eyes sparkled with her joy. "Come on," he said as he grabbed her by the hand and made a beeline to a large garage close to the house. Mother was tall and slim. This enabled her to match steps to his quick pace. I felt pride swell within as I watched her lithe form swing along beside him, then I ran to catch up. I scrambled through the door as I heard Mother's excited voice. She sounded as if she were crying and laughing in the same breath. "A real washing machine, darling, how did you manage this?" I skidded to a halt to admire the shiny white machine with the wringer on top. It was the first I had ever seen. Daddy handed Bo over to Mother, then crossed his arms and looked down. He seemed to struggle to control his mirth. "You are not going to believe this," he answered. "Up the road, at the top of the hill, lives Miss May. A retired old maid school teacher. I was mending the pasture fence on that side when I heard this God awful scream. I grabbed my hatchet in case I should need it for protection and went on up the hill fast as I could. When I got there, I saw Miss May on the porch. She was bent over this washer, screaming her head off. I snatched the plug out of the socket to stop the rollers till I could figure what to do next. Her tit was caught in the rollers. I found this lever beside the rollers, see here?" He showed Mother the release lever. She stared at him, slack jawed with amazement. "Well," he shrugged his shoulders as if he felt a little embarrassed. "Got her loose, didn't I? I loaded her up in the truck and carried her all the way to Thorsby before I found a doctor. It was dark before I got us home. She wouldn't have the washing machine after that. She insisted I come and take it away the next morning. I offered to set up her wash tubs and draw her water when she gets ready to wash. Fair trade I say." "I am flabbergasted," said Mother. "I never heard such a tale. I do hope the poor woman is alright." Daddy put his arms around her and answered. "She will be fine as soon as the bruising and soreness goes. Dr. Rose comes to town on alternating weeks of the month. I will take her for a follow up visit then." Turning her to face him, he placed his hands on her shoulders. "I have been working hard, but Jane, I don't have the wiring in the garage or the house yet. You will have to wait before you can use the machine. We will make do with kerosene lamps for a while. I have someone to come and help you on wash days. You will need her when you start canning too." She is a colored women who lives' on the other side of our back field. Her old man Sam helps me around the place when I need him." Mother assured him she was well pleased with all he had accomplished. Arm in arm, they strolled toward the house as I followed, and we entered our new home. Daddy asked Mother to leave the unpacking for tomorrow. She would have help, and as for supper, there were sandwiches' in the icebox already made up. In the house, only three rooms were unremarkable and sparsely furnished, but the kitchen was a country women's dream. It was spacious and cheerful with its mint green walls, white trim and red accents. It would seem, my new Daddy had an artistic side to his nature. There was a black wood burning stove, a mahogany dining table and eight chairs. There was a walk in pantry filled with Mason jars of all sizes. He had built a work bench and a large cupboard, but the pride of it all, was the big pressure canner sitting in the middle of the work bench. "Now Jane," he cautioned, "Be careful with this gadget. It can kill you. When you see that gauge going into the yellow line you turn the damper down on the stove, then you loosen the pressure gage here. Once it goes across the yellow zone and into the red, it will blow. If you see that happening you hit the back door running. Don't worry about the canner. Keep the kids out side while you are canning. They don't need to be in here under foot anyway." I would like to say she made it through her first canning season intact, but alas it was not to be. Mother left her canner to make a quick trip to the chicken yard with a pan of tomato peelings. She became enthralled with talking to Dominecker and let too much time elapse. Just as she stepped into the kitchen door, a resounding boom rent the air. Her scream raised the hair on my head. Daddy came from the corn crib and passed me in a dead heat. By the time I made it into the kitchen, he had taken Mother in hand. He was trying to peel her apron from her head. She kept shrieking but held tight to the apron. His voice shook as bad as his hands as he begged, "Come on honey, let me see." He managed to uncover her face. She was fine, but she was jittering and percolating like a lid on a boiling teapot. Placing his hand on her round tummy, he asked. "Hey, are we having a baby or a squealing worm here?" Her face turned redder then the tomato splash on the walls and ceiling. She shushed him and shooed me out the door. "Stay out till we get the glass cleaned up. I don't need any cut feet today." I sat on the porch and heard her wail. "Oh Louie, what a mess I've made, and oh! Just look at my canner, it's ruined," Then I heard his answer. "Sweetheart, I don't give a damn about the canner. I can buy another one of those. I am just glad you and the baby aren't hurt, and I tell you right now, you are not to can any more with a canner unless someone is here with you to help. We might not be so lucky next time." I wandered off the porch and went to play. "Shu-shu-shu, a new baby," I hummed.

It was almost twilight time on this first day on the farm. We had ate our sandwiches. Bo had been bathed and put to bed. I could hear the low murmur of Mother and Daddy's voices from the kitchen. I went into the packing box that contained our toys, and removed Sarry, Lill and Fair Fey along with my teddy bear. I carried them outside and sat down on the porch steps. Everything was so beautiful and mysterious. There were little black winged things darting very fast in the air. They went to and fro. Moving too fast to see from whence they came or went. All the lovely green colors of day were given way to the shades of night. A bird was singing a song of many tunes from Miss May's hilltop. I drew a deep satisfied breath of air, redolent with the fragrance of different and unknown blossoms. Oh, if only Mama and Mac could see this, everything would be so good.

When speaking in my mind or to my make believe family, my speech was clear and acceptable. The problem only appeared when I stressed to make myself clear to adults. Missouri, whom I was forced to call grandma, poked fun at me when I spoke. Her criticism was cruel and made me feel awkward. I had regressed to using pantomime and as few words as possible again. I avoided speaking at all when I could get out of it.

While I was hugging Teddy and my dolls, I apologized for leaving them in the box so long. I told them of all the wonderful things they would see tomorrow. "Let's bless this land tonight," I told them. "Tomorrow, we will find the most beautiful stone there is, and put it in a secret place in the front yard. It will welcome all of our friends from across the Bridge of Twilight. This is a magic place. They will like to visit us here." I picked up Fair Fay and waved her back and forth at the yard. "Blessing of the Danu, yiie," I screeched. I got more magic then I bargained for! I watched as tiny lights began to appear. First a few, then many came from the wooded area around the yard. Blinking lights went off and on everywhere. It's a shame to say, but I dropped Fair Fey. It was every man ah, child for herself. I boogied across the porch and made a mad dash for the kitchen. Wide eyed, and beyond even my limited speech, or maybe because of it, I hummed and buzzed like a berserk bee on the warpath. Mother grabbed me by my shoulders and turned me. "What is wrong? Will you stop chittering and bouncing so I can understand you? Do you have ants on you? Have you been bitten?" She was turning and looking all over me. I grabbed her hand and tugged her toward the front of the house. She and Daddy followed me. As we went out the front door, I pointed. "Ook," I said. "See, magic." Mother began to laugh. She set on the top step and pulled me down between her knees. "Oh Louie, she has never seen a lighting bug before." Daddy never said a word, but went back into the house. "Not magic," I ask as my bottom lip trembled. "Of course they are," she whispered. "And God sent them tonight just for you to enjoy." "Will dey always tum?" "At this time every year," she promised. "Like all of Gods creations, each have its own time and season." Daddy came outside with a lidded jar in his hand. He captured a few bugs in the jar and screwed the lid back on. He had punched holes in it. "You will have to turn them loose in the morning, so they can go home. See, they have little lights in their tails that flash. That's why they are called fireflies," He put the jar in my hand. I cocked my head, as the bird twittered from the hill. "That is a mocking bird, listen."

He began to whistle. The bird imitated his every sound. There came a whistle from the woods on the other side of the yard. Daddy set down on the step beside Mother. "Do you hear that one?" He asked. I nodded my head, yes. "That is a quail. She is calling for her mate. Here her say, Bob White? When he hears, he will answer and say, chip fell out the white oak, like this," then he whistled. "Be real still and quite," he said. Each time the bird called for her Bob White, Daddy answered her till he called her right into the yard. I decided my new Daddy had magic too. I pointed at the small winged things that darted about the yard in the dusk. "What?" I asked. I was told they were snake doctors. When Mother said it was bed time, I went gladly and said my prayers. I wanted to thank God for everything and tell him I could hardly wait for tomorrow.

Chapter 6

THE BLACK PEARL

I scampered away from the man, who had toiled all day behind a mule and plow beneath a merciless sun. There had been no water to slack his thirst, nor food to appease his hunger. There was no remorse within me, for I had suffered no cost for my actions. I only felt relief that I had escaped without being held to a higher price of accountability. Like the hide off my back. It begun with Mother calling me from the back door. "Betty June, come in here." I went into the house and found my dinner on the table. Noon meal was called dinner. The night meal was suppertime. "Come eat your dinner," said Mother. "Then I want you to carry Louie's to him." I said, "No." Then swept my hand across in front of me and slapped the air to sign, too far away. "Gits lost," I said. Then I sat in the chair and stared at my food. "No, you won't get lost. I will tell you how to get there."

I was not really upset with taking Daddy his dinner. I was angry because she called me Betty June. I was Pat. Pat brought memories of hugs and kisses. Of teasing voices and love. I am Pat, my heart cried. Call me Pat, but I spoke not a word. I hated the name Betty June. It sounded like a name you would give a tumble bug. I came by this childish notion, through an unpleasant word association. I played with what I mistook for a June bug. Mother hollered, "Put that nasty thing down. That's a tumble bug." Then she showed me these gruesome insects tumbling the cow paddies. Thus June bug, Betty June, tumble bug. Go figure, a child's thoughts. What I really wanted was my name back, and the happy things that went with it. I had been robbed! I heard Grandma when she chastised Mother for calling me Pat. "Why do you call her by that silly name? It's ridiculous. She is old enough, you need to stop molly coddling her," she grouched. I had not been called Pat since that day. Mother and Daddy were both up tight when Grandma came to visit. It was always a long two weeks. "You are a most impossible child," said Mother. "If you are not going to eat, come here and let me show you the way." I picked up the lunch pail, a jug of water and followed her outside. She pointed the way and said, "Just remember when you get to the edge of the corn field, walk the fence till you come to the butterbean patch. From there you will go through the fence to cross the little pasture. You will find him behind the trees on the other side." I sat upon my journey with a feeling of happy adventure. My imagination kicked in and I became an Indian princess. I struggled against many perils to deliver food and medicine to my handsome brave. He was injured and hiding from his enemies, in a secret cave behind a waterfall. When I came back to my present mind, I stopped to take stock of where I was. I reckoned this was the butterbean patch. Who Knew? The only butter beans I ever saw were the dried kind cooked with fat back and on my plate. I did not like them there, and I cared even less about them on the bush! Mother was canning all sorts of fruits and vegetables, but we were not allowed to eat them yet. She said they were for winter time.

I bent to set the lunch pail and water jug on the opposite side of the fence, preparing to go under it. As I dropped the pail, I heard a snort and felt a breath of hot air on the back of my neck. AURG, Egore! He trotted away a short distance then turned to face me. He lowered his head, and pawed the ground while rolling his eyes. He was sending a definite challenge. Just try it girllie. While I kept my best eye on him, I eased the lunch pail and jug back to my side of the fence. "Bastid," I muttered. "Daddy's goanna saw you horns off you sumbitch. He say so. I goanna gits it and blow it up you arsh." It felt good to abuse something with ugly words. I shook my fist at him. I was happy to see this angered the snorting bovine even more. As I contemplated the situation, I realized I was very hungry and thirsty. I drank of the water and poured the rest on the ground and then I ate the sandwich. This deed was not done, allowing me a thought about the consequences of my actions, nor did I care. I carried the pail and jug home and sat them in the kitchen. Mother was rocking the new baby to sleep, so I had every right to tiptoe and be quiet. I went out to play, still refusing to face the reality of what I had done.

It was a very angry man who returned home from his labors that night. His face looked chiseled and drawn. Making his sandy eyebrows and hair stand out in stark contrast to his flushed color. His voice was tight as he ask of Mother. "What happened to my dinner and water today, Jane?" I stood outside the kitchen door and listened. It was Katie who bar the door time. "What is wrong dear? I sent you your dinner. Fred woke up and needed attention so I sent dinner on to you by Betty June." He pulled a chair out and sat. "Well I didn't get it. Come in here girl." I took a deep breath and walked into the kitchen and just stood there. My mind was a complete blank. There was no plausible excuse for what I had done. "What happened to my dinner?" He asked. "Bull," I answered. "What?" His eyebrows shot up. I wrung my hands. I needed words. This man did not understand my signing. It was my own creation and worked only with people who knew me well. As a rule, I did not care a fig about those who did not understand. I helplessly fluttered my hands. He stared at me from keen blue eyes. "You are smarter than people give you credit for," he said. "There is nothing dumb about you. Now answer me. What did you do with my dinner?" I squared my shoulders and stood straight. "Ate it," I replied. "Ate it?" He repeated. "Louie, I am sure there is a reasonable explanation." Mother intervened. "I am sure there is Jane. I would just like to know what the hell it is." "Hungry," I blurted. "You were hungry, so you ate my dinner." I vigorously shook my head, yes. "Bull." I tried again, making the sign of horns on my head. He leaned back in his chair and crossed his arms while he quietly studied me. Then the light of understanding began to dawn. "You found Egore in the pasture?" I nodded, yes. "Jane, you didn't think of the bull when you sent her out. He had her blocked. So she had herself a picnic with my dinner and come back to the house." He threw back his head and roared with laughter. "Jane, get me some supper. I am starving to death, and you," he sputtered. "Go find yourself something useful to do. I'll tell you what. Go bring in the pot before it gets dark. I am too wore out to stand watch for you tonight, so you better get it while there is still some daylight, else you will find your butt out in the dark by yourself." I did not have to be told twice. I raced for the pot and made it back from the garage fast. As I stepped to the porch, I heard Daddy say, "No whipping, Jane. It wasn't done out of meanness to me. She is just timid and spooks easy." "She didn't used to be," said Mother. "There was a time, she didn't believe cow horns would hook, and she would have found a way to outwit that bull. Now I hardly know her. She has changed to a hardheaded, stubborn, sneaky scamp that is scared of her own shadow. Maybe your mother is right and I have let her get out of hand. Maybe I should bear down. Missouri says I have spoiled her." "If something is bothering the girl Jane, you need to find out what. I don't think you can beat it out of her." Why could they not see? It was as plain as the nose on your face. My whole life had come apart. I never knew when I was going to be beat or for what. I was let go when I should have been corrected or chastised to severely to fit the crime when I had no idea of what wrong I had done. I suffered terrible nightmares. I was deathly afraid of the dark. I did not feel loved anymore. I did not fit in Missouri Coffman's world, and what's more I did not want to fit. I felt anger and total contempt for the adults in my world.

Grandma had recently spent one of her extended visits. When she was in residence, life was miserable for everyone. The after effects of her visits lingered on after she was gone, like a curse to haunt the house with her dictates. Mother came under fire for everything she did. Missouri Kauffman was always full of advice and willing to dispense and enforce it on all who would bow to her will. She held her own daughter up as a perfect reflection of good breeding and nurturing. In this, she was correct. Louie's sister, Aunt Ester was the epitome of beauty and goodness. Her husband, Sam Faller was a gentleman and good provider. Each time they came to visit, they came bearing gifts, and they made no distinction between us children. Bo and I loved them, and in return felt accepted by them. The only problem being, Grandma lived with Aunt Ester and

Uncle Sam. When they came to visit, they brought her and left her till the next visit. Grandma's nature was spiteful and abrasive while in our home. How she managed to rear such a lovely person as Aunt Ester surely would be a marvel for genetic science. I think Aunt Ester was just born to be a lady and thrived in that atmosphere. I was not and did not thrive at all. My spirit began to grow crooked.

After any one of her tirades against Mother for whatever reason, she would end with, "But then, what could a body expect with no better raising than you had." With a sanctimonious sniff and self-sacrificing sigh, she would turn away, leaving Mother fighting her tears and choking on her anger and disappointment. For this, she gave up her own people. The longer Grandma stayed the grimmer Mother's visage and the stricter with me she become. The unhappy stress in the home, caused Daddy to disappear to the corncrib for his white lightning jug fairly regular. This was one more thing to make Mother sad.

Upon Grandma's advice on child rearing, my dolls were taken from me and hung on the wall like whatnots. I was allowed to take them down to play only when my hands and clothes were clean, and only then in the house for a short period of time under strict supervision. I kept Fair Fey hid out in the garage. While at play, my imagination inspired me to be quite graphic in my actions and sound effects. With my imaginary sword in hand and my winged stallion beneath me, I fought my giants and dragons. I would suddenly feel the hair on my neck rise. When I turned to look, she would be peering at me from around the corner or from behind a bush. With her pale watery eyes full off malice and disapproval, she would scurry away to make it known that I was up to my heathenish games again.

It was due to her influence that I lost my room. "You can't trust little girls when they reach that age, you know. They do things. She is too old to sleep in the same room with her brothers." I was not even school age yet, but my bed was moved to the living room and set up in one corner. Fred's crib was moved from Mother's and Daddy's bed room, and in with Bo. Had this been given as the reason, I would have been fine with it. Fred was such a delightful baby. I certainly did not mind giving up my room for him and Bo. I loved them with all my heart. The lascivious reason, I heard spoke to Mother by Grandma sickened me. It made my face burn with shame. I felt dirty even though I was totally innocent.

Grandma would scare me. Her actions were not like Mothers. In times past, when I became a little to rowdy or fussy, mother would set me on her lap and whisper, "Shush listen, I hear that old Whompus kitty. She is coming after a noisy little girl. Shush listen." I would become very quiet and still, while I strained my ears to listen for this creature called the Whompus kitty. The next thing you knew, snuggled safe and secure on my Mother's lap, I would be sound asleep and Mother would put me to bed. Grandma's scaring was different. She would listen for me to tiptoe across the floor to the pot. She would give me time to get settled, then scratch and rap on the wall and go woooo. Hysterical with fright, I would flee the pot, leaving a trail of piss from the pot to the bed. She would cackle and say, "If you weren't such a little heathen, you wouldn't be a scardy cat. If you trust in God, you don't have a fear of boogers under the bed." I think in her own self-righteous way, she felt it to be her Christian duty to accept this tribe that she found foisted upon her and lead us into the enlightenment of the white man's or Christian way. Which in her mind, were one and the same. I would think any new daughter-in-law wishes for love and acceptance from her husband's mother. Mother wanted desperately to fit in Missouri Coffman's world. Daddy's answer to the conflict was to imbibe in alcohol. Thus softening the edges of his mind, enough he did not have to address the problems of quarrelling women folk. He kept his head to deep in the bottle to notice. The more miserable things become the more he drank and the angrier Mother became, with no outlet for her anger but toward Daddy, Bo, and me. Till it became a vicious cycle. Abuse became a way of life. In the name of spare the rod, spoil the child. You may ask me, how I can forgive this. Read on and please understand.

There was more than one type of brutality at work here. The delicate human physic can be destroyed beyond repair without ever lifting a hand in violence. I know this due to the fact, I found myself in the same position in later years of my life, long after I watched it done to my Mother. In retrospect, I examine the past as an adult with a clearer vision, and understand now, what I could not understand as a child, and yes, I can and did forgive Mother.

Mother's self-esteem was damaged in the early years on the mountain by her in laws from her first husband. The mistreatment by the man at the spring coupled with the disparaging, prejudiced remarks made by other's was so mortifying it scarred this gentle women's soul for life. She thought she was bettering herself by cutting lose her past and her family to embrace Louie's family. She believed this was something she must do to be a dutiful wife and began a new and better life for her children. Grandma and Daddy convinced Mother, we would all be better off if she separated herself from our previous life before we ever moved from Birmingham. Whether consciously or unconsciously, Missouri recognized this weakness of low self-esteem and used it to browbeat Mother into subjugation to her will, and attempt to make me into her idea of a proper little lady. She was in simple words, a control freak of the cruelest nature. The strain of trying to measure up to her mother-in-law's ideals; deal with an alcoholic husband, do the work of a farm wife, and stay pregnant nine months out of the year, while trying to retain some of her own human dignity, broke my Mother's mind. I feel sure the way Mother treated Mama, prayed on her conscience and played a part to some degree of Mothers break from reality.

I have noticed at most of the extreme pinnacles of hardship in my life, there has been someone or some outside influence to buffer me from the worst of the pain and conflict.

I do believe in guardian angles. They are other human beings God places along the most precarious routes of our lives to assist us. Pearl was such a one.

On wash days or days when the work was extra heavy, a black women named Pearl came to help with the work. Mother was expecting her and Louie's second child. I was most curious about Pearl but leery of her. She was the first black person I had ever known personally. I gave her a wide berth but watched her from the corner of my eyes. She never approached me or spoke to me.

She treated me much as one would treat a wild creature. She was pretending to ignore me till I was curious enough to approach her.

In our neighborhood, the women rivaled each other on the whiteness of their bed linens. Mother boiled and blued her sheets with Rinso White to a fare-thee-well before she hung them to dry. Pearl declared Mother's sheets to be the whitest, brightest sheets on any line, anywhere.

If I wanted Mother's permission to do something, I would motion the action and asked, "Hum Mudder, hum." If it was agreeable to her, she would answer um-hum, if not she would say no. On this occasion, she was standing over the big iron pot used to boil white clothes. Punching stick in hand, lost in her little dream world, she slowly punched down her boiling sheets. Along comes I, red socks in hand. I motion toward the pot with the socks and asked, "Hum Mudder, Hum." "Um-hum," she answered. I tossed the socks into the pot. By the time she realized something was wrong, the boiling water was red, and so were the sheets. Mother was the first to ever own pink and red, paisley bed linens. The party line was busy and it did not take long for word to spread of the strange phenomena hanging on the Gentry clothes line. Cars began to slowly cruise up and down the road and one could see the ladies craning their necks to get a good view of this unbelievable sight. Pearl visited a few households that afternoon inquiring about work for herself and her man, Sam. While at the back door of these homes, she dropped a bit of gossip about Mrs. Gentry and her wish for colorful décor in her home. Miss May walked down the hill to personally congratulate Mrs. Gentry on her originality and daring do. Mother accepted all praise with iced tea and graciousness, then showed the pattern for the matching doilies she was about to crochet.

The town of Jemison was a relatively safe place to live in the 1940s era as were most small country towns in the south. The KKK was active but not much was ever said about them, except whispers now and then. So and so got a beating because he neglected his family, or that uppity young colored boy was threatened with a cross burning because he didn't know his place.

There had been no problem with Bo and me disappearing for short periods of time as long as we stayed within calling distance of the house. I honestly do not know what set Mother off this time. I had learned to watch her eyes. There would be a certain look there. They would sparkle darkly and manifest an intense snapping look. Almost as if she was having trouble holding them steady. When I saw this look, I tried to keep Bo and me out of her way if possible. Sometimes, Daddy took the brunt of it. She would fly off the handle and go for him with her punching stick. It was not always possible to avoid her.

We had left the yard to watch the pollywogs in a ditch, by the road. I told Bo, we might get to see one turn to a frog. We did not stay long. Upon returning to the house, I knew one or both of us were in trouble. One never knew with Mother. You might be wakened from a sound sleep at daybreak, being pounded in the face or having a switch whacking you from one end to the other, and never know what you were being beaten for. You might be a little late getting home from wherever you had been sent, oh, any excuse would do. It did not matter. These beatings had begun after the birth of Fred and Mother became pregnant again with her and Louie's second child, Chester. As time passed, they escalated and became more severe.

Upon our return, we stood in the edge of the yard and watched as she calmly plated three long, knotty switches together into a braided whip. Oh dear Jesus, surely she was not going to whip us with that. I felt Bo tremble beside me. I put my arm around his shoulder and together we slowly walked across the yard. He was such a small little feller, at the age of three. Built like his daddy, he was of a small stature with light blond hair. He was just a quiet little boy who followed his big sister and was obedient to my smallest request in his loyalty to me. Once we drew close within her reach, her hand shot out and closed around Bo's arm. I should have walked across the yard without him by my side. It might have made a difference. I will never know. She dragged him into the house and to the side bedroom. I ran around the house to the bedroom window. It was open but I was too short to see inside. I could hear the whip

65

whistle through the air and Bo's screams when it found its mark, till he passed beyond screams and there were only moans. What to do? I had to stop it. I hit the side of the house with my fists and screamed over and over; "I hates you, hates you, hates you." When I realized everything had grown quite except Bo's moans, I looked up. Mother was standing in the window with the worn-out and broken whip switch in her hand. She reached out the window and grabbed me by the front of my dress, lifting me to the window ledge. She then delivered a clout to the left ear that rang my bell before she dropped me to the ground. I crawled away toward the corn field till I was able to stand. Then I ran into its cover to hide. I waited a long time and fretted the whole while about Bo, I did not know how bad he might be hurt. After a while, I crept out of the corn field, and back into the house. I found my Bo bathed and dressed in clean overalls and a long sleeved shirt. The only sign of his ordeal was the long bloody whelp on his neck and the side of his face, and the hurt in his haunted little blue eyes. He did not move or speak. He sat there all afternoon still and quite till Mother called us to supper. He went to the table and ate all on his plate without a word. Then he went to bed without saying his prayers. I went to bed and pulled the covers over my head and cried for him. I had failed my little brother.

My ear hurt for three days from the blow I had received. The ear and left side of my head was bruised. By the end of the third day, the pain had become so intense, I cried continuously. Mother heated a box of salt. She put the hot salt in a pillow slip which she put under my head. Sometime during the night, something inside my ear ruptured. The relief was tremendous. After that popping sensation, the ear drained and I quit crying and went to sleep. By morning, my hair and bed linins were covered with the bloody drainage from my ear. Mother had to set up the wash tubs a day ahead of time to scrub my head and do laundry. We had electricity now but she still boiled her whites and rinsed everything through the tubs three times. The children got bathed in the rinse water. After scrubbing my head, she came after me with a comb. We did not own a hair brush. As a matter of fact, I never saw a hair brush till we visited Aunt Ethel and I saw my cousin Bonnie use one. I took one look at the comb and decided I had enough. I screamed, "No," and dove under the bed. "Come out and get it combed now or you will be sorry. The tangles will be worse once it dries you know." I crawled farther toward the back of the bed which sat against the wall. "Don't tare. Oo huts me. Go way," I wailed. Mother went out to wash the sheets. I napped under the bed for a while, then woke to the call of nature. I went out the front door to make a roundabout tour to the little house out back. There was no way to get past Mother on the return trip. I raced down the hill and tried to dodge her but she caught me. "Now you behave, little miss. Sit down on this bench and let me get the tangles out of that hair." Pearl stepped up to the bench. "Umm-umm. It do looks like a stump full O granddaddies, don't it? If you would likes Miss Janie, I got the sheets all wrung out and laying over the line. I could take care of the child's hair fou you. Not good, you be lifting yo arms up so long to be combing out tangles, and mind you Miss Janie the line is down low. Soon as you git the sheets spread and pinned I will heft the pole line up so them sheets be high enough not to drag tha ground. Don't want no mud on dem pink sheets. No ma'am." Mother seeming relieved to relinquish the task handed the comb to Pearl. She sat on the bench and motioned me to come closer. I stepped a little closer but not to close. I left myself a little running room, should I need it. The black women pressed her lips tight but one corner turned up and her eyes twinkled. "Now, you knows you to perty a baby to leave yo hair in thet kind o mess." I put my hands over my hair and shook my head no. "Hut Mith Purl." "Now, you don't be callen me Miss, little Missy." "Well what I call?" I asked her. "Call me Aunt Pearl," she answered. "Why? Not my aunt." She reached for my hand and drew me closer while turning my back to her. "I will tell you while I gets these tangles out." Gnarled but gentle fingers began to untangle the snarls in my hair painlessly, bit by bit. As she worked, she questioned me. "Why do you not want to call me Pearl? Just answer me. You don't got to pay no mind to how you says it baby. Aunt Pearl don't hold with proper talk no how." I did make an effort to speak slowly that I might articulate as clear as possible. "You grownup," I said. "I not call you first name." She picked up the comb and began to use it on my hair. As she ever so carefully detangled she explained farther, "You can't call me miss cause you a white child and I am colored. That's plain as I knows how to put it, but you going to be my little white angel and I be yo aunt Pearl. That means I gonna takes care o you best I can." "Why?" I asked again. "Cause God said so, but Lawd, Lawd, how comes he puts such a test on old Pearl, I don knows. Now you do like Aunt Pearl say. Pay tention, no more miss to me, and no more yes mam and no mam, cause that's the way things is." "Okay." I agreed as Aunt Pearl began to braid my hair. She then pulled me closer and asked. "Would you like to visit Miss May some? She gets awful lonesome on thet hill. She got lots of fun things little girls would like up there. You start school next year. Do you good to talk to Miss May. You got lots to learn, and it do Miss May good to. She got lots to teach you." I said it might be a good thing to go see Miss May, at least once. Aunt Pearl said she would speak to Mother about the matter.

I did not forget the warning Aunt Pearl gave me. I was careful to adhere to her request; for I sensed an under layer of caution, and yes, fear in her voice. I did not understand why it should be so. I only knew there was something terribly wrong when someone as good as Aunt Pearl had to fear anything as innocent, as a little white girl speaking to her elder in a respectful manner. There was a lot of good, and some not so good in small southern towns. Let the tapestry show, this was my life in the south in 1945.

Chapter 7

MOCKING BIRD HILL

Mother packed a picnic basket. I watched her fill it with good things to eat. "Get Jimmy Ray and come with me," she told me. She led us up the hill toward the end of the road. It was my first trip to that mysterious place from whence came the songs of the mocking birds. What, I beheld was breathtaking. The yard was filled with the splendor of every gender of plant and blooming flower that could grow in that area. A sight boasting all colors the imagination could conceive greeted the eye. The outside parameter of the property was surrounded by a forest of trees and shrub. It resembled a delicate bowl of many colored jewels settled in a nest of green. Everywhere my eyes chose to feast; I saw birds, butterflies, and bees of every color. Nature's children rustled and peered from the lush foliage. The crowning glory in the scene was the simple log cabin set in the middle of all the splendor.

Mother delivered Bo to her friend who lived across the road from Miss May. He and one apple pie was dropped at Mrs. Bartle's. Mother and I crossed the road and walked across the yard on a path of slate stones to arrive at the front porch steps of the log cabin. Pausing at the foot of the steps, she smoothed my hair and straightened my dress. "Mind your manners or you won't get invited back," she admonished. Then she led me up the steps to the porch and knocked on the door. Miss. May opened the door. I had seen her before but not up close. She was a tall slender woman, as tall as mother but that is where all resemblance ended. Miss May had a large bosom. She stood straight with her shoulders back and head

69

up. Her hair was like white thistledown piled atop her head. She was a formidable sight at first look. Her chin and lips had a stern appearance about them, till one looked in her eyes. A twinkle there, gave her true nature away. "Hello Mrs. Gentry. How good of you to come, I was about to have tea. I would be most pleased if you would join me." Her manner was gracious as she welcomed us into her home. She spoke with a fluted bell like quality of voice. Overcome with shyness, I leaned and hid my face against Mother's leg. She nudged me and I knew this meant, stand up straight. I did but ducked my head and played with my fingers. Miss. May reached down to place her fingers beneath my chin. Firmly but gently she lifted my head till she could see my face. Looking down at me with a smile, she spoke with that extraordinary voice I eventually come to trust and love. "And you are," She trilled. I gulped a deep breath, "Betty." I answered her. "Ah yes, the little girl with the big imagination," she said as she ushered Mother and I into the kitchen. "I have heard good things about you, and I look forward to us getting to know one another. Your mother tells me you read very well all by yourself. That is a great accomplishment at your age. Won't you-all sit here at the table while I fix the tea? Betty, would you like cookies and milk?" To answer her questions would have been redundant for she had everything on the table even as she spoke, "Mrs. Gentry, may we dig into this basket? It smells wonderful." Mother looked very pleased and asked Miss May to call her Jane. Agreeing Miss May asked mother to call her Eleanor. I had never known Mother to drink hot tea before or since unless visiting Miss May but she seemed to enjoy it. I made up my mind, should I ever come back, I would ask for a cup of hot tea. I enjoyed my treat. Believe you me, it was a treat. Fresh thick baked tea cakes filled with roasted sugared pecans and jellied fruit candies. My heart gave a funny little jump when I noticed the red and white checked table cloth. Could it be? No, it cannot be. This was not the mountain. It is best to forget it and Noah's Ark too. While we ate, Miss May and Mother talked. Somewhere in the course of their discussion, I heard Mother say to Miss May, "We don't encourage her with her make believe." My ears perked up as I brought my mind away from the mountain and the lost yesteryear. I decided it might be in my best interest to pay attention to the present. "I don't believe I understand," said Miss May. "What is wrong with a healthy imagination?" Mother looked a bit uncomfortable as she sought words to explain. Miss May laid her hand on Mothers and gently patted as she spoke in a soothing voice. "I understand Jane. Little pitchers' have big ears. May we discuss this later? I would like to help in some way. It would be good to be allowed to brush off my teaching and counseling skills to use once again." I looked around as I drummed my heels against the chair rounds. Miss May had lots of pictures hanging on her walls but I did not see any ears. Maybe, she meant tea pitchers. They had one ear on one side. I would have to give this some thought later. Maybe I could ask Aunt Pearl the meaning of this statement.

The conversation turned general as Mother gathered up the empty picnic basket and covering cloth. Miss May asked me if I would like to come visit twice a week. I looked at Mother. She smiled and nodded yes. "Now Betty, what do we say to Miss May?" I ducked my head and mumbled an incoherent thank you. Miss May stooped to my level, placing her hand once more under my chin, she brought my head up and looked me square in the eyes "I am a speech therapist as well as a teacher. Have you ever worked with a therapist before?" I shook my head no and ask. "What that?" She smiled as she answered. "Someone who helps another learn to speak. You see, I used to stutter when I was a little girl. It is called a speech impediment. A lot of people have it, but you can and will learn to speak, if you really want to. How old are you?" I held up five fingers. I had just turned five, and some time I would forget to stick out my thumb. Miss May took my hand in hers and counted, "One, two, three, four, five, the bear stole honey from the hive." She tugged on each finger as she stroked downward, the same way Mother did when she milked Bossy the cow. I could remember this. Five and hive sounded alike. I could put sound alike words with numbers. That would make the numbers easy to remember. Hot diggadee dog! I could learn to count fast. I felt so smug in my ignorance. How little I knew. Math was to be my downfall. No matter how hard I try, numbers would always lie to me. My checkbook is proof of this failure. I am much like the lady who stood in front of the judge and explained, "But your Honor, I could not have been out of money. I still have checks." The written word was to be my forte'.

We picked up Bo on our way home. As we ambled down the dusty road, Mother pointed out two Robins doing a courting dance. "When they mate, they mate for life," she explained, "Till death parts them. That is when you see the robin cry." This was a lesson, I was to remember years later when I witnessed the death of a female robin. She had been struck by an automobile. Her mate stood guard over her with his head and wings drooping. I feared for his safety. He was too close to the traffic in a busy work area. I picked up the small broken robin and moved her farther from the road. The next time I drove by, I was amazed to find the male bird building a bower of flowers over his mate. He stayed by her side grieving the rest of the day. By the next morning, he was gone.

Mother was a shy woman about a lot of things. I knew it was not wise to get to personal with my questions, else she would scold and send me off to my own devices, but on this day she seemed relaxed and at ease. I took the opportunity to ask questions about the things she was telling me. "What is courting, Mother?" Mother looked down as we walked a ways while she thought best how to answer my question. "Why, I guess you would say it is two people getting to know each other with the notion of getting married, if they decide they like each other. If its critters, they mate. Some mate for life. Others mate, then go their separate ways, and don't ask about mating till you get old enough to understand." "Yes ma'am," I answered. I did not tell her I already knew about mating. Aunt Burma had explained about the birds and bees to me. Even though, I was a bit confused as to just what bees had to do with it all. I did not feel I should tell mother about that. I knew when to let well enough alone and not foul someone else. Aunt Burma had come down for a visit. She had lured Mother back to Birmingham for a short visit by telling Mother a lie. She told Mother, Mama was really sick and about to die. Mother reached Birmingham and found Mama well and hearty. When called to accounts for the lie she told, Aunt

Burma excused it by saying she just wanted to bring her sister and mother together again. She felt this would be the only way Louie would let Mother come to Birmingham. Now Aunt Burma and Mother would write each other sometimes. I did not want to start a big hullaballoo between sisters and I sure did not want Grandma to get her teeth sunk into that kind of information. Her old hide was tough as wilt leather but Mother's feelings were to tender for Grandma's criticism. Also, I had learned to my sorrow who the backlash struck when Grandma took the tomahawk after Mother.

Sometimes, Mother walked with me when I visit Miss May. Sometimes, I went alone. The times Mother walked to top of the hill with me, were special for the both of us. Miss May taught me language skills, the alphabet, and how to count by one, fives, and tens. Mother showed me the different plants in the woods and ways they could be used for food and medicine. She taught me the way of God's wild creatures. She showed me how to examine the scat and foot prints to determine the size of an animal and how long since it had passed that way. Did it eat flesh or was it a harmless vegetarian? She told me of the different stages to watch for in rabid animals. Mother told me of the time, her mama was attacked by a dog. I listened avidly as she began her story.

"Daddy came from plowing that day and said to Mama. "Git up before sunup in the morning Dovie, pack us some dinner and we'll go fishing. I saw a whost nest out back and the grubs init are just right fer bait. You young'uns make hast and fetch all the worms and crickets ye can find." Daddy would smoke the wasp of the nest, tear it down and put it in a sack to carry the larvae to the creek to bait our hooks.

We were all scattering out to find our favorite fishing spot. Mama got her hook in the water first and was laughing because she beat Daddy. He was bellowing at her while he ran with his fishing pole in his hand. "No fair Dovie, but ye jest wait and I git rid ah this dang basket oh yors and I bet I show yah how to catch a fish first." A large dog came running and staggering from the woods. He was making a strange moaning sound in his throat and foaming at the mouth. He seemed to be trying to get to the water but Mama was between him and the creek and could not move fast enough." Mother stared at the ground with a pensive look as she seemed to gather her thoughts. "I saw Daddy break a heavy limb from a tree while he screamed at J.D. and Tommy. "Mad dog, mad dog! Stay away. Keep back! For God's sake Dovie, run!" It was too late, Mama was on the ground and Daddy was terrified the children would be bitten trying to help Mama. He beat the dog to death to get him off her. She had bites all up and down both legs. I remember Daddy trembling and crying as he said, "You know what we have to do, Dovie." Mama was shaking and crying. "Yes John, I know." Daddy took her home to the wood shed and locked her in. Mama remained there in the shed for I do not know how long. It was my responsibility to take her food and slide it through the slot in the door. After some days passed, she would beg and cry for me to let her out. She would plead, "Jane, you can see I'm not mad, please! Unbar the door." I would not do it because Daddy warned us he would have to lock us away too if we let her out. Oh, I wanted to so bad but we were all scared to. Finally after weeks in the shed, I do not know how long, Daddy let her out. After that, it seemed Mama and Daddy were never close again. She was pregnant with John L. when it happened and, well your uncle John L. just was not right when he was born. It was like Mama blamed Daddy and kept him at arm's length. Seemed to take the fun out of her and Daddy was unhappy. He also blamed Mama when someone carelessly left a bottle of lye water sitting on the window seal. John L. had just learned to walk by that time. He pulled up to the window and got hold of the bottle of lye water. He was drinking from it when Mama caught him. How he lived through that, no one but the good Lord himself knows. I thought to myself, I don't blame Mama. If someone locked me up and left me, I wouldn't want to be around them ever again." "Why Grandpa mean," I asked. "He wasn't mean," she answered. "He was just ignorant. Back in those days', people who lived on the mountain didn't go to doctors. No one knew there was such a thing as shots for rabies. When a body was bitten by a mad animal, it was certain death but before they died, they would go mad and they would bite anyone they came in contact with and that person would have hydrophobia. The ones who loved those sick ones most were afraid of them but wanted to stop their suffering. So most of the time, they would keep them locked up until they were sure they did not have rabies. If it proved out they did have it, it was sad but the sick person must be killed as merciful as possible. Most often, they were smothered between two mattresses. It would take some time for the infected human to get sick and show signs of illness. Daddy didn't know how long, so he kept Mama locked away until he was sure she wasn't infected with rabies." I accepted this explanation but I still felt a good bit of resentment toward Grandpa Walden on Mama's behalf. I knew he had caused her much sadness. I took note of this story and learned from it. Never walk down a road or wooded area without carrying a long sturdy stick or a gun, if you are a grown up. Do not pet strange animals.

Mother taught me to be thankful for the gifts I received from Mother Earth. They were put there for the benefit of the children of the Great Father of all creation. Each living creature and plant was important in the scheme of life. No matter its size or inclinations, it has the right to live when at all possible. All life is sacred. Take it only for food, clothing, or self-protection. When you have the need to take an innocent life, ask its forgiveness and commend its spirit to the Great Father. These are things my mother taught me.

Mother wanted some time away from the house. She planned to take me exploring. Aunt Pearl would take care of Bo, Fred, and Baby Chester. Daddy had left to haul a load of produce to Birmingham and was not expected back until tomorrow. "Go relax for a while, Miss Janie. Don't you fret over a thing. I'll make supper, so's ya'll kin wait til the cool of the evening to come home." "Thank you Pearl, What would I do without you? I really need a little time away." Mother told her. Aunt Pearl reached with a worked worn hand and patted Mothers back. "I knows you do, Miss Janie. Why don't you come and sit? You got time. Let me comb and plait yo hair." She patted Mother while she guided her to the wooden rocking chair on the front porch. "It will make you feels better," she declared as she eased upon the screen door and tip toed inside to fetch the comb. We sure did not want to wake up the sleeping children, especially the new one. Daddy named him Chester and that young'un could break your heart with those pitiful sounds he made when he cried. A body just could not resist stopping whatever they were doing to pick him up "I swear Pearl, a hair fixing is your answer to every angst and complaint known to woman," laughed Mother. "Make me sleepy is what it'll do!" Aunt Pearl did not answer till she was outside again with the screen door eased closed. She stepped behind Mother's chair. "You git woke up when you start walken. Hep you walks easy, it will." She puckered her lips and gazed with incredulous bug eyed wonder at the back of Mother's head. I sat on the steps with my face hid against my knee. I bit my lip to keep my shoulders from shaking with suppressed laughter "Gots more pins in it en Carter's got little pills," she grumbled. "En ain't no wonder! It twisted up in corkscrews all over yo hade, Miss Janie. Why you wants to go twisting it in knots dat way? Um, um, umm." She shook her head as she pulled hair pins from Mother's hair and put them in her apron pocket. "Feels good that way," said Mother. "Keeps it from straggling down in my face in that hot kitchen." Aunt Pearl fussed as she patiently worked out the knots with her fingers. "Well, it will feel jes as good put up neat and sho look a lot better." When Aunt Pearl had finished, Mother's hair lay in a soft coil atop her head. The stress lines had eased from her face. "Now shoo! Get gone!" Aunt Pearl smiled as she shooed us like recalcitrant chicks from the porch. Mother giggled like a carefree girl. She took me by the hand and danced across the yard.

Mother went to the edge of the woods where she showed me how to look for a sturdy limb, and then break it in a way to leave a point on one end. "Always carry one with you when you walk alone, especially in a wooded area. You need something to stir the debris as you walk to scare away such things as snakes, even if you have a gun with you. It makes a good weapon against some other types of critters, if you will learn how to use it.

"Your Aunt Merty lost her boy Harold, because of a pack of wild dogs. The little feller had a weak heart. When the dogs attacked him and his brother they ran and climbed a tree, but Harold who was only eleven years old, fell from the tree. The fright was too much for him. He had a heart attack. His brother Gerald fought the dogs off with a stick. By the time help come, it was too late, Harold had gone to heaven. Our eldest sister has had a tough row to hoe where her children are concerned. She lost a little girl when she was a tiny babe. She was only three months old when she took with the fever and croup and nothing Mama could do, saved her. A white dove came and sat on the well curb and cooed three times. Mama stood like a statue, so still. Seemed like she stared all the way to heaven. Then she laid the baby in Merty's arms. Three hours later, the babe breathed her last breath." We stood quietly for a moment while Mother remembered. Then with a shake of her head, she seemed to collect herself and moved deeper into the woods.

"The point on the stick is useful for more than protection. They can be used to dig roots that are edible. I will show you lots of plants that are edible or can be used to make medicine and teach you how to use it. You must promise me, you will not eat or take anything from the woods till you have learned the correct way." I solemnly gave my promise. Mac had taught me well. If I break a vow, I will lose the trust of others. Trust was very important. I understood the concept and reason of this value, my good word was my honor. To break it was unthinkable. Mother taught me a lot on those walks.

There were many fun things too. She showed me maypops and the sleep bush. When I brushed it's fronds with my hand, it would curl up and sleep. We laughed together as she picked beggar lice and cockle burs from my clothes and hair. It was fun to tease the Betsy bugs and watch them rear up on their hind legs and look so fierce, knowing they were totally harmless. This is where the expression, crazy as a Betsy bug originated. Those were good times. This was the Mother I loved.

Alice Virginia Coe Walden,
and (Grandson) Tommy Walden

Betty Lowery telling The
Story of forget me not

Chapter 8

FORGET ME NOT

I awoke one morning to a racket that sounded like a hell haunt in full cry. I could hear screaming, wailing, and banging coming from the kitchen. I thought I was having a nightmare. I pinched myself. No indeedy, I was wide awake. Now you and Fair Faye have done it, I thought. You have messed around and brought one of your banshees to life. I saw the door between the living room and kitchen was closed, and that was unusual in itself. I left my bed and tiptoed to the door. I opened it just a wee crack, just enough to take a peep see what was going on in there. I did not need to get my ear to the door, I could hear very well what was said. Daddy was sitting at the table. He looked like a whipped puppy. He would open his mouth and rare back as if to say something in his defense, but he could not get a word in edgewise. Mother was whirling around the kitchen like a dervish, screeching terrible things at Daddy. Things like, sorry, good for nothing, low down. "Your Mother acts like the Gentry's are so high and mighty," she shrieked. "Me and mine are not good enough for ya'll. Why, she's got her nose so high in the air, if it rained, she would drown." She put her hand on her hip and stuck her nose in the air as she delivered this statement. "Now you got tha nerve to come in here, in my face and tell me you have lost all of the money you made from our produce, even the share we owe Mr. Deel? You should've been home two days ago. I have sat here and worried. If I found the truth of the matter, I would probably find your sorry tail has been laid up in Tin Pan Alley spending our survival money on whores as well booze." There was that Tin Pan Alley again. It truly must be a terrible place. She was always threatening to send me back there if I did not behave. As she let loose with this last diatribe, she hurled a cooking pot across the kitchen. I had not seen Mother in a state this bad, since the day Daddy was speaking to a friend of his and referred to her as his old squaw. You might gather by this time, she had been made to feel very sensitive about our Indian blood. So had I, but I told myself, I did not give a tinker's damn, so there! That was the way I dealt with it. Mother did not deal so well. As the cooking utensil sailed across the room, Daddy made to rise from his chair. "Uh-oh," I said when I saw Mother reach beside the stove for a stick of stove wood. I ran as quick and quietly as I could to the back bedroom. I knew Fred and Chester would be alright. They could not get up and get in the way, and I knew Daddy would protect the babies with his life, if necessary. No matter what he might be or do, that man loved his boys above all else, with the exception of his whiskey, that is. I also felt secure that no matter how out of control Mother got, she would never hurt one of her babies, but it was possible Bo could awake, and he was subject to run right in the middle of the free for all. Though, he was hardly more than a baby himself, he still felt a protective instinct toward his Mother. Neither had he learned to duck and cover yet. If I stuck around, Mother would tell me to run to a neighbor and get someone to call the sheriff. Daddy would block me or grab me, if he could get his hands on me, and tell me to stay. I wanted none of it. After the hoopla and tears were over, things would be all sugar and honey anyway, that is, if she didn't kill him first. I did fret about that, but for right now, Bo and I had to head for high timber. I drug him out of bed and raced through the house with him in tow. I did not take time to maneuver the porch steps. I made for the end of the porch and swung Bo to the ground, then jumped down behind him. I threw him none too gently into his red flyer wagon. He whimpered and I took time to give him a quick hug. "Sorry sweet," I whispered, "be quite. Everything fixin to go to hell in a hand basket round here, an I gotta make damn sure we ain't in tha basket." My teacher had called Mother to the school several times now about my colorful language and I did try to adhere to Miss May's tutelage but in times of stress, I would revert back to my no-no speech and the expletives I had picked up with it just popped out. Still does for that matter. "Hold on tight now." I said as I grabbed the handle of the flyer and ran as hard as my stubby little legs could go. I headed across the yard for the back side of the barn. I knew today was the day for Aunt Pearl to work for Miss May. If the fracas ended up in the yard, Aunt Pearl would hear it and come fetch us across the pasture to Miss May's. Daddy would be displeased because he would be embarrassed for the neighbors to know but I did not care. While we hid out behind the barn, I taught Bo to sing School Days with me. I did not want him to hear what was going on in the house, so I kept egging him on to sing louder and louder, till he was shouting. He drowned out the noise from the house. After a while, he began to complain. He was hungry. I ordered him to sit in the wagon until I returned. I went to the edge of the front porch and listened. I could hear Mother softly weeping. I went around to the back door and slipped into the kitchen and peered into the living room. Mother was sitting in her rocking chair. Daddy was on his knees with his arms around her, his head in her lap. There was blood on the side of his head, on his blind side. He was pleading with her to give him another chance. I tiptoed back the way I came. On the way out, I lifted a couple of leftover biscuits from the warmer on the back of the stove. I slipped out the back door, and stopped at the well, where I drew up the bucket containing a cake of butter wrapped in corn shucks. I used my fingers to open the biscuit and smear butter on them. Mother would skin my hide, if she saw me do that. One did not put their fingers in Mother's butter! I smoothed the butter, wrapped and put it back into the bucket, and lowered it into the well, then tied the bucked off. As I ran past the edge of the yard, I stripped off pepper seeds from the wild pepper grass and put it in the biscuits. I fed us, and then distracted Bo for a while longer, by showing him how to pick honeysuckle blossoms and suck the nectar for dessert. I guessed by this time, it was okay to go back to the house.

Mother and Daddy were sitting at the table drinking coffee. I sat in the living room with my ears perked. They were discussing the best way to salvage the situation. Daddy wanted to sell one of the cows. He said he could do this and sell his truck to come up with enough cash to satisfy the debt to the landlord. "When planting season comes again," he explained, "the beef calves will be ready to sell for seed money." Mother nixed the idea about the cow and the truck real quick. I did not understand why. I took it to mean she loved her cows so much, she could not stand to let one go. I thought this was a ridiculous attitude, considering the dilemma we seemed to be facing. It took my daughter, Sandra, after all these years to educate me about this. A family needed two cows. You breed one. Once she calves, she will give milk for her calf. When it can eat on its own, you wean the calf from its mother, but she will keep giving milk as long as you milk her every day until she goes dry. By this time, the other cow has gone through the same process and is ready to milk. That is why Mother refused to sell one of her cows. She said to Daddy, "I will sell some of my chickens. I will keep enough to give us eggs till next harvest. I can sell my canned goods, I have put up. I think I can get us through. Louie, we will need that truck. What if one of the children gets sick? We have to go all the way to Thorsby to find a doctor. It will take all we can do to get by, but we can make it. We will pay Mr. Deel. If we are careful, there will be enough to buy feed for the stock and chickens with enough left over for seed money comes time to plant. Your check will feed us and pay the electric bill and take care of any emergences that might come along." Mother sold all of her wonderful jams and preserves, all of her canned vegetables. She even sold the dried fruit. She sold her canned cracklings and the meat from the smoke house. Word spread and the town ladies were in and out, for several days. I watched her take out her crocheted doilies and sell them. Mother was an extraordinary seamstress. She designed and cut her own pattern to make herself a suit. The material was a tiny gray and black check. The lining was red and sewn in a way to turn out and make the collar and lapels, so they were red. Also there was three gold buttons on the front, she had filched from Daddy's button collection that he had started while he was in the army. I still have that button collection till this day and the rest of the buttons that matched the ones on Mother's suit. She made the skirt to match, with a white silk and lace blouse to bring the suit together. Mother made this on an old singer peddle sewing machine. I remember hearing her make exasperated sounds as she struggled with the silk. It was the first and only time, I ever heard my Mother swear. She looked so elegant to me when she wore it. It was the only nice clothes she had. Mother sold that outfit for thirty dollars. She grabbed me back, when I screamed no and tried to rip the coat from the lady's hand. The woman seemed flustered and remarked, "Well I have never seen a child take on so." Holding me fast, Mother answered. "The child is angry," but she made no apologies. I cried as the woman walked out the door with Mothers suit. "It's just clothes, Betty June," Mother soothed as she wiped my tears. "I can make more." "Mother, don't we have nough money now?" I ask as I buried my head against her. Mother sighed and said, "Come with me. I have something to show you." She led me to her bedroom, where she lifted me up to sit on her vanity stool. "I am going to show you something. This is a secret between you and me. You must promise to never tell anyone. Do you understand?" "Yes Mam," I whispered. "Do you promise?" She knew her girl well. Once a promise was given, the creeks could raise enough to flood the Pearly Gates and I still would not tell. Mother took the top of her powder box off. She then took the thirty dollars and worked it beneath the powder. "There is more money in there," she said, as she pulled out a piece of paper which she brushed off and handed to me. "Look at this. If anything happens to me, you take Jimmy Ray and this money and note. Go to the bus station. Give the note to the person at the ticket window. They will sell you two tickets to Birmingham. The person that gives you the tickets will make a phone call for you. The number is written on this paper. Then, they will put you on the right bus. Someone will meet you at the bus station in Birmingham. I have already made arrangements with the ticket agent." I asked Mother who would meet us. "I don't know but it will be family. You will know them when you see them. You will be safe." With trembling lips, I asked her. "What about Fred and Chedder? Can't I take them too?" "You can't handle two babies, but they will be alright. Louie will see to it they are taken care of." I tried to be brave for I felt a lot was depending on me, but I could not stop the tear I felt slide down my face.

We made it through that winter and spring living on dry beans, fatback, and cornbread as our staple, butter biscuit, and Golden Eagle syrup for breakfast. All that good food Mother had worked so hard to put aside for her family, and look what we had to eat. I hated the sight, smell, and taste of dried butter beans and fat meat. I gagged on the fat meat when I tried to eat it, but Daddy forced it down me with threats of a whipping if I did not eat it all. He would lean across the table and say, "Its better then you had before I came along." I hated him then. I thought he was being mean. I realized when I grew older, he was hurt because it was all he had to offer us, but it was his fault. In his alcohol soaked mind, he knew this and felt guilty. My refusal to eat pointed out something to him he did not want to accept. His family was going lacking because of him. When someone is guilty and in denial, and another person points the guilt out with their action and attitude, it creates strife from one toward the other. I cut my teeth on strife. It made me strong.

It was in the early spring, Mother received a letter from her Aunt Mae Watts. It read, "Jane if you can, come to Alabama City as soon as possible. I took Mother from John and Kate and brought her home with me. She is very sick and asking for you. She won't tell anybody else what she wants. She insists she will, 'tell Jane when she gets here'." The letter had been sent to Noah's Ark, then forwarded twice before it reached Mother. Daddy agreed to let Mother go. I saw him hold her tight while she promised she would come back to him. He purchased train tickets for us all to Birmingham. He could not go. He was getting the fields ready for planting.

As the train sped down the tracks, I watched the landscape swish by and listened to the wheels. Clickity clack, clickity clack, till the sound became, going back, going back. Once again, the mountain called. Way up on the mountain where they bury the dead, I wait for you. I caught the scent of red dust and wild flowers. Suddenly, my memory came startlingly clear. I remembered the meaning of the call, the dust, and flower scents. There was a grave in a copse of trees. I knew who, where, and what I should do. With a strange calm and contentment, I fell asleep to the clatter of the train wheels, going back, going back. I awoke and the understanding of the call from my mountain; where I must go, and what I must do, was lost. It has never returned. Though I have struggled to remember, I cannot retrieve it. I hear only the haunting call, the wind sighing through the trees. I smell the dust and flowers. I have a tender feeling of something, or someone so lonely and so sad.

From Birmingham to Alabama City, we traveled in a truck. Bo and I rode in the back of the truck with some of our cousins. I do not remember which ones. I only remember hay in the truck bed, and fighting to keep their hands out of my Cheerio box, while I hung on to Bo with the other hand.

Allace Virginia Coe Walden, Mother of Great Aunt Mae Walden Watts, and Grandpa John Walden had passed on to her reward, and laid to rest before we arrived. Mother and Aunt Mae tearfully embraced and Mother explained the misfortune of the late letter. "I only wish I knew what she wanted Jane." Aunt Mae exclaimed. "Do you have any idea of what on earth it could have been?" Mother sat down and motioned Aunt Mae to sit on the sofa beside her. Mother put her arms around her and spoke softly. "Aunt Mae, you remember how Grandma would get sick and call me to her bedside? Every time she got sick, she thought she was dying and called for me. She always asks for the same thing. She would say, don't forget me Jane. Put a bouquet of Forget-me-nots in my hand. Tie them with a blue ribbon and when you get to glory land, I will wave them at you, so you will know me. That is all, I can think of Aunt Mae. All I know to do is find some Forget-me-nots and plant them on her grave. She wanted to be remembered. She wanted to leave her mark on this earth that said, I was here. I will plant her Forget-me-nots, Aunt Mae, and I promise you as long as there is a Walden standing, she will not be forgotten." So began the tradition of the Forget-me-not. When I lose a loved one, it is in memory of Allace Virginia Coe Walden and for my Mother's promise. I place a bouquet of these little blue flowers in their hand.

When my Aunt Lilly died, I went to Mother's house to go to the funeral with her. "Betty," she said. "Go look out the window at Lilly's back yard and tell me what you see." Looking out the window, I wondered just what it was I was supposed to be looking for. "Well," I mused. "I see lots of pretty flowers." She pinched me. "You can't see the woods for the trees. Don't you see the blue flowers? I swear Betty, they were not blooming yesterday. But today, they are solid blooms." I could only marvel at the sight. The back yard beds were full of the little blue flowers. "I want you to make a bouquet for Lilly and put in her hand. Tell the story of For-get-me-not, least some might forget. Will you do that for me and her?" "Yes Mother. I won't forget," I promised as I kissed her cheek and went to gather the flowers. I smiled at the blue sky and the blue flowers and remembered Grandma Coe as I gathered the blossoms.

Grandma Allace was a very tiny woman. She was loved by all, for her kind and sweet nature. She was also one of those who imparted knowledge from the distant past with her stories of times gone by. I personally do not remember my Great Grandma Coe, but I listened avidly to the stories my Mother, aunts, and uncles passed down from her. Her Great Grandparents had migrated to America from Wales, to escape the English tyrants, the starvation of famine, and death that was upon the land of Ireland and Scotland.

Grandma Coe told Mother, the Walden's ancestors had left Europe, fleeing the inquisition to take sanctuary in Holland. Upon researching the origin of the name Walden, I was able to my satisfaction to verify this.

In the twelfth century, a group of people called the Waldiens, who took their name from their leader, a man named Waldo, were accused of being heretics. They believed that all men should have the right to preach and spread the word of God according to the teachings of Jesus Christ when he lived on this earth. Reading the bible was only for the rich leaders of the Catholic Church. The lower class masses flocked to the preachers of the gospel in large numbers. The Pope was petitioned to allow these ministers to preach to the common man. The petition was denied. The persecution of these people was so dire, they were forced to separate into smaller groups and flee for their lives. Some hid in the mountains of the Swiss Alps, some escaped into Germany, and others to Holland. They were run to earth like hunted animals. Afterwards, they were either murdered or placed in captivity/dungeons to face torture and slow death. The plight of these people was so pitiful; the blind poet, John Milton 1608-74, was moved in his compassion to write a poem of their sacrifice and a chastisement of shame to the catholic pope.

On The Late Massacre in Piedmont

Avenge oh Lord thy slaughtered saints, whose bones lie scattered
On the Alpine mountain cold; even them
who kept thy truth so pure of old
When all our fathers worshiped stocks and stones, forget not;
In thy book record their groans, who were
thy sheep and in thy ancient fold
Slain by the bloody Piedmonts that rolled
mothers with infants down the rocks
Their moans the vales redoubled to the hills and they to heaven
Their martyred blood and ashes sow o'er all the
Italian fields where still doth sway the triple tyrant;
that from these may grow a hundred fold
Who having learnt thy way early may fly the Babylonian woe.

It was the offspring's of these first protestants, the great twice grandparents of John Walden who made their way, finally, from Holland to America, where they settled in Coal County, which was a Coal mining country in the Appalachian Mountains. There is no place known as Coal County, but all counties in coal mining parts of North America are called Coal Counties, even now. It was Grandma Allace, who taught Mother to grow the Coal Miners Flower, or as some referred to it later, the Depression Flower. Grandma Allace was forever wishing someone would take her back to Coal County. Sand Mountain could not compare with her beautiful Appalachian hills and hollows. The shine was not as good either! It was used only for medicinal purpose, you understand. Grandma Allace's favorite pastime was fishing. Even after she grew too old and frail to go on her own, her son would carry her and a chair to her favorite fishing hole. He would sit her in her chair and bait her hook. There she would be content to sit for hours. One day, she asked her son to take her fishing. "Aww Ma," Grandpa said, "Not today. Maybe tomorrow, okay? Today, I have plans." As he went out the door, he saw his Mother wipe her eyes with her apron and heard her softly sigh. He ignored the prick of his conscience and kept going. Grandpa must have been hunting that day. Otherwise, why would he have been in the woods? He never said, but he came home out of breath from running. He was scratched and bruised from one end to the other. Mama looked at him with dismay. "My Lord John, what in the world happened to you?" He stood in the middle of the kitchen and looked at Mama with a confused expression on his face for a moment. Then he answered her. "I don't know what the hell happened to me, Dovie. I Thought the devil were after me. I heard somein in the bushes but I couldn't see nuthin. I guess I panicked and ran. Those tree limbs and bramble bushes seemed like they whipped me and tripped me up all tha way home." Mama wiped her hands with her apron, then using it as a pot holder took the coffee pot off the stove and poured him a cup. "Sit down, John, before you fall down. Now why would you take such a notion in your head that the devil would be after you?" Grandpa fiddled with his cup then with a sheepish look said, "Well I felt so damn bad sayin no to Ma and leavin her here. Maybe I thought the devil ought to take me. Guess, I punished myself. Mama smiled and said, "I done told you about that Whomphus Cat, John. She don't take kindly to those who don't give the right attention to their dependents." Grandpa made a wry face and asked. "What is this Whomphus Cat, you have been scaring my kids with all these years?" The children gathered close to hear Mama's answer. "It was passed down from an old Cherokee story of a young Indian maid. She was so pleasing to look upon, everyone spoiled her. She grew to become a very demanding and strong willed young woman. She resented staying in the village doing what was considered woman's work, while the men went on long hunting trips. She ask to go but her husband refused. It was taboo and unheard of for a woman to go hunting. She dressed herself in a panther skin and followed the braves on the hunting trip. As the men made camp, they discovered her in her hiding place. She was carried before the counsel. Their decision was to cast her from the tribe. She could be heard at night screaming and wailing, as she roamed the wilderness alone. She became a creature half cat and half woman. The Whomphus Cat. Her spirit wanders the wilderness places of the mountains till this day." "Well you can be sure whatever it was, you won't catch me ever sayin no to my Ma agin."

While I am on the subject of Grandpa, I will tell you this. He and Aunt Mae stayed on the outs, most of the time. Those two carried sibling squabbling to new dimensions. They did come together, once in later years, at the wake of a close family member. Someone had purchased an unusual funeral wreath. The wreath was made of glittery black foil decorated with red and white roses. A black telephone was mounted in the bottom of the wreath. At the top there was a white ribbon streamer with gold letters that announced, God called and he answered. Grandpa and Aunt Mae were overawed with the beauty of this wreath. As they stood there and gazed at it, like two starry eyed children looking upon a lollipop tree, Grandpa said to his sister, "Mae, I'll make a deal with you." "What kind ah deal," she asked suspiciously. "Well," said Grandpa. "See, we can make a pact. If I die first, you buy me a wreath just like that one. If you go first, I will buy you one jes like it." Aunt Mae snorted, "John Walden you lying old skinflint. You ain't never bought nuthin fer nobody, much less me." "I swear Mae, say truth. I highly admire that wreath, an I figure it's a sure bet you gonna outlive me. What ya say, Pax?" Aunt Mae studied a moment then said, "John, you swear if I die first, you promise you gonna buy me that same wreath, right there." "I swear it Mae, truth, I promise." Aunt Mae slapped Grandpa on the back. "Okay John, but remember you will have to face me in eternity and I would follow you all the way to hell just to jab you in the rear with a pitchfork, if you play me false." As it turned out Aunt Mae died first. Cousin Gerald made Grandpa get out of his overalls and put on pants to wear to the wake. Grandpa stood by his sister's coffin to make his last farewells. Looking down at her, he slowly shook his head and said. "I know what I promised Mae, but ya gotta understand. I can't afford that wreath. It's too expensive." It was right then his suspenders snapped and his pants fell to the floor. To Gerald's chagrin, not only had he lost his pants, he had on no drawers. "Mae!" Grandpa howled shaking his fist at the coffin, "I know you did that. I heard you laugh." Poor Gerald was so out done. He struggled to get Grandpa's pants up. It wasn't an easy task, for Grandpa in his rage, was raving and jigging like a bug on a hot griddle. As Gerald drug him away, Grandpa was heard to say. "She done that. Keep laughing, bitch. Wait till I catch up with you."

I am proud to be able to tell you, before he died, Grandpa turned his heart and life over to God. In his last years, he was diabetic. He lost one leg, due to this condition. He insisted on keeping the shoe to his missing foot in his pocket at all times. As time passed, the doctors needed to amputate his other leg. Again, he insisted on carrying this shoe in his other pocket. One day while giving him his bath, the aid misplaced Grandpa's shoes. He had nurses and aids running thither and yon, searching for his misplaced shoes. They were turning the nursing home upside down. There was no peace to be seen, till they were found. The shoes finally turned up in a dirty linen basket. Mother asked, "Daddy, why do you insist on carrying those old shoes in your pocket." "Because," he replied testily. "I want them put in the coffin with me. Jesus promised me a new body when I arise. I don't intend to traipse through eternity barefoot." Such simple faith, from a man who lived so hard a life, is a testimony to all of the Lord God Jehovah's loving capacity to forgive, and grant the peace of passive understanding to the worst as well as the best of us.

Chapter 9

GOD'S LITTLE BLESSINGS

I played with our dog Snowball. This was his name because he was snow white and he came to us with the first winter snow. Mother heard crying outside. Daddy went out to investigate, and there in the snow was a beautiful puppy. Daddy said he was a Feist. That is a small dog developed for hunting in the southeast United States. I thought God sent him to us with the snow for Christmas. Daddy said he bet old Sam left it there for us kids. Sam denied any such thing. We taught him to fetch and when we clapped our hands to the music on the radio, he would dance.

It was a Saturday night treat to gather in the living room, turn the radio on and listen to the Grand Old Opera. Snowball loved it as much as we did. Believe it or not, his favorite singer seemed to be Jimmy Rodgers, the singing brakeman. He would dance to, All around the Water Tank, whether we clapped our hands or not. It seemed to be the yodeling that turned him on. My favorite was Cowboy Copus singing, In the Eyes of That Strange Little Girl. Bo and I got to stay up late those nights. I do not remember missing it, except once. Daddy carried us to the movie theater to see, Steamboat Round the Bend. He promised we would go, once a month. That promise was never to be kept. I do not remember ever going to another movie, until I was old enough to slip out the window, while Mother was on the night shift at Albright and Wood drug store. Mother had got that old time religion, some years back and movie theaters were a sin. So were lipstick, cutting your hair, wearing shorts or pants, and do not mention a football game. It was the devil's own invention to slide you straight into hell before your feet got cold. Seven Brides for Seven Brothers, was worth a beating if I got caught. I did not that time.

While I played with Snowball, I listened to Grandma and Aunt Ester. Grandma sat in Mothers rocking chair, where she could lean forward and spit her snuff into the yard. I would have to make sure Bo and Fred did not play there for a while. Aunt Ester pushing with one foot, swung slowly back and forth in the swing. Grandma leaned toward her and whispered loud enough for a deaf person to hear. "She's breeding again, disgraceful if you want to know what I think about it." Aunt Ester's mouth trembled. This usually preceded saying anything not in agreement with the other person. "Well Mama, you know the Lord decides these things, not us." Grandma snorted. "The Lord my foot, he's got nothing ta do with it. If she spent more time tending her family and house, she wouldn't stay with a young'un in her belly. She just does it to git out of helping out in the field, and have that old Pearl here doing most of her chores." "Well in this case, it takes two to make one, you know." Aunt Ester replied. "There's no need to criticize one and not the other." Grandma spit and sniffed, "humph," she grunted. "Ain't fare an you defend her when she pops em out like peas from a pod and you can't have even one." Aunt Ester's face seemed to turn to wax, it looked so pale and still. "Oh," she exclaimed as she jumped up from the swing. With her hands clenched at her sides, she glared at Grandma, then seeming to marshal her temper, she walked to the end of the porch where I sat. I felt as if I would choke on the lump in my chest. I knew what breeding was. That is what happened with Egore and the cows, so the cows could bring calves into the world. It made me furious for someone to make that kind of comparison to my Mother. It was nothing like the pretty birds and bees, Aunt Burma told me about. Aunt Ester took something from her pocket and leaned down. "Here darling, take this and go share it with Jimmy. I have some candy for you, but you should wait till after dinner." She handed me two sticks of gum. I bailed off the end of the porch and ran as fast as I could go. I left Snowball tumbling behind me. I made it to the barn before I turned my wolf loose. I threw and slammed everything

I could pick up, and cursed until I felt depleted. I slid down the barn wall and into my other world. I chewed my stick of gum and gave Bo's to a large black cat, who said his name was Womphus Cat. He introduced me to all his strange friends. Then he danced with boots on his feet and a crown on his head. Miss Perky Opossum, in her gingham dress, stepped on Mr. Womphus Cat's tail and made him drop his scepter. She picked it up and kept time to the music of a fiddle and fife, while I played the drum on an old syrup bucket. Aww, how it made me laugh. After dinner, I was questioned about Bo's gum. I insisted the cat got it. Aunt Ester emptied the Suzy pot next morning, she grinned and remarked. "Well, look what the cat drug in." She had found a very large wad of gum in the bottom of the Suzy pot. She and Mother seemed to think this quiet funny, but Grandma thought I should be punished. Once for stealing and one for lying.

Everyone was surprised, while at the breakfast table, Aunt Ester announced to all that Grandma would be going back home with Uncle Sam and her today. Daddy raised his eyebrows at his sister but no one ask why, and Aunt Ester never said why. Grandma sat and viscously punched her biscuit to death with her fork. I think, probably for the first time in her life, someone stood up to her, and won the contest. Aunt Ester got an extra big goodbye hug and a bouquet of wild flowers from me.

After they were gone and Daddy went to the barn, I wandered into the kitchen and sat down at the dining table. Mother was washing dishes. I took a deep breath and asked, "Mother, are you breeding again." With a gasp, she whirled from the dishpan, soap suds flying everywhere. "I will slap the wadden out of you, Betty June. What ails you, cumin in here, asking me a thing like that? Have you lost what little sense you wus born with?" I ducked my head into my shoulders and squeezed my eyes closed. Then I began talking ninety to the dozen's to get it all out before I did get slapped. "Well, that's what Grandma told Aunt Ester. That's what made Aunt Ester mad, cause Grandma said you could have em and Aunt Ester couldn't and that's why Aunt Ester got mad and made Grandma go back home with her and Uncle Sam." "Well, well,

well," said Mother as she poured herself a cup of coffee. She ambled toward the table with her lips puckered, her tongue in her cheek, pulled out a chair and sat. "Do tell. Now, what exactly was said? This I want to hear." I related all I had heard on the front porch. When I finished, Mother got up and poured another cup of coffee adding lots of cream and sugar, which she put on the table in front of me. Now this was a never before heard of wonder. "You can drink this, while I explain some things to you," said Mother as she sat back down.

"I want you to know, each baby God has sent me is a treasure. Bringing a new baby into the world is not something to scoff at or dread in any kind of way. It is something to rejoice and be glad about. It is God's blessing upon the joining of a husband and his wife. I am pregnant, not breeding. I am a human being, not an animal and I can promise the world from now on, I will be treated as such and so will my children. Stay here and finish your coffee. I will be back directly."

I sat and drank my coffee, while I worried over what kind of war I might have started now. Mother returned from the barn with a pleased smile on her face. She kissed me as she took my empty cup. She went back to her dish washing and told me to go play. "I don't have anything to do Mother, will you tell me a story?" This is when she told me of the beginning of my life on Sand Mountain. She told me a little about her Grandfather Kelly who taught her mother how to survive off the land, and her mother passed this knowledge to Mother. I was too young then to grasp the idea of genetics. It was not till I grew old enough to follow the blood line that I realized, someone did not tell it quiet like it was. There could not have been an Indian princess, for the name Kelly came from the male side of Mama's family. There was only Grandpa Kelly, my Great Grandfather, better known as Bed Kelly, because he never slept in a bed. He was a hunter, trapper, and probably a moonshiner. He only came home occasionally and when he did, he slept in his bedroll outside. His was a dying breed, for the era of the mountain man had passed. His father was an unknown Cherokee Indian. Maybe he was a chief. We were told, he was. I now know, he was a renegade for he had escaped going on the trail of tears. He would have been a small child at the time of the Cherokee removal. My Grandmother, Dovie Kelly, married John Walden to avoid being placed on a reservation. The federal government listed her as a Choctaw, but Mama was Cherokee.

That night, I prayed for our father in heaven to bless my Mother, for all the good things she did, and to forgive her for the things she did that were not right. I explained to God that Mother was not mean. I was beginning to realize that at times, she was driven by something she could not control. I noticed Grandma Coffman's visits were less frequent and when she did visit, she did not seem to have much to say. After she got mad at Daddy, she stopped coming at all, unless Aunt Ester and Uncle Sam came down for the day. The last time I remember an overnight visit from her at the farm, Daddy had a little too much corn squeezing before he came to the supper table that night. Grandma, just trying to make light conversation I suppose, made the remark, "You know, I heard and I believe, it's so as people age, their tastes changes. I know mine has." Daddy reared back in his chair. With a twinkle in his eye and a wide grin on his face, he answered her. "Well now, I don't know about that. Seems to me, I remember when you were young, you sure did love fried chicken and I don't see that has changed. That's the third piece you have ate and reaching for another." Daddy thought this was so funny. He roared with laughter. Grandma threw her piece of chicken back on her plate and jumped from her chair. Mother covered her face with her hand and I contemplated sliding under the table, before the crockery began to fly. "You drunken oaf," Grandma leaned across the table and snarled. "I didn't raise you to act like the rear end of a mule. I don't have to stay here and be insulted by a drunken sot. I tried to raise you right but you have turned out to be just like your sorry daddy. I wouldn't put up with trifling ways from him and I won't put up with them from you." Daddy's face lost its joviality real quick. He laid his fork down and calmly replied. "Well Mother dear, don't think you can make me sleep under the porch, like you did my dad. You won't run rough shod over nobody in this house no more." Without another word, he went back to his supper as unruffled as Mother's old rooster after he ran a quarrelsome hen from the barnyard. Grandma threw her napkin on to the table and marched to the back room, where she proceeded to pack. Come daylight, she was up and demanding to be carried to the bus station. Even years later, every time I would hear that old country song, Thank God and Greyhound she's gone, it would bring to mind, Missouri Coffman. Seems to me, the whippings were not as often for a good little while after that, and they were usually deserved, even if they were too severe in my opinion.

Daddy's drinking had slowed down the past year and things seemed to be better. He even made his trips to Birmingham and sold the produce, without the drinking problems he had the year before. The veterans had a benefit for one of their own. They played baseball on the backs of mules. All agreed Flimflam was the star of the show and Daddy was as big a comedian as Flimflam. We children had a fine Christmas that winter. Mother and Daddy decorated a beautiful tree after we went to bed and put presents under it. The spring came, went, and it was crop gathering time again. Mother and Aunt Pearl worked hard to do the canning and food preparations for the coming winter. Mother, however, did not look well at all. Though she was swollen with child, she was not near as large as the other times she was pregnant. Her arms and legs were skinny. She had ringworm that had started on her chin and went all the way around her face. Her eyes were badly swollen. I had put my arms around her while she sat in the living room and asked, "Mother, don't you feel well. Are you tired? I can make sandwiches for us and I can wash the dishes too." "It's just this old ringworm's got me feeling poorly," she said. "Pearl is going to come back in and feed ya'll when she finishes milking. You can wash the dishes, if she don't have time to do it. Dr. Rose is coming today. He is going to bring me some medicine for my face. I will be alright, don't fret over me." I watched her for a few minutes then asked. "Are you sad cause your butterfly is gone?" She shook her head and gave this story with a lesson in the telling.

"Baby, some creatures were created to be free. The butterfly only has a small bit of time on this earth. God made them a thing of beauty, for the joy of man and for his own pleasure too. I think he knew he was going to have trouble watching us make a mess out his handiwork and just took a whimsy one day and said. 'I know this creation called man is going to try my patience. I think I will make something that will not cause me so much heartache.' Then he calls his angels together and says. 'Design for me a thing of beauty that is quiet, delicate, and completely innocent, with no need for enmity or malice toward any other creature. Make it pleasing to the eye. Maybe, mankind will see it and appreciate all the wonderful things I have given them.' When the angels finished, they brought the design to him and he created the butterfly. They live just long enough to mate and lay their eggs, so there will be another butterfly the next season. We must protect the cycle of life with any of our Fathers creations."

The butterfly situation came about when walking in the woods picking blackberries and gathering some moss, Mother found a cocoon on a golden rod stem. She brought it home and laid it on the window sill. This morning when Aunt Pearl came in, she looked in the window and called, "Oh Miss Janie, come look. Hurry do." She was bouncing up and down on her spindly little legs and pointing at the window. There was a very large, beautiful butterfly sitting on the little bowl of moss that Mother kept on the window sills. "My heavens, isn't it a sight?" Mother exclaimed as she sank into her chair. Aunt Pearl patted me on the shoulder and laid her finger against her lips. I stood back and kept real quiet and still while Aunt Pearl hurried to the kitchen and fixed a cup of coffee, which she brought to Mother. Handing it to her, she said. "Sit right here, Miss Janie. I'll pack Mister Louie an ole Sam some vittles, so Sam kin take it on out to tha field. Then I feed the chilluns they breakfast, after I milk dat ole lowing cow. Doc be makin his rounds. He be here, tarectly." Mother sat and drank her coffee, while she watched her butterfly. I sat at her feet and watched Mother. It was seldom I saw her so at peace. Mother reached over and laid her hand on the window sill. She seemed to hold her breath, while the gold and black creature crawled upon her finger. She slowly brought her hand back to the arm of the chair. It sat for a time, moving its wings slowly up and down. Mother said, it was drying its wings. In a hushed voice she ask, "Betty June, can you open this window for me." I got up and raised the window. Mother reached over and rested her hand on the window sill. "Good bye, little beauty," I heard her say. "I wish I could keep you safe but that's not the plan." Soon after, the butterfly lifted from Mothers finger. It took flight toward the woods and out of sight.

Mother sat and rested till the doctor came. She went into the bedroom with him and closed the door. I sat in the floor and waited. Doctor Rose went to the kitchen, where Aunt Pearl had a pan of warm water and a clean hand towel set out for him. He told Aunt Pearl he needed to speak with Mr. Gentry before he left. She went to the back porch and vigorously yanked on the bell rope that was used only in case of emergencies to call the men folk home. In a matter of minutes, I saw Daddy sprinting across the field. He and the doctor sat on the front porch. Aunt Pearl went into the bed room with Mother. No one seemed to be paying any attention to what I was doing, so I stayed in the living room. I could hear Daddy and the doctor, as they spoke. Doctor Rose said, "Louie, she is only in her seventh mouth and the baby is very small, but she can't carry it to term. She can start labor at any time now. If the child is to be saved, she needs to be where I can take care of a premature baby. I can't do that here. Your wife and the baby need hospital care." Daddy agreed for mother to go to the hospital. Doctor Rose also advised Daddy that mother should never try to have another baby and they should let him take care of that problem, while Mother was in the hospital. Daddy said he would sign the paper work as soon as he could make arrangements for the children and get to the hospital. Doctor Rose was tall and slender with real long legs and he went by me in a hurry. I jumped up and went right behind him. I ducked into Mother's room before he could close the door. I knew where the hospital was. That is where they took me, when they took my tonsils out. I knew that place was a long way off. I grabbed Mother by the hand and clung for dear life. "I want to go too," I wailed. The good doctor took time to comfort me and promise me, my mother was only going for a little while and would bring me back a new baby. "Can I have a sister?" I sobbed still clinging to Mother. I figured I had a good bargaining ace here and I intended to play it for all it was worth. Doctor Rose scratched his head while he thought of the best way to answer this. "Well," he drawled, "I tell you what. If there are any baby girls there, I will make sure you get one. It depends on what the angels have left there." "Well don't bring it back till you find one," I sniffed. "And make sure she looks just like that." I pointed to Lil, where she hung on the wall. Doctor Rose seemed a little skeptical, but he agreed to try. He bundled Mother into a quilt. He then picked her up and ran to his car, where he put her next to him in the front seat. They left in a cloud of dust and I went about my business, firmly believing I had made myself clear and there would be a pretty baby sister on the way for me. I was one mad little girl, when some weeks later, an ambulance came bringing Mother and a blue bassinet. I met them on the front porch. "Is that my new sister?" I asked. "Sorry honey, it's a baby brother." I was told by the man carting the bassinet. "Well hell," I muttered. Then anger getting the best of me, I stomped my foot and shrieked, "Take it right back. We don't want no more boys around here. I ask for a sister. Take it back." "Look honey, he's real pretty." I turned my head and looked the other way. The man sighed and set the bassinet in the bed room, then returned to the ambulance, to assist bringing Mother in. I looked over into the bassinet, at the tiniest speck of humanity one could imagine, and I pinched him. He cried and I felt my heart break, so I cried to. Then I ran out the back door. I popped myself down on the steps, trying to keep my anger going but I only succeeded in feeling like the terrible brat I was. Aunt Pearl stepped out to the porch. "What you did to dat baby?" She demanded. I hung my head but did not answer. "Ain't you shamed? He jest a tiny mite an can't take up foe his self. En you big sister posed to look out fo him. Who gone love dat poor lil thang?" I begin to cry in earnest. "I will Aunt Pearl. I won't be bad no more. I am so sorry I won't ever pinch him again." She stood for a moment, staring out across the field then making up her mind, she said. "You go roun hind da barn. I gets Miss Janie settled, I come an tens to you." Without another word, I ran for the barn. It was not long before Aunt Pearl came with a switch in her hand. It was the first and last time, she ever found it necessary to switch me. When she had welded the switch enough to say the job was done, she asked. "Now duz you know why I switch you?" I nodded my head yes, "Cause I was bad," I sniffled. She broke the switch and flung it away. "No, cause you knows you done wrong an now you be punished, sos you kin forgive yo self. Not be punished no moe. God bless you wid dat sweet baby, but member dis. God gives an God kin take away. Aunt Pearl hugged me and went back to the house. I went down on my knees behind the barn and asked God to forgive me and thanked him for my new baby brother. I promised to forever love and take care of him, even though he was not a girl.

Chapter 10

THE PICKLE BARREL

After the birth of Louie Jr. and Mother's surgery, her physical health improved greatly. For a while, she seemed happy and life went through the winter and spring in a peaceful and content manner. This was in the year of nineteen forty eight. I had finished my first year in grade school. Jr. had overcome his premature start in life and was on his way to being a healthy child. Though still a small delicate one, his coloring improved and he did not scare us to death by turning blue and struggling for breath anymore. He became a joy in my life. I could hardly wait to get home from school to assure myself he was still with us and well. Mother said, "Enjoy him while you can Betty June. He is the baby of our family. When he grows, there will be no more babies for you till you have your own." He continued to gain weight and strength. Though quieter than the rest of us, he was a cheerful baby. Mother commented, "One would think with this kind of blessing in our life, Daddy would have been grateful enough to find the strength to fight his alcoholism with a bit more zeal." This did not seem to be the case.

He worked hard in the spring to plow and plant his crops, but he drank more and more. When it came time to gather those crops and take them to Birmingham, he was totally out of control. He suffered with a very bad case of alcoholic withdrawal when he tried to sober up enough to tend to the gathering and selling of his crops. Mother discussed her concern with her doctor. His advice was to make Daddy understand he needed medical help. He and Mother together talked Daddy into letting them make arrangements for him to go into a medical facility and undergo treatment for his condition. Under pressure from Mother and the doctor, Daddy agreed.

What I am about to relate to you is true. I assure you, it really happened just this way. The story passed around was so unbelievable, it spread far and wide as a joke. I have heard it told as a joke, since I have become an adult. The person doing the telling never realized it involved my family and was an actual happening. I am here to tell you it was no joke. The good doctor made arrangements for Daddy to present himself to the hospital and admit himself. He also arranged the transportation, through a friend of his, who was a mortician. His driver needed to deliver a cadaver, to the same city where the hospital was located. He agreed to furnish transportation for Daddy, who did not mind riding in a hearse with this silent companion.

I think Daddy began to chicken out, as the trip started. He begged the driver to please stop in the next wet county and buy him a pint of whiskey. "Look," he explained. "I am real nervous about this. I never did anything like this before. I am scared. I need just a little drink to calm my nerves. Do you realize, I will never have another drink as long as I live? That is a long time to think of fighting this monkey on my back, buddy." He wheedled and begged until the driver gave in. "I need a pack of cigarettes anyway," he said. "If you need it that bad I will get you a pint of some kind of whiskey, while I am at it. I never touch the stuff myself. That junk is poison as far as I am concerned." While the poor unsuspecting driver was in the store, a hitchhiker ambled up to the hearse. He asked Daddy if he could catch a ride to the next town. Daddy being the amiable man he was, answered. "Well sure, if you don't feel squeamish about riding in the back with a body. The casket is closed and I am sure the feller in it won't mind atall." Daddy obligingly jumped out. "Just crawl over the seat and go through that curtain. I can't open the back doors for you. They are locked." The hiker gave a mighty thank ee sir, then over the seat and through the curtain he went. The driver returned with the pint and cigarettes. He opened the pack and lite up as he cranked the hearse and pulled on to the highway. "Mind if I smoke one of those," Daddy asked. The pack had just been passed to him when a hand reached through the curtain and taped the driver on the shoulder. "Don't mind if I do meself," spoke a timid little voice from the back. Screaming the driver lunged for the door. Daddy clamped his liquid courage between his knees and grabbed the fleeing driver by his collar with one hand, while guiding the hearse to the shoulder of the road with the other. Attempting to calm the driver, Daddy handed him the bottle. "Take a swig or two of this," he advised. "I think you need it worse than I do." The shaken man grabbed the bottle and chugged. It was not long before quite calmly and with a happy chuckle, he climbed to the passenger seat and passed out. His troubles had just begun. Daddy took the wheel and continued on to the hospital. Upon their arrival, Daddy and the hitchhiker checked the drunk driver into the hospital, as Louie Odell Gentry. Daddy then parted company with his partner in crime, never to see or hear from him again. He drove the hearse back to the funeral home, parked it and walked home. He simply told mother, he had changed his mind about going in the hospital. That was the end of it, until the wife of the missing man and the doctor showed up at our door to ask Daddy, where on God's green earth, might the tearful woman find her missing husband. Daddy's explanation was, "Well, I'm not sure I know. I left him at the hospital. He seemed in a right worse shape than I was at the time. I would have thought he would have explained his condition to the doctor's satisfaction and made it on home by now." The outraged doctor sputtered. "I have called the hospital. They inform me, YOU were left there by two men unknown to them. Although Mr. Gentry insist he is not, who they think he is." Daddy raised his eyebrows and shrugged. "Well, I feel sure there is just a small misunderstanding. Just tell the hospital to turn Mr. Gentry loose and send him home." He even generously offered to go pick him up. It was an irate doctor who put a hysterical wife into his car and disappeared in a cloud of dust. "Well! She sure lost her religion in a big hurry. I never heard such language from a lady in my life," I heard Daddy mutter, as he slammed the screen door. Mother sat on the front porch for a long time, with her apron over her head. I never knew if she laughed or cried. Maybe she did some of both. Daddy fetched Aunt Pearl. She made supper that night. Mother went to bed early. After supper, Daddy slipped into his and Mother's room. I am not sure what transpired in there. I could only hear muffled voices through the closed door. However, in the shake of a lamb's tail, Daddy made a hasty exit from the bedroom, with a blanket and pillow under his arm. I heard a crash against the door, as he closed it behind him and sprinted for the back porch. Daddy slept in the barn, the rest of that week.

Not many days after the hospital fiasco, I awoke one morning to find Mother in the kitchen with boxes and clothes scattered everywhere. I watched as she pulled dishes and various kitchen utensils from the cabinets. The metal ones, she haphazardly, threw into a big box. The breakables were wrapped in our clothes and packed in separate boxes. All of her home canned jars of food were sitting aside in one end of the kitchen. I watched as with grim eyes, she silently packed our belongings. It was not long before some men and women came in and proceeded to pick through the canned jars of food. They boxed them up to carry to their vehicles. I watched money change hands as Mother's canned goods went out the door. When the food and the people had gone, Daddy came into the kitchen and tried to put his arms around Mother. She shrugged him off and turned her back. In a very soft voice, I heard her say, "Go away. I am trying not to love you anymore." With a deep sigh, he whispered. "Oh Jane, darling." With slumped shoulders and dragging feet, he left the house. "What is wrong Mother," I asked. "What are you doing?" She straightened up and turned toward me. I could tell she was fighting hard for self-control. Her eyes had that strange snapping look in them. Instead of running to hide, I went to her and wrapped my arms around her hips. That was as high as I could reach. She pulled me toward a kitchen chair and sat down. Placing her hands on my shoulders, she looked me in the eyes and answered me. "We have lost the farm, Betty June. Daddy has found us another place to go. We will be okay. With his monthly check, we will at least have rent and food money, so don't you fret." "Of course we will," I comforted her. She smiled at me as she patted my face.

"Your teacher told me how you came to her when she received word that her fiancée's plane went down. She said you were a very special little girl and I do believe you are." "She cried. Mother, he was lost behind enemy lines. She was so sad. I just let her know, I love her. I told her what you said, about how we must all be thankful for those men, who are giving their life to keep us free." She studied my face for a moment before she answered me. "I didn't know you understood what I was trying to tell you. You are to grown up for your age, I think, but I believe you are going to be a strong woman someday. Lord knows you will probably need to be. Go now and let me get done with this packing. Your Daddy will be ready to load up soon." I went outside and began to gather our toys while I thought about what I had seen and heard. For the first time, I got an inkling of the pain my Mother lived with. Only eight years old but I understood broken dreams and lost hope. The abuse of alcohol hurt the abuser as well as the abused ones. Why, oh why, would people throw their lives away for a bottle of golden fire that made them do stupid things? I could not and still do not understand. Watching my Mother cope, did help me understand this one thing, if nothing else. A dream may shatter but hope is eternal. As long as there is breath one goes forward.

Daddy returned later with two men, who drove a large truck. They loaded all of our possessions onto the truck. Daddy drove us, in his truck, to our new home. Mother had been there the day before and scrubbed the place down; floor, walls, and all with lye, turpentine, and corn shucks. I had noticed that morning as she packed, her hands looked red and raw and now I knew why. A body had to be real particular when moving into an old wood house in those days. There was the ever present risk of disease such as seven year itch, called thus because at that time there was no cure. It was caused by contact with bird or animal mites that lived in the cracks and crevices of old wood where fowls or mice had nested. In this day and age it is known as scabies. Scarlet fever could be carried by fleas from rats to humans. There was also the possibility of horrid little critters, known as bed bugs. I turned in a circle and gazed about with dismay. There was a large potbellied wood heater sitting square in the middle of the front room with a smoke pipe going straight out of the roof. I could see daylight between the boards of the walls. I think my horror must have shown in my eyes, for mother placed her hand on my shoulder and said. "At least it's clean, Betty June." Then she swished her skirt tail and donned her apron with a huff and exclaimed. "No self-respecting vermin would deign to live here."

While moving in the furniture, there was a loud commotion on the front porch. As Daddy and the men moved Mother's refrigerator from the truck to the porch, the roof fell on them. There commenced a lot of cussing and scrambling, when the debris was finally cleared, Daddy leaned against one of the remaining support post. Mother, who had ran to the front door when she heard the roof falling, stood in the doorway. With her hand clapped over her mouth to stifle her laughter, her eyes were stretched wide and sparkled like sun dappled creek water. Daddy glared at her and the refrigerator. Then up to the roof, while he wiped the blood from his brow. "You know, anybody living in a place like this, got no business with a damn Frigidaire no way. Know anybody might want to buy it," he asked. One of the movers stepped forward and asked. "How much you want for it?" "One hundred dollars," Mother declared holding out her hand. "Sold by the pretty brown eyed lady," said the man. "I will take the money for the truck while we are at it," answered Mother. Daddy began to stutter, "But, but." The big man licked his thumb and grinned, as he stepped around Daddy and begin to count out the money from his wallet. He placed it in her outstretched hand and with a flounce, she put it in her apron pocket and went back in the house. The man slapped Daddy on the back. "Come on, Cotton," he said. "And let's get this job done sos I kin git this here contraption home to tha little lady. She will say it's ah grand thing I have done this day. Hot damn, theys gonna be a good time in the ole barn tonight," he sang. "Cheer up buddy. You'll git out tha dog house someday. We will even help you mend the porch roof," the other mover said. With much laughter and teasing, the three went back to unloading the truck and repairing the roof. When they had finished, one drove the big truck away while the other drove away in Daddy's truck. "Well hell, hard to come, easy go. Ain't that right," he said while cocking one eyebrow at me. He sat down and bit a plug off his chunk of bull of the wood. I stood and watched, while I tried to conjure a way to swipe a bite. Sure enough in a few minutes, he leaned against the wall and his eyes closed. The tobacco lay on the porch beside him. I sat down and slowly inched my hand toward the tobacco square. I eased it to my lap and waited a few seconds, while I kept my sight on Daddy from the corner of my eye. When he remained still, I bit the tobacco and laid the rest back by his side. I vacated the porch swiftly and went in search of a comfy hiding place in the back yard. I found it high up in an old apple tree. I purred with sweet contentment and nestled there for a good little while, before I went back to the house.

Mother saved the cardboard boxes as she unpacked. She put daddy to ripping them down one side with a butcher knife and flatting them out. I stacked them aside, while wondering what she intended to do with all those boxes. I heard daddy tell her, they would make good insulation. "They will help," she agreed. "But they won't be enough. I need to chink these cracks. Sister summer is going to sleep. Old man winter is coming around the corner. The hair on the wooly worm is thick and solid. The squirrels are fat and bushy tailed and the hornets are building burrows deep underground. I want you to go to the pickle barrel this afternoon. Take Betty June to help. Use Jim's wagon. I saw stacks of old newspapers there. See if they will let you have all you can bring back. Betty can pull the wagon back, while you carry all you can." Daddy looked a bit dubious. "That's two miles there and two back, Jane." Mother said, "I know but I think she can handle it." Daddy winked at me and answered her, "I don't doubt that. Wasn't her, I was thinking about."

After dinner, Daddy took the red flyer off the porch and called to me. "You better hope in and ride there girl. Save your legs while you can. It will be easy going but it's gonna be a tussle gitten home with all that paper your mother wants." As I got into the wagon, I wondered why we needed so much paper and what was this pickle barrel? I did not ask. I figured I would find out sooner then I wanted to. He pulled me in the wagon until we were out of sight of the house, there he stopped and reached into his shirt pocket and took out his tobacco. He then took out his pocket knife and cut himself a big plug. Placing it in his jaw he leaned his head back and looking up toward the sky he said, "Um-um-um." Then he squinted down at me with his one good eye. I huffed and squirmed a bit but kept quiet. Looking real solemn and thoughtful, he began to trim off a smaller piece while he said. "Just between you and me and the gatepost. How many times have I blistered your fanny over my tobacco?" Pulling my dress tail down over my knees and wrapping my arms around them, I scrunched them tight to my chest and mumbled. "Lots." Leaning forward with one hand cupped behind his ear, he shouted. "What cha say?" "Lots," I shouted back. "Yes, I sure have. I did try to discourage you from a bad habit. Never told your mother though, knew what she would do to you." Handing me the plug of tobacco, he continued. "I guess if you want something, you want it. I do understand that. But see here girl. Don't you ever steal from me again. I'll not have you being a sneak thief. If something can't be done up front then its best not to do it at all. Course, there is times when it is best not to let your right hand know what your left hand is doing. Like while you are chewing that tobacco. Understand?" I happily poked the plug in my mouth as I nodded yes. He said no more, just pulled the wagon while I chewed and spit. I studied on this double standard he had presented me with. I come to the conclusion, it was okay to hide what you wanted to do but not okay if it was something like breaking one of the Ten Commandments. I never heard anywhere in the good book that said, thou shall not use tobacco.

About a mile into our journey we passed a large house built of pale yellow stone. It was trimmed out in white and brown, with a green roof the color of the moss Mother liked to gather. The property was isolated in the midst of the woods but open to face the road with a long curving driveway. I gazed with admiration at this house, so much like a fairy tale castle. It set back from the road on flower studded rolling green lawn amid large shading oak trees. The front porch ran the length and around the sides of the structure supported by sturdy ornamental columns. The broad width of the front was complimented by high arched glass double doors and wide windows. I could see delicate drapes made of white and yellow dotted Swiss material crisscrossing the windows. The top of the house was built with gabled turrets and a veranda above the lower porch. Daddy said this was called a widows walk. I wondered what kind of person lived in such isolated splendor. Surely, it was a king and his queen. At night, I lay and dreamed up different scenarios, where I might someday live in such a house. I even went so far as to tell the school bus driver, I lived there. She would drop me off in front of the beautiful house and I would amble slowly up the drive way. Once the bus was out of sight, I would turn around and with a last wishful glance over my shoulder, I would run home.

Upon arriving at our destination, I found the Pickle Barrel to be a small colorful store. In the far corner of this little store, was a large potbellied heater. You would find in the winter months should you happen by, a never ending pot of coffee brewing on top and a huge pot of soup bubbling merrily. It was there for anyone to sample a generous portion, provided one bought a gourd with their name on it from the proprietor. This you were welcome to wash at the well and hang on a peg board to use the next time you came. There was a water bucket with community gourd on the back porch for drinking and a pan for hand washing. The outhouse was a far distance back behind the store, thus a reason I supposed, for all the saved newspaper and Sears Roebuck catalogs. In the summer months; as it was the first time I visited the store, there were large pots of boiled peanuts, and cold cider. In the corner was a wooden brine barrel filled with pickles. There were benches and chairs sitting about, occupied at most anytime, you were of a mind to go there with laughing men, swapping stories or playing checkers. I noticed a tall thin man sitting in a straight back chair by the door. He was noticeable due to the fact that he was quietly whittling on a small piece of wood. Though he sat there calm and quiet, he would smile every now and then at some of the other men's more outrageous behavior. A big jovial faced man with black hair and a fascinating handlebar mustache that twitched sideways when he smiled shook Daddy's hand. He introduced himself as Casey, the hired help around this here establishment. Upon ascertaining Daddy's need he said, "The boss is in the back," then he bellowed at the top of his lungs. "Come out here Honey Pot and meet your new customer." A small buxom woman with rosy cheeks and blue eyes, her face framed with a halo of red curls bounced through a door leading from another part of the store. I said bounced because that was the best way I know how to describe this small bundle of energy. She seemed to sizzle and percolate. "What ye be caterwauling about now Mr. Casey? For sure and ye kin be heard to tha other side o perdition. I'll not have ye making out I'm a deaf ole bat, I won't." With a smile, she swatted at him with her dishtowel. I felt my heart soar to hear that beautiful Celtic lilt once more. Mr. Casey beamed as he placed his arms around the woman. "This is my Mary. Sweetheart, Mr. Gentry here wants some of those old newspapers you have been hoarding for most of the years you have frazzled my life and nerves. She drives a hard bargain Mr. Gentry. I will leave it to you to talk her out of her newspapers. Then you can have a cup of cider and sit a spell, while I introduce you to some of your good neighbors. I will get acquainted with this pretty colleen first. Come along princess." He took me by my hand and led me toward the pickle barrel. Lifting the lid, he fished out a big pickle, which he presented to me with a courtly bow. He led me back to the front of the store. He lifted me up and set me on the counter by the cash register. "I understand why my Mary, being the packrat she is, would horde newspapers. Though I don't know why anybody else would want with so many, would you?" I banged my heels against the counter and cleared the pickle from my throat, while I tried to think of a reasonable answer. I could not so I opted to tell, as much of the truth as I understood it, without being to informative. "Insulation," I said with a wise nod of my head. "Aww, I see. Very good for insulation, I hear. Lots of stuff to be insulated, is there?" I shrugged and chewed some more on my pickle, while I thought about what I had heard Mother and Daddy say about the boxes and newspaper. I was reluctant to tell our business but I would have stood on my head and stacked BBs with boxing gloves rather than let anyone think I was uninformed about anything. Sometimes, I think Mother rued the day I ever learned to talk. "Keeps away the winter wind," I declared. "Keeps old houses warm, but some day, I am going to live in a big yellow stone house with lots of flowers." After a moment of thought, I added, "And widderwalks." Mr. Casey seemed at a loss for words as he turned his back to fiddle with a few objects on a shelf. After a moment, he pulled a large red hankie from his back pocket. He wiped his eyes and blew his nose before turning back to face me. It was then, I noticed the whittling man had left his chair by the door and was standing beside me. He took a coin from his pocket and laid it on the counter. He nodded at the candy jars then walked back to his chair by the door, where he took up his whittling once more. "How many brothers and sisters you got, sweet heart," Mr. Casey asked. "I have four brothers," I answered. "I don't have any sisters." He began to fill a bag full of candies. "Good gracious, you have all those brothers and not one sister? What's your favorite candy?" I did not even have to think about that. "Liquorish, cause it taste like paregoric." He made a face but put lots of Liquorish sticks in the bag. "I just bet you will never have to worry about being well protected with that many men around. Brothers take care of their little sisters." "I am not little sister. I am big sister. I am the oldest and onlyest," I bragged. He handed me the bag of candy. "Well today, I bet you are going to be the most loved big sister in town when you get home with this." Miss Mary came to the register to ring up a sale. She nudged Mr. Casey with her elbow and said, "Do ye kin tha need O all that paper, Mon? Himself nere did say." "Insulation Dear," her husband answered. Drawing back with a disbelieving look she repeated him. "Insulation? Well he insisted on paying for the dratted papers, Mr. Casey." "The Gentry's are the new family just moved in the old Dawson place," he informed her. "Aye," she replied, without another word she took a brown bag from underneath the counter and began to fill it with cans of fruit and cookies and other various foodstuffs. Once the bag was full, Mr. Casey carried it and placed it in the wagon with this explanation. "Mr. Gentry, this is a welcome to the community gift from me and the missus. We hope you to be one of our regular customers." Daddy looked of a mind to protest but Mr. Casey raised his hand and said, "Mr. Gentry, My Mary is loved by all, for she is a wonderful lady, but she rules all her own, heart and mind. Now if she is a mind to claim you as one of her own, it would behoove you to accept. You do not want to stir her ire. No sir, you don't." Daddy thanked the man and said, "Mr. Casey, you will call on me when you need someone to lend you a hand from time to time, I hope. I am a jack of all trades." Mr. Casey agreed and I for one was glad to see that bag go home with us.

Mother lined those old walls with newspaper and then nailed the cardboard over the paper. Daddy nailed boards around the outside to stop the wind from going under the house. He cut and stacked firewood outside the back door. With the wood stove going in the kitchen and the potbellied heater in the front room, we stayed warm through that winter. Daddy found Bo and me lying on our stomachs with our eyeballs squinting through the cracks in the floor one day, when it was too cold to go outside to play. "What are you doing there Jabo?" Bo who spoke with a long drawn out sonorous speech answered. "Wee waachingg tha raaatss plaay chhaase." Daddy scowled down at us and called to Mother. "Jane, come and see what these young'uns are talking about. Mother came from the kitchen and asked. "What." He motioned toward the floor with his head. "Look under the house. They say there are rats under there." Mother knelt and looked through the crack. "Iiiee!" She screeched, as she jumped up from the floor. "Louie, there is hundreds of rats under there. They will be in the house next." Daddy left with the promise he would be back soon. A short time later, Mr. Casey drove into the yard. "Casey to the rescue," he shouted as he and Daddy jumped from the truck taking two boxes from the truck bed. As they set them on the porch, we could hear a lot of growling and yowls coming from both boxes. The men ripped a board loose from one end of the porch. They took two of the biggest cats I have ever seen before or since, from the boxes and pushed them through the hole. The Female was a marmalade and white calico. The male was as black as pitch. Their names were Mammy and Pitch. Their heads were huge and the eyes large and round. Daddy often referred to Mother's biscuits as cat heads. Now, I knew why. Mr. Casey said they were main coon cats and declared them hell on rats. They placed traps inside the house. Bo and I watched through the cracks in the floor as the cats scattered rats to a fare thee well until there was not a one left. I listened to traps go off all through the night for the next two nights until there were no more rats.

Mother was the one to suffer most that winter, for she had two babies in diapers. There was no electricity to power her washing machine, so it was back to the rub board and washtubs. The diapers would freeze and stick to her fingers as she hung them on the clothesline. Her hands were so raw and bleeding, she would have to use a spoon to mix her biscuit dough and make drop biscuits. There was no Aunt Pearl to help now. In the month of December, we ate syrup and biscuit three meals a day till we ran out of flour. Then it was syrup and cornbread till we ran out of syrup. Daddy had enough money left to buy one jar of syrup. He gave it to me and sent me to the Pickle Barrel. We always used Golden Eagle but oh my, how expensive that brand was. Looking up and down the shelf that held the different brands, I spied a gallon bucket of syrup that caught my eye because the bucket had pretty pink roses painted on the tin. It was named Briar Rose sorghum syrup and was real cheap. Good gracious, there would be enough of that to last a long time with enough money left over to buy Daddy a square of Bull Of The Wood. Wouldn't he be pleased at my thoughtfulness and of course, I could enjoy a chew on the way home. Now folks, let me tell you. Syrup and cornbread three meals a day is rough on anybody to take, but try it with soggum, as Daddy called it! Mother ask Daddy. "Whatever possessed her to buy tobacco with the extra money when she knew I needed flour?" I heard Daddy grumble as he sat down to the table, "I don't know but if I ever think to send that girl back to the store after syrup, I hope you will kick my ass down the road before she gets off the porch."

Aunt Ester and Uncle Sam always come down for Christmas to visit and bring presents to us. They had always made sure we had a good Christmas. They were not coming this year. As a matter of fact, they had not visited since we had left the farm. Mother said they were disgusted with Daddy. They had left us on our own to sink or swim. I found Mother sitting at the kitchen table wiping her eyes with her apron, while she read the letter from Grandma.

"I don't blame them Louie," she sniffled. "It just seems so unkind to the children. All of them still believe in Santa Clause, except Betty. They will have nothing for Christmas." Daddy seemed at a loss for words for a bit. Then he said, "I found a pretty tree back a ways behind the house, Jane. It's not too far to walk. Let's take the kids for a walk in the woods this afternoon and cut it. It will be fun for them to decorate it. I will go to the store. I would be willing to bet Mr. Casey will let me put some fruit and candy on the tab. They even have a few little hand carved toys, Slim has whittled. I can pay them back with fire wood. Mr. Casey asks me about that yesterday. He says he needs all he can get." Mothers face seemed to brighten. "You think so? Oh wouldn't that be a blessing." She seemed to come to life. While she laughed, she shed her apron and began to dress us all in coats and scarfs. We made it home with the tree about dusk/dark and decorated the tree that night.

It snowed off and on that week, so we knew we were in for a white Christmas. We did not mind, we enjoyed playing in the snow. What we did not know, was on the night before Christmas, it was going to freeze and all the snow was to become a solid sheet of ice. The morning of Christmas Eve, we awoke to find boxes of food sitting on the front porch. Later that day Slim, the whittling man, came by and left a fresh killed turkey on the back porch, feathers and all. He helped Daddy for a time with the wood chopping. Daddy invited him in for a cup of coffee. He sat at the kitchen table and held first one and the other of the boys on his knee. He smiled and patted them each in turn, as they chattered at him in their baby talk. Daddy told Mother, "Mr. Slim was a good ole soul but he was a mute who lived alone. Having the children pay him so much attention, was probably the best Christmas anyone could have given him." Mother insisted that Daddy go first thing the next morning and invite him back for Christmas Dinner.

Christmas day was an iced winter wonderland. Rainbow hued ice sickles hung from the roof and tree limbs. The sun struck fiery sparks from the ice each direction I looked. The beauty was a breath stealing miracle till I tackled the hill going up to the outhouse. It was a solid shield of ice, I found to my sorrow when I tried to make my morning visit in that direction. I slipped and fell backwards smacking my head on the ice. I sat there on the ice and threw a royal tantrum, kicking my feet and turning the air blue with my outraged bellows and curses. Daddy walked up behind me. "Hey," he said, "dry up that racket and quit that language before your Mother hears you. She will give all your presents back to Santa." "Ain't no Santa," I screeched and kicked the ice again. "Oh yes there is and I am him. I'll burn every damn one of them if you keep that up. Now come here." He picked me up and deposited me at the top of the hill. "Now go on and tend to your business." Only a bit mollified, I rubbed the back of my head and sniffed "How will I get back down?" "I will have that taken care of by the time you come back," he answered. When I came back, he had used the ax to chop steps in the side of the hill. At the top sat one of Mothers big dish pans. A rope was tied into the hanging handle on one side. "Hop in and push yourself off," he encouraged. I did not have to be told twice. Down the hill I swooped with a joyous shriek. Grinning from ear to ear, he showed me how to hold the rope and drag the pan behind me as using the steps I climbed the hill to come down once more. He went back in the house and a short while later, he was back with Bo and Fred. Fred could crawl his way up the ice steps but Bo and I decided it was more fun to put him in the pan and pull him hand over hand up the hill. I sat him in my lap. "He's a humdinger," drawled Bo, as he shoved us down the hill. Only problem was, Bo forgot to turn go the rope and he came all the way behind us. He lay at the bottom of the hill, and then slowly sat up, blinking his eyes. I waited with bated breath, to see if he was still all of one piece. He looked at me with a most beatific smile as the sun made a white halo around his white hair and said, "I'm a humdinger too, and so is my sister." We played until Mother called us in for soup and hot chocolate with marshmallows yet! Yea! The smells coming from that old wood stove were fragrances sent from heaven above. Mr. Slim sat at the table, entertaining Mother and Daddy with his squeeze box, while they prepared Christmas dinner. That afternoon just before time to eat, Mr. Casey drove in with a load of restored toys on the back of his truck. He told Mother and Daddy he had been delivering all over town, the day before and that morning. He asked them to let us come to the truck and pick as much as we wanted. He said the men at the store had great fun restoring those toys. It would seem, they had themselves a regular little Santa's workshop in the back of the store and had worked like little elves for a couple of months, to get all those toys ready for all the children in town. I found quite a few things I liked on the truck but the one's that stand out in my memory after all these years, was the red tam-o-chanter with the gold shamrock pinned on the front and a music box that played Zip-A-Dee-Doo-Dah from my favorite childhood movie, Song Of The South. My Aunt Ester had carried me to the theater, while on a visit to Birmingham to see this and Annie Oakley. I carried the music box in and straight away took one of Mother's kitchen knives and ever so carefully, praying it would not fall apart, I popped the back off. I wanted to see what made the music when I turned the crank. I could see the crank and a roller with a tiny gear on each that meshed and worked together to turn the roller when I turned the crank. On the roller was a rubber sleeve with little bumps on it. As the roller turned, the bumps on the sleeve would slip past and strum the ends of metal tines that were different lengths, thus giving forth the different sounding notes to make the tune. Fantastic! Marvelous! I crowed with pleasure, as I snapped it back together perfectly. It was a tired but happy little girl, who went to bed that night. Following a day filled with precious memories that a lifetime would never dim.

Window Wandering

I say there road, where do you go,
As you wander far and wide,
Do you travel to the ocean, or up a mountainside?
Maybe you end on a small wee trail.
In a wood land still and green,
Where little creatures play and hide,
And I might stop and dream.
You wander on so restless, leaving me behind,
Gazing out my window, wandering with my mind.
But hey now road, I'll grow someday.
Then I can follow you, and surely there along your way,
I'll find adventure too.

Betty June Gilliland

Chapter 11

SMALL WARRIORS

Early on in 1949, we were moving again. I was eight years old. The nights were still cool but the days were just beginning to be pleasant. Daddy took a job at a saw mill. He found a house so far out in the woods, they had to pipe in the sunshine. The well was dry but if you crossed the road and went down a path for, oh I would say about a quarter of a mile, you would come upon a spring. My gracious that water was so cold and sweet. If you left the house turning left, you would eventually find Jemison. I knew this because that is the way the school bus went. It drove in from that direction then made a turn in my front yard and went that-a-way again. Where this road went if you turned right from my front door, I have not a clue. I tried to follow it one day for half the day before I gave it up and went back home. I never got out of the woods nor saw another living soul. I knew that little dirt road went somewhere because that was the direction the rolling store came from. It came down the road from the right and stopped at the house before it rolled on down the road, the same way the school bus went. Farther on, in that same direction, was a little brown church. They would have an all-day singing and dinner on the ground, once in a great while when an itinerant preacher came along, which was not too often. A couple of miles farther on past the church lived a family of Pollock's. At least, that's what Daddy called them. They were kind of a wild bunch because it was just a house full of men without the touch of a woman's hand. This was declared by Miss Velma. I did not think she favored them too highly because they spiked her tea pitcher at the last church social. There was no harm done. One old timer got caught up in the spirit. He commenced to dancing the buck and wing and shouting so loud, that his false teeth flew out across the church yard. They landed, yep you guessed it, right in Mrs. Velma's tea pitcher. I heard Daddy tell Mother, "The whole shebang was saved by the skin of old man Jorgen's teeth, but I was fixing to accidently knock it off the table anyway. The little bastard's laced old lady Velma's teapot with Spanish fly."

On a ways, past the church, the road eventually forked. The left side went on to town. The right fork led to a dead end. This is where the Pollock's lived. It was there you would find a little pig trail leading off to the left. If you follow it through the woods a piece, you would come to another dirt road. On that road lived Mrs. Velma. It was a short cut, you see. Back to the other road, the one that went to town. Do not try to figure it out, I could not. What makes you think you can? Daddy said that I had no more sense of direction then a rabid bat. That was said after I led him and Mother on a merry chase all over the woods, trying to call them home when they got lost. Every time I called to them, I was in a different place. Well I was not the one lost, now was I? I walked to Mrs. Velma's once a week, to get a gallon of milk for Mother. Mother went with me, on the first trip, to show me the way. Mrs. Velma was a kindly lady, who made sure I never left her house empty handed. She always fed me before she sent me on my way and gave me a bag of rock candy, which I would stop and share with the Pole boys. That's what I called them.

"Poor Hettie Mae," Mrs. Velma said to Mother. "She had fifteen boys and hoped for a little girl so bad. The last one was a little girl but it just weren't to be. She were breeched she were, and the midwife lost Hettie Mae and the little one. According to the midwife, Hettie could most likely been saved but it would have cost the babe's life and Hettie wouldn't agree, so trying to save the babe, she lost both. Now them boys got no ma and they just raising themselves." Sometimes Joackum, the youngest one, would meet me out in the woods and we would wander and play, while his daddy and brothers would set their traps and hunt. Jock made sure I knew where the traps were, so I could roam free. We did not live there long, but what with helping Mother and Daddy hunt lightered pine wood for the fireplace and wood stove plus roaming with my friends, I grew to know those woods like my own back yard. He taught me the call to guide others quickly to me, should I need assistance. I could hit a high C note that would rise to the tree tops and ring clear as a clarion call. I just needed to learn to stay in one place when I sent out that call. Jock gave me a little gyp dog. She was a pretty little brown and white Feist. She was not as smart or special as Snowball, but he was long gone. Daddy gave him away when we lost the farm. Anyway, she was my dog because Jock gave her to me. She must have been with pups when I got her, because it wasn't long before she presented us with a litter. Then we all had a dog apiece. On wash day, Mother would take all of our dirty laundry down to the spring. She did not have to worry about what her laundry looked like to the neighbors now. There was no one to see. Fred would hang on to her dress tail and stumble along behind her. Bo and I would carry Louie Jr. and Chester. Chester could walk but he could not keep up. Once we reached the spring, we would put the little ones on a pallet and Gypsy would lie beside them and never move while mother washed clothes. Bo, Fred, and I had a grand old time playing and swinging on the monkey vines. We did not have to worry about the babies. Gypsy would not let so much as an ant crawl on that pallet.

Mother managed to hang on to some of her chickens and a smart move on her part that was. She could kill a young pullet once in a while, so fried chicken was a special treat, but now hear this. Do not ask for one of her eggs. They were money to her. She used them to trade to the rolling store for flour, sugar, meal, whatever staples we needed, and even a bit of cloth for her a new dress, once. Her dresses' were too large to make out of the pretty printed flour sacks that my dresses were made from. Sometimes, she would choose to buy her flour in plain white sacks when she noticed, we needed new under drawers or princie slips. It could be downright depressing when your draw string on your underwear quit working and gave way at the wrong time or place. No sir, Mother never wasted an egg. You ate biscuit and syrup with fried fatback for breakfast or nothing. Our school lunch was a biscuit with a piece of fatback or tripe. I usually traded mine off for a lunch ticket and ate in the cafeteria. There were free lunches but we did not want anything free. "We can't help being poor," said Mother. "But we can help being beggars. A patch on your overalls is a badge of honor, but patches on the top of patches are a disgrace." Yes, we had pride in ourselves if nothing else. We did not go hungry, as long as she had her eggs to barter for what was necessary. That is how it came about, the day her old Domenecker hen laid her egg in the wrong place. Mother took advantage of the situation, to do something special for Daddy. I heard that old speckled bird down in the outhouse, raising such a fuss she could have rivaled Hinny Penny. The rooster was scratching in the wood pile for his morning snack. I went to the outhouse and looked in. The hen seeming very worried was quarreling and walking around the hole in the toilet seat. When she saw me, she gave a loud squawk, jumped about two feet high and off the seat. The way she ran by me, anybody would have thought, she was being bird dogged by a hungry fox. I ran behind her, as she went tearing down the path toward the house, cackling all the way. The rooster, upon hearing the commotion, had come running to the foot of the path. When she reached him; he began to make deep soothing, chirring, and clucking sounds. With his head cocked sideways; he, for all the world, appeared to be listening and giving strong consideration to the plight of his missus, while she hopped and flapped and continued to squawk. She then turned and hi-tailed it back to the outhouse with him in hot pursuit. I ran on to the house to get Mother. When we got back to the outhouse, both the rooster and his old hen were goose walking around on the toilet seat stretching their necks, and peering down the hole while carrying on a raucous quarrel. I thought she was trying to explain how it happened and he was telling her what a hen wit he thought she was. Mother sent me to the house to bring back a rake, a bucket of water, and a clean cloth. She used the rake to drag the egg from beneath the outhouse. She rinsed it off then picked it up with the rag and carried it to the back porch. She placed it in a pan of clean water with soap and red Lysol. She washed and rinsed it real good then boiled it. "Not a word about this," she admonished me. "You keep your mouth shut." She made Daddy an egg sandwich the next morning and sent it to work with him. "Waste not want not," she said. Boy, did he ever think he rated.

As time went by, things were good and I dared to hope, they would stay that way. We had all accompanied Mother and Daddy to the woods, in search of lightered wood. Our search had been fruitful and on our way out of the woods, we come across a whole lightered stump, down by a small creek. Mother said, "Louie, I think we got about all we can tote and Jim and Betty are tired. They been lugging these babies over an hour." Daddy looked up at the sun and said, "Yea, it's getting on close to supper time. Ya'll head on home. I want to take a closer look at this stump. I think I have found a bee hive." I looked back over my shoulder before I completely lost sight of him. I saw him swing his axe once. He slapped his ear and yelled Bingo! Then he ran toward the creek and dove in. There was a swarm of bees behind him, with their little bee brains set on vengeance. When we got home; Mother mashed up some feverfew, mint, and snuff. When Daddy came in, she smeared that gunk all over him. He and the Poles went back another day and robbed the bees. They left the stump and some of the honey intact for posterity. The Pole's did more than help Daddy rob the bees that day, they showed him where they had their whiskey still set up. It was a wonder, I had not already stumbled on it. The only reason I had not, was due to the fact that it was set up on the far side of the creek and I did not know how to swim. Mother was of the notion that one stayed away from the water till they knew how to swim. Jock had never showed me a safe fording place, so they were still safe from little prying eyes. I would most likely have took the hatchet to it, had I found it unattended. It caused too much dissention between Mother and Daddy. One day, he did not come in from work at all, nor that night. I guess it just was not in the makeup of a Walden woman to put up with a drinking man. I do know, Aunt Mae sewed Uncle Leroy up in the bed sheet while he was passed out and took the razor strap to his hide. It did not stop Uncle Leroy from drinking but he damn well did not dare to come home drunk anymore.

Mother called me to the kitchen and sat me down at the table, the day after Daddy lay out all night. She loomed over me, while she asked me some strange questions about Daddy and me. At first, I was bewildered. When I understood what she was asking, I felt shamed and angry although fearful, for her eyes had taken on that strange look. I was hemmed in. There was no place to run and hide. I crouched down into the chair and wished with every ounce of my being, I could disappear. "He can deny all he wants to but if you will tell me he is molesting you, I can have him locked up and we will be rid of him. I will get his check and we can live better. I could afford to buy you the things you need, like store bought dresses and nice shoes. You won't have to put up with his mistreatment anymore." I began to cry in earnest. "He doesn't mistreat me," I said. "Tell me Betty June, where did he put his hands on you, inside your panties? Has he ever felt of your breast?" My teeth chattered so hard, I could hardly answer her. "No, no, the last time I saw my real Daddy, he showed me a bullet. He said it had Daddy's name on it. He would shoot him. He told me so. I saw the bullet. I told Daddy what he said. He knows what my real Daddy would do. Besides, Daddy loves me. He would never do anything like that." I lay my head on the table and cried for us all. I was sorry for Mother but I would not lie on Daddy. I heard her open the back door and I lifted my head. I saw her take her punching stick from the porch and carry it toward the front of the house. I knew it was going to be a bad trip this go-round. Bo was in the back yard when I went outside. He put his arms around me and asked me. "What are we gone do, sister?" I shushed him while we held on to each other. "I don't know, Bo. There's going to be a killing. I know it's going to be real bad." "Be quite," he said. "I will slip into the kitchen. I will take all the butcher knives and the hatchet and hide them here, under the back door steps. Can you get into the bedroom and get the shot gun?" Nodding my head against his shoulder, I whispered. "Maybe I can. I will try." He squeezed me close for a second, "Okay, do it." I went for the gun with my mind winging ahead of me, planning the next move to protect the family. Little brother was finally growing up. I was not alone any more. Mother was sitting by the fireplace in the front room. She did not see me take the gun from the bedroom and slip through the kitchen with it. Bo was waiting outside. He took it from me and laid it with the knives under the porch steps. "You get em all," I breathed. He gave a short nod of assent. "Now, I think we better clear out," he said. I stood there in the late evening and looked at the sky to judge how much light we had left. "Bo, it may get dark on us before it's over and we got no light. We will be out after dark." "Humph, you think anybody's going to notice?" I sighed. "Well no, I guess not. Are you scared?" "Not of the dark," he answered. I made my decision then. If Bo could be brave, I could too. "Okay, let's get the babies. We will go to the woods where my playhouse is. There is a big bush there that grows and leans over. It's like it makes a hut. You take the kids and go. I will meet you there. If you hear anything happening before I get there, take the boys and go deeper into the woods." I went into the house. I could see Mother still sitting in front of the fireplace, as I gathered blankets from the beds in her bedroom. I did not go anywhere near her. I knew she was waiting for Daddy to come home. I knew she was in a bad way. She was to still and quiet. I felt real sad for her but I was all my brother's had. I could not afford to put myself in harm's way. I was dreading it but I hoped Daddy would come on in tonight. I did not want to be in the woods with the babies during the night. I bagged up biscuits and whatever I could find eatable. I think it was cheese and fried fat back. I put all into a flour sack. I fixed baby bottles of milk and a jug of water, grabbed a box of safety matches and headed down the road. Bo and I met, where he waited for me and we took the boy's into the woods. Bo fixed beds with the blankets, there under the shelter of the old wild yaupon bush. I knew it had to have been there, since time out of mind for it was tall and wide spread. Its limbs grew so thick and tight and curved down to the ground, it was impossible to see under it. I thanked the Father for the shelter of this safe hiding place, he had provided. I left Bo and the babies there and went back to the house. Mother was still sitting where I had last seen her. I sat down on the steps of the back porch and waited.

The twilight shades had given way to the dark shadows of night, before I heard footsteps in the front yard and then heard Daddy walking across the front porch. I held my breath, as I listened to him fumble with the door. I jumped up from the steps and like a silent wraith, slipped in through the back. I heard the whap of the punching stick, and the sounds of struggling. A few steps carried me from the kitchen to the bedroom, where I could see into the front of the house. There was blood pouring down the side of Daddy's face. He and Mother were wrestling over the stick. The breath I had been holding, hissed through my teeth as I saw him wrench the stick from her and crash it down across the side of her neck and shoulder. He threw the stick across the room and stood reeling with a dazed look on his face. I flew across the room and went down beside her. "Have you killed her," I screamed. He leaned over and held his hand toward her and questioned, "Jane." Then he stood up and squinted at me, through his sighted eye. "This is your fault," he said. "You and your lies. What did I ever do to you, little girl? Why would you hate me so?" I shook my head back and forth in denial. "No Daddy, she just made it up in her own mind. I didn't tell her that Daddy, I didn't." He stared at me for a minute then cursed and slammed out the front door, his footsteps retreating across the porch. Then all became quiet. I washed Mothers face with a wet cloth, as she lay on the floor then helped her up into her chair. I brought her a glass of water and encouraged her to sip. She cried and accused me of trying to poison her. After a bit, I was able to talk her into lying down. I checked her shoulder and prayed it was not broke. It hurt but she was able to move her arm and fingers. I stayed beside her till she became quiet. I sat in the dark and thought over what Daddy had said to me. She must have accused him before she questioned me. No wonder he did not come home. That was enough to make a teetotaler want to drink. I went back to the woods for Bo and the little ones. He was there under the old yaupon bush humming softly and a little off key, while he cradled Jr. in his lap and Chester and Fred under each arm. We brought the babies home and put them to bed. He agreed to stay home and watch over them the next morning, so I could go to school.

Morning came, as gray and downcast as I felt. The clouds hung low and angry, with a sullen atmosphere. I heard Mother in the kitchen and smelled coffee. I went in and fixed myself a biscuit to go. I asked Mother if she thought she would be okay, if I went to school. "Bo is going to stay home and help with the babies, if that's alright with you," I told her. "Yes," she said. "That would be best. I suppose I will need him today." I went outside to wait for the bus. I went to school but I just could not keep my mind much on studies. We had been studying about centrifugal force and gravity and I fairly well grasp the idea of it, so I just sat there and let my mind wander. It was a relief to be away from home for a while and just relax. That is why, I did not notice Mother when she first came into the class room. The sound of her voice drew me back from my wool gathering with a start. I wondered how on earth she got there, but I never got the chance to ask. The teacher motioned me to come to the front. Mother did not say anything to me but my teacher said, "I am so sorry to see you go Betty, but your Mother tells me you are going to Birmingham today and most likely will not be returning." She hugged me and said, "I am sure going to miss you." I could sense the reluctance in her. I do not think she wanted to release me but she was not in a position to hold me against Mothers will. Once outside the school building, I looked around me and asked, "Where is Bo? Where are the rest of us?" She took me by the hand and said, "They will be alright, till I come back for them. I can't take them right now. I am taking you to Birmingham first, to see a doctor." I was totally bewildered. "But Mother, I'm not sick. I don't need to see a doctor." She kept walking. We had reached the highway by then. A car was coming toward us and she stuck her thumb out. The car went on by. "Mother, what are you doing?" "Just come on and be quite," she said. "I am trying to catch us a ride." The sky choose that moment to open and pour. Lightning struck close by and the thunder reverberated across the sky, like rolling war drums. A car pulled up beside us. The sheriff hauled his considerable bulk out and said, "Mrs. Gentry get in here before you and the child get struck by lightning." Mother hesitated. We were both already soaked to the skin and the sheriff was not getting any drier himself. "Come on Mrs. Gentry," he urged. "This is a dangerous storm. It is going to start hailing any moment." The words were no sooner spoken then the hail began to fall. The sheriff picked me up and put me in the car and Mother got in beside me. The sheriff leaning into the car said to Mother. "Now Mrs. Gentry, we have something we need to discuss. I want you to stay calm and talk to me. Now if you don't, I will have to handcuff you and I don't want to do that. Will you cooperate with me?" "Yes sir," Mother gasp. She clutched my hand and I could feel the waves of fear coming from her. Her voice was shrill as she demanded to know what was going on. The sheriff closed our door and got in the front seat. He motioned for the deputy to drive and I heard the locks click. He turned toward Mother, and handed her some folded papers. "Mrs. Gentry, your husband went before the judge this morning and he signed this court order to put you in Brice hospital for treatment." "He can't do that," said Mother. "Yes ma'am, he can and he did." "I am just trying to get my little girl to a safe place and get her away from him," said Mother. "Well you went the wrong way about it Mrs. Gentry. Your husband had to have stitches put in his head, and I would say it doesn't speak well of your state of mind, to think you can hitchhike all the way to Birmingham. Having a young child with you makes your situation appear even worse. Don't worry about your little girl. We will check everything out before we let her go home." They took me back to school and the sheriff talked to my teacher. She then took me to the principal's office and they questioned me. I denied the things they asked about Daddy and me. I told them it was not true and I did not know why my mother would think such a thing. I went back to class, till the end of school day. I caught the bus home that afternoon. I noticed a change in the people at school the next day. My little friend seemed uncomfortable and embarrassed when I approached her on the school ground. We never played together anymore after that. I became a true loner. I told myself I did not care. I do not need any of you, I thought. To make matters worse, if they could be, Daddy brought an old boy home with him one afternoon. He was about as scurvy looking piece of trash, as I have ever clapped my eyes on. He said his name was Leonard. Daddy brought him there to supposedly baby sit our little brothers, while he worked and Bo and I were in school. He tried to cause dissention among us and teach Fred bad things in the doing. He would give

Fred a switch and tell him to whip Bo and me. Fred was still a baby. He did not know any better. He just thought it was a great game. Truthfully, he was too little to hurt us physically but it was meant to hurt us emotionally with the cruelty of the act. I did not feel it was the right thing to teach Fred either. How did I reason this at the age of eight? I do not know. I just knew it was not right.

A few unhappy weeks like this went by. Then one day, something happened to bring it to a head and Bo and I fought back. We got of the school bus that day and were not greeted by our dogs as usual. I began to question. "Where are they?" Leonard would look at me with that smug grin on his face but he would not answer. I called and I hunted. My little gyp never showed. I finally turned on him and demanded, "You know something and you are just dying to tell me. I can see it's about to kill your soul to tell me, so out with it." "Do you really want to know," he asked. More than a little exasperated, I replied. "Course I do dummy. You better not be give my dog away." "Come on, I'll show you." I followed him into the woods never dreaming the extent of his cruelty. There lay my poor little Gypsy. He had chopped her head off, right there by my playhouse and left her there for me to find. OH! The fiend. Till this day, the horror of it is with me. I fell there beside her. "Why? Why did you do this?" I raged at the unspeakable thing he had done. "Your Daddy told me to," he shouted. Afterwards, he laughed and ran from the woods. Once I was able, I picked myself up and went back to the house. He was sitting out by the wood pile. The axe was leaning against a tree, back behind him. He was facing the road. I went through the house and out the back door, so I could slip up behind him. I had every intent and purpose to kill that bastard. It was the first and only time, I really planed for and cold bloodedly wanted to kill. I slipped up to the tree and picked up the axe and moved up behind him. This was a large double bladed man's axe. I tried to lift the axe and get a running start. It only angered me more, that I could not lift the damn thing. It was too heavy. I remembered the lesson in centrifugal force. I spun in a circle and let the weight of the axe and the air pressure lift it away from me. As I came out of my spin, I released the axe. He had turned his head and saw what

I was about. He had presence of mind enough to jackknife himself
forward from his perch on the log and flattened out face down. The
axe skimmed over him and landed with a thunk on the other side.
He jumped up and faced me. "You crazy little bitch," he stammered.
"You would kill a man?" I answered him. "Don't see no man, but I
would kill a snake in a heartbeat. Might be best for you, if you left
here." "You skinny little piss ant," he snarled. "You couldn't swat a fly.
I'll have your ass locked up with your crazy Ma, you see if I don't."
My body ceased to tremble with its impotent anger. I felt something
akin to molten steel rise up in me, turn cold and solidify. That red
haze danced around me like flame and I let it take me. I felt as if I
could project the flames from my eyes and let him see the wrath of
the hell, I was condemning him to. I raised my hand and pointed
my finger at him. "Curse you," I said. "Let the hounds of hell take
you. They will strip the meat from your bones." He laughed but he
did not sound so cocky anymore. "Just who do you think you are?"
"I am the one that's going to send your black soul to hell before it's
over. Stay, I want you to. I may not be able to lift the axe but I have
a hatchet. You have to sleep sometime. There are plenty of butcher
knives around or how about a little rat poison in your coffee. A few
black widows tangled up in your bed sheets. Oh yea, there are more
ways to skin a cat then one, and I know all of em." I do not think I
am an evil person but I do have my breaking point. I believed by that
time, I had reached it. I was declaring all-out war. I'd had enough.
I think, I made my point. It also was not idle threats. I did intend
to carry them out and think he knew it. He grabbed Bo's bicycle
and straddled it. "We will see what's what, when your old man gets
home," he said and started to peddle off. "That's my brother's bike,"
I yelled. "So what," he answered. "Louie gave it to me." Bo had been
searching for his dog too. He was not to find it because Leonard
had put the puppies in a sack and drowned them in the creek. The
Pole's found them later. Bo and I never talked about it. I do not
know how much he saw and heard, of what went down between me
and Leonard that day, but as he started to peddle away, Bo came out
of nowhere like an avenging angel. He had a large round lid. It was
sharp around the edge. I do not know where he got such a weapon.

I would have had a fit, if I knew he had access to something that dangerous. He made good use of it though. He sailed it across the yard. Had he been tall enough, he would have succeeded where I failed and that boy would have been bad hurt or worse, right there. Well, Angles must look after fools and children, I guess. Bo's aim was to low to get Leonard but he caught the bike in the front wheel. Believe it or not, the bike slewed sideways. It blew both tires and broke the chain and all the spokes in the front wheel. It also took quite a bit of skin off old Leonard's noggin and elbows and tore a hole in the knee of his jeans. When he managed to get himself up out of the road, he left hobbling and pushing the bike. As Bo turned and walked back to the house, I heard him taunt. "You may leave with it but I guarantee you won't leave riding it." Way to go little brother, I thought to myself, you are learning what it is going take for you and me. I felt sad about it but it seemed, everything we loved or that loved us had been taken. We had to learn to fight our own battles.

I went into the kitchen and poked some kindling into the red embers and then laid a log on top of it in the stove. I put the kettle on, to heat water, to wash up the dishes and set the coffee pot on the back eye. While the water heated, I tided up the beds and sweep up. My mind was such that when I poured the hot water into the dishpan, I stuck my hand in the pan and poured the boiling water over the top of it. A large blister covered the top of my hand before I could even set the kettle down. When I screamed and grabbed the top of my hand, the blister burst. Bo came to my side and looked at my hand. "Aww sis, how did you do a thing like that?" I was so hurt, I took my pain out on him. No way was it his fault but I berated him up one side and down the other anyway. He said not a word of recrimination. He sat me down at the table and put some of Mothers menthol salve on my hand. Then set about washing the dishes for me.

Daddy come home and went straight to the wood pile and began chopping wood before he came into the house. Leonard must have been hiding in the woods, for he came to Daddy at the wood pile. I stayed by the bedroom window and listened, as he told Daddy all about how I tried to axe him and made him leave. He showed him the busted bicycle. "That girl is dangerous, Mr. Gentry and that damn boy is just as crazy. He is right behind her in everything she does." Daddy laid down the axe and leaned against the tree, while he cut himself a plug of tobacco. "Well boy, who told you to axe the girls dog almost before her eyes? Any fool would know better than that. When I said get rid of the dogs, I meant carry them off and you know it. You just didn't want to take the time to do like I asked you to. You should know you couldn't leave them around here. The girl knows these woods like the palm of her hand. You can't hide nothing from her. You can be thankful, she didn't call that bunch of Pollock's down on you. They would put a bullet in your head and swear they thought you were a deer over that girl and who would there be to say different." Daddy stated as he spit across the wood pile. "Mr. Gentry, I wuz just." "You wuz just trying to be a mean smart ass, is what you wuz," Daddy barked. "I don't think it's going to be too healthy around here for you Bub. I spect the best thing you can do is go on home, and I would stick real close to home for a while, if I were you." Leonard pushed the bike on down the road and that was the last we saw of him.

Daddy brought a load of stove wood in and deposited it behind the stove. I saw him watching me out of the corner of his eye, as he stacked it beside the stove. I poured him a cup of coffee. When he sat down at the table, I handed it to him. "Heard you and Jabo raised a bit of hell around here today," he said. "We raised a lot of hell and will do more than that, if we see him back here again. Why did you have my dog killed?" "I didn't, he was supposed to take them back where they come from. I got to many mouths to feed, to be giving food to dogs. What happened to your hand?" I shrugged my shoulders. "I spilt hot water on it," I answered. "Well that don't speak to well for what you are going to be handling around here, does it?" "I can handle it," I said. He sipped his coffee before he asked. "What do you intend to do about school while I am at work?" I threw the dish water out the door before I answered him. "You know I can't miss school. The truant officer will be out here. You will have to stay home. You will have to do the cooking. I don't know

how. But I can do everything else." "Yep, yep," he grunted, guess that
is the way of it.

The household fell into a routine that was livable for us all.
Mother was away for three months before we went to visit her. That
was the only visit we made during the six months, she was there.
She seemed glad to see us. I commented on how pretty and shiny
the floors were. I had never seen this type of floor before. It was
hard and so glossy, it looked like marble. "Yes it is pretty, she said,
"but hard work. We have to get on our hands and knees and scratch
the old wax up with snuff box lids, before we put new wax down."
How often do you do that," Daddy asked her. "Once a month," she
answered. "Oh!" She said to brightly. "I am not complaining, we
need to keep busy, you know." We heard a loud sound of someone
with a high pitched voice, crying down the hallway. "No, don't do
that. That's nasty. Don't do that." It made me nervous. "What are
they doing to her?" "Oh," Mother answered me. "That's Granny. She
is alright. The staff wants to wash her clothes. We go through this
every week. She has two dresses. She wears one and carries the other
rolled up under her arm. They let her carry her old umbrella when
an attendant can be with her. She is subject to swat someone with
it, if they get to close. When they give her a bath and take her dirty
dress to laundry, she thinks they are trying to do something ugly
to her and steal her dress. She will quite down in a little bit, when
they threaten to take her to the tubs." Bo was looking about and
taking it all in. "What are tubs," he asked. Daddy cleared his throat
and raised his eyebrows at us. I could tell, he did not want us to pry
into the hows and whys of this place. Mother answered us anyway.
"That is where they take you, if you are unmanageable. They strap
you in tubs of water and make you stay there, till you calm down."
She shivered. "Nobody wants to go there. They keep you almost all
day, if nobody has time to take you out. That lady is all the way from
Mobile. She has someone who takes care of her there, so she will be
going home soon. They say, they have done all for her they can and
she is harmless. The state won't pay your way after so long, if you
are not a threat to others. I have a friend who has been in and out of
here a few times. She told me, Granny lost her mind when she lost

the man she loved at sea years ago. Poor thing. I feel sorry for her some time. She says, she needs to get on home. There is someone she must meet, when his ship comes in. She talks about finding the key to Davey Jones locker. Maybe she will go soon. I hope so. We all are happy and celebrate when someone leaves this place."

"What do you think about your mother, girl?" Daddy asked me one day. "Do you think she is getting better? I will bring her home when the doctors say she is ready." I busied myself tidying the dish washing counter, while I thought about my answer. "Daddy, I want Mother to come home, but I want things to be different. Did you get the feeling she is trying too hard to act normal? Like to bright, to perky somehow. Like her good humor was forced." He sighed and fiddled with the salt shaker. "Yea, I got that, but her boy's need their Mother." I hung my dishrag and sat down at the table. "Look Daddy," I said. "I love these woods. They are more home to me, then this house is but for Mother, it is different. You moved her out here, where she is shut off, without a living soul around. We have no family anymore. How many years since she's seen Mama or her sisters and brothers. Uncle Sam and Aunt Ester don't come to visit anymore. She has no grown up people around at all. She needs to be closer to town, at least somewhere that has water and electricity. She doesn't need to have to drag our laundry half a mile down a pig trail to wash it. Do you even know how many times her and me have had to dodge that old mammy moccasin that holes up by that spring down there?" "Well hell," he said, "I can get rid of her." "Daddy, that's not the point!" He grinned then. "I know girl. I understand what you're saying and I will see what I can do." "Well there is one other thing," I added. "You're drinking. You have stayed sober the whole time Mother has been gone. If you would stay that way after she comes home, it would help a whole lot." He looked down at his lap and blew a heavy breath through his lips. "No I haven't," he replied, "I still drink. You just don't know it because you don't meet me at the door with a stick when I come home. It's peaceful and I just go on to bed and sleep it off. You're easy on a man's nerves girl. You keep growing the way you are, you will be a treasure to some man, some day." He began to stir sugar into his coffee. Daddy never drank sugar in his coffee. I reached for his cup and poured it in the slop bucket, then poured him a fresh cup and set it in front of him. "I'll go gather the eggs and feed the pig," I said as I picked up the slop bucket and went out the door. He hollered at me. "We will have to leave the pig. I can't butcher it till winter." "Sell it," I yelled back and heard him muse to himself. "Jane, I wish I could tell you, our little gal is something else." I smiled and went on down the steps.

Chapter 12

GOOD BYE IS NOT FOREVER

Winter was coming up by the time the doctors released Mother. Christmas was just around the corner and I had turned nine years old. We were so close to some of Mother's family when we brought her from the hospital, Daddy decided to take her to visit her family in Birmingham and Sand Mountain before we went home. That was the visit when Uncle Tommy's mule kicked me over the barnyard fence. Bo got a belly full of crab apples that caused a big stink and Chester fed one to Aunt Ethel's hen and near choked her to death. The way Aunt Ethel hollered, one would have thought it laid golden eggs. When working a farm, poultry and livestock are precious commodities. Mother saved the old hen by grabbing her up by the feet and jiggled her till the apple popped out.

After we returned home, Daddy found a place to live close to town. It was a little shotgun house with three rooms and a kitchen but it had electricity and running water. It just so happened to be right next door to Aunt Pearl. Only two large fields and some pasture land separated us from Mocking Bird Hill. Mother would be able to visit Miss. May and Betty Lou once again. I had hoped with the helping hand of Aunt Pearl this close and renewing acquaintances with her old friends, would go a long way toward helping Mother stay happy and settled.

Aunt Ester, Uncle Sam, and Grandma came down for Christmas. It was only the second visit they had made, since we had left the farm. That was also the first Christmas, I did not receive toys. I got clothing and a purse. At least, the purse had Rudolf on

135

it. If you pulled a string, his nose would light up and Mother did not hang it on the wall. When I cried, I was told I was too grown up for toys. Aunt Ester gave me the cash to send me on my first trip to the beauty parlor. The Shirley temple hairdo was all the rage back then and I was real happy with my head, full of curly locks. Aunt Pearl baked me a sweet potato pie. She would bake pies for me and set them on the window sill. When I come in from school, I would steal it from her window sill and she would chase me with a brush broom. I would run away laughing, to hide on the back side of the field, under a weeping willow and eat pie till it was all gone. Thank goodness, they were always little pies. Otherwise, I would have made myself sick, I am sure. She carried the big pie to the house, for the rest of the family.

Mother seemed withdrawn and quiet. I did most of the chores and tending to the boys and Aunt Pearl did the cooking. Sometimes, Mother would pitch in. She spent most of her time crocheting. She slept a lot too. I thought I would get a rise out of her, the day I spanked Louie Jr. She did ask what I was doing. "I have told him to ask for what he wants and not climb, Mother," I explained. "He was standing on the chair, drinking from a glass of water. Right recently, a little boy fell from a chair doing that very thing and cut his face. Now, he will be scared for life and blind in at least one eye." "I heard about that," she said. "Jr. mind your sister." Aunt Pearl assured me, she would watch over the three little ones while Bo and I were in school, if Daddy was not there. The only accident that occurred was, when Chester wandered to close in behind old Sam while he was chopping wood. The top of his head got split. He seemed okay though. He was whiney for a few days. He would cry for the doorknob because he thought it was a biscuit. It was an uneasy time. I could not say exactly what was wrong. Not then or now. Things were just out of sync someway. Then it blew up in my face.

I do not know what kicked it off. The fight was going full blast when I walked in from school. As I walked in the door, Mother swung Bo's baseball bat. It caught Daddy across his kidney and he went to the floor. He tried to rise but he could not. She raised the bat high over her head. I dropped my school books and threw myself across him. Mother stood there with the raised bat in her hands. While I shielded him with my body, I lifted my right hand to her and pleaded. "Please Mother, don't. They will lock you up and you will never get out. Please put it down." Her eyes blazed at me as she spat such spiteful words. "Don't think I don't know what's going on behind my back," she shouted. "You must like it. You lie to cover up for him." "No Mother, you're wrong, please," I pleaded. The fire left her eye's then. All color drained from her face. She made a strangled sound and dropped the bat before she fell backwards across the bed. I stood up and began to wring my hands. I was beyond knowing what to do this time. When Daddy was able to get up from the floor, he was about out of his head himself. "No more," he roared. "You hear me, no more." Then he blasphemed while he took the bat and put it under his foot. He broke it and shoved it in the heater. Then he spied mother's punching stick. It went the same way as the bat. Then oh my God; my Fair Fay, Lill, and Teddy, he burned them all. I ran out the back door and across the field. I curled up beneath the weeping willow and cried until I could not cry any more. That is where Aunt Pearl found me. She crawled under the tree with me and pulled me up on her lap. She combed my hair away from my face with her fingers and held me for a while. My teeth were chattering but I was not cold. I felt hot. Aunt Pearl said, "You stay here. I be right back." I clung to her. "It okay angel. I not gone leave you, but you needs tending. Aunt Pearl will come straight back." When she returned, she brought a cool rag and washed my face. "Now here, you drinks dis." I swallowed what she gave me and shuddered. "Dat Bromo Seltzer," she said. "Help you calm yo little frazzled nerves. Help you sleep too." She pulled me into her lap again and rocked me while she hummed rock of ages. After a while I said, "I got no place to sleep Aunt Pearl. I can't go home." She pushed me away from her and looked down at me. "Cose you can. You gone sleep in yo own bed." I shook my head no. "I don't think I am wanted there, Aunt Pearl." "Chile you needed there is what you is. Yo ma don't even know she in dis world po thang, an yo daddy is gone. Dem lil chill'un got nobody but day big sister. An you talken bout you can't go home. You gots ta go. Ain't nobody but you. Now you listen to yo

Aunt Pearl. Hear what you an Bo gots ta do. I come in tha morning
an fix breakfast. Den you an Bo go on to school, but you tell dat
boy, he got to member he don't tell no body bout nuthin. If he do
dem welfare folks gonna come and take y'all all away. Day splits ya'll
up and sends y'all away from each other an day locks yo ma back
in dat hospital. Maybe, never see her agin. She done tole me bout
dat place." "But Aunt Pearl she said" "Shh," Aunt Pearl shushed me.
"Don't matter what she say. She can't hep what she say. Yo po ma, a
right sick lady. Aunt Pearl gone hep you hol yo lil family together,
till yo daddy come to his senses agin. He come around. You see, give
him time." "Aunt Pearl, he burned up Fair Faye and Lil and ohh my
Teddy," I wailed. "Now you gots ta stop dis," she scolded. "You big
girl now. Can't be crying like a baby over toys. You gots ta live in the
real world now." She wiped my face once more then took me by the
hand and led me home.

Mother stayed in her twilight world for two weeks. Aunt Pearl
would prop her up and feed her broth and wipe her chin when she
dribbled. She kept her body and bed clean. She furnished our food,
cooked, and cleaned for us kids.

When I came home from school one afternoon, Aunt Pearl
was sitting on the front porch. I laid my books down and sat on
the steps. "How has she been today, Aunt Pearl?" She smoothed
her apron then folded her hands in her lap. "Bout tha same. I gots a
notion she might git better if Mr. Louie was here, an she could hear
his voice talk to her." "Well he aint here and I don't know if he will
ever come back," I said. "Sam know where he be. He come cross him
this morning, down at ta feed store. He stayin cross town at a frien's
house while he plants a garden fo her. Sam tell him bout yo ma. He
say, ax you what you want him ta do." I did not even have to think.
"Send Sam after him," I said, "Now."

Daddy arrived about dusk/dark. He came in and sat on the side
of Mother's bed. He picked up her hand and leaned over and put
his head on the pillow. He lay like that for a moment then sat up
and wiped his eyes. "Janie," he said. "Jane, can you hear me? I would
have been back before now. I wanted to but I was afraid. Jane honey,
I didn't know you were in this kind of shape or I would have done

been back." He turned to Aunt Pearl and me and said. "It's a good thing Sam found me. I would have been headed for Mobile as soon as I got those tomatoes planted. I got me a job down there. I am trying to get my foot in the door at a place called Brookley Field, but I will be working at a dairy farm to start off." He turned back to mother. "You hear that, Jane? Would you want to go with me?" We all sat up that night. Aunt Pearl, Sam, Daddy, and I. It was way in the wee hours that Mother began to respond to Daddy's voice. Daddy and I could not make much sense of what she said. It took Aunt Pearl to tell us. When Mother finally opened her eyes she said, "Just lay me there." "What are you talking about honey? Lay you where?" She raised her arm and pointed, "There," she mumbled. "It's wet, put it on my head and turn it on. Then I can walk under the trees." Daddy seemed perplexed. "Do you know what she means?" He asked and Aunt Pearl nodded her head. "She think she back in that hospital place, Mr. Louie. She talkin bout treatments they give her while she there. Somethin bout tubs." Daddy soothed and talked to Mother all night. He promised her, she would never go back to that place again. He told her all about his new job he was taking and what a beautiful place Mobile was. He promised he would not leave. He would stay with her till she got well. It took well over a month to get Mother up and some of her strength back. Once that happened, she did give her consent and we moved to Baldwin County, Alabama.

The packing was finished. There was nothing left to do but wait on the man, who was going to load us up and move us to Mobile, Alabama. Mother had hugged Aunt Pearl and said, "I will be better now Pearl, don't you worry about us. At least I won't be cold any more. Louie says it don't ice up down there like here. Why! He says winter only last about three months and are usually mild." Aunt Pearl patted Mother on the back and wordlessly nodded her old gray head. She placed a cane bottomed straight chair on the porch and sat down. Uncle Sam had replaced the cane straps in the bottom of the chair, so many times over the years that Mother laughed and said he had a vested interest in it and gave the chair to Aunt Pearl. I sat at her feet with my head in her lap. I tried not to cry as she alternately stroked my hair and patted my back. We knew this was our last goodbye. She sat me upright and softly sang, I'll Meet You in The Morning, as she braided my hair. "It's not fair Aunt Pearl," I protested. "It just ain't right." I bit at my bottom lip as I fought to hold back my tears. With a sigh, she slipped her arms around my shoulders and laid her head against the side of mine, as she nestled my back snugly to her knees. "Is right my baby. Time you move on. Bout time ole Pearl move on to. I done my part fo you. They be others waiting to help you learn what yo Auntie can't teach. Yo Mama done tol you bout they be a time an a place fo ever thang under God's sun. Mine an yo time an place was here an now but chile, you knows we see each other in another time an place. Aunt Pearl be waiten fo you wit a smile, an a how do you do. The good Lord give you me fo a time. An I allus been grateful fo my lil white angle. Now, you go an members all I teaches you bout how to live right. You member tha golden rule an all Miss May done teach you. I be watching over you an live in yo sweet lil heart always. You hear me now. Go make ole Pearl proud. You is wise past yo years, an you gone be a fine lady someday." She said no more. She just sat there in that old cane back chair, stroking my hair and humming Golden Bells till with my head on her lap, I began to doze. Aunt Pearl shook me awake some time later and with a big smile turned me toward the road as she said, "Lookie here, who we got commin." I knuckled the sleep from my eyes as I stood up and looked toward the road. Miss May and Mrs. Betty Lou drove into the yard in an old Packard, Mrs. Betty Lou's husband had bought her when he came home on leave. They were the proud parents of a new baby boy and Mr. Barttels wanted to make sure his wife had transportation, should she have need of it. She had not quite got the hang of clutching and shifting gears yet. The car bunny hopped into the yard, scattering dogs and disgruntled chickens. Miss May handed over the baby to his mother and stepped from the car. Drawing herself to her full height, she turned a gleeful eye toward the red faced Betty Lou. "Well dear, I must say, that was most educational. I hope you won't mind, if I take a short cut across the back fields and walk home. I will take the child with me, of course." She dusted and fluffed her skirts then proceeded to straighten her hat. She soon gave this up as a lost cause. The awesome floral arrangement had torn lose and one large rose dangled before her eyes. She simply removed the hat pin that appeared lethal enough to use in a sword fight, turned the hat backwards and repined; leaving the rose to dangle at will. That was my inimitable Miss May. Should an earth quake level the place where she stood, she would simply dust her hands and asked, "One lump or two." One would never guess, she had spent the majority of her adult years, waiting for the love of her life. He was M.I.A. since world war one. Though Miss. May never gave up hope, she made a busy and fulfilling life for herself by serving others. In my mind, I noted the difference between her and the wasted life of that poor soul in Brice Hospital. Though I might lose my perspectives from time to time and for a brief period stray from those lessons of Aunt Pearl and Miss May, I learned, never accept defeat. Never turn your back on life. Keep going forward. Keep believing tomorrow is going to be a better day. Above all else, do what good you can for others and do not dwell upon your own woes to the point, there is no room for joy in your heart.

With a smile; Miss May presented Mother with a basket of sandwiches, cookies, and fruit to sustain us on our way to our new home. "It is so kind of you to come to say goodbye," Mother told them. "Indeed, we did not come to say goodbye, but to wish you well till we meet again. Never say good bye. We will always remember you and be praying for you. No matter how far away you may be, you are forever near and dear to us Jane," said Miss May as she embraced Mother then me. They stayed with us, those three dear friends, till the moving man came and loaded everything on the truck. Mother put the three younger boys in the front with her. The moving man secured the load with ropes and bailing wire. He put a mattress down in front of the wooden tailgate for Bo and me. I could not see over the top but I could see through the slats. I watched as my friends grew smaller and smaller, then mere dots before they faded from my sight, the song Aunt Pearl sang spinning through my mind. Yes Aunt Pearl I will meet you in the morning and I will know you by the crown that you wear. It will be the brightest one there. Though they grew small to my sight then. Today, they are larger than life as they stand beside me, nodding with approval and smiling to see the essence of my memories of them woven into my tapestry.

Chapter 13

A SLICE OF SPICE AND SOMETHING NICE

We lived the first year in Baldwin County. Therefore, I did not get the full ambiance of the city of Mobile to begin with. Baldwin County at that time was laid back, and is till this day in a lot of ways. Its flavor flows like sugar cane syrup; sweet, somnolent, with its slow consistency of time and life moving inexorably forward at its own un-hurried pace.

Near the edge of the yard was a spreading oak tree, heavily draped with Spanish moss. This, a never before seen phenomenon to me, was the first sight to greet my eyes as I peered through the tailgate from the back of the truck. Like a mysterious lady garbed in drifting gray skirts, it shivered and feathered softly as the breeze whiffed through the branches of the tree. As soon as the tailgate was removed, I headed straight for that tree. The moss was light and airy to the sight but when I tugged on it, I found it to be of a tough fibrous consistency. I recognized it as a separate living entity, needing the tree only as a place to house it. Humming birds alternately hung in flight or darted among the blossoms of a large Mimosa tree. It was my first sight of a Mimosa tree. It spread like a huge umbrella made of lacey green leaves and pink feathery blossoms. Standing beneath it, I cocked my head sideways. As I breathed the heady fragrance of The Gulf Coast air. I listened to the shrill buzz of the July fly and the throaty chorus of bull frogs, blending with the peeps of tree frogs. A virtual symphony welcomed us with joy to our new home. I smiled as I realized there was a branch or creek close by, for I could hear the sound of fish flipping their tails in the water. I was to learn later, to stay away from that creek, for it was not a creek as I knew them at all. It was what is known in south Alabama, as a bayou. In my new paradise, there was danger. Creatures called gators and cottonmouth water moccasins dwelled there. They were just as mean as and a lot more deadly, than Egore the bull. Unlike the friendly highland rattlesnake, which gives a warning before it strikes or the shy dry land moccasin that stays well hid, the cottonmouth will swim right up to you or drop from an overhanging tree limb, to say hello close up and personal as it strikes, and the gators are not a bit friendly either!

The front half of a large red barn trimmed in white, had been modified to a home dwelling with electricity and running water but no bathroom facilities. This was no hardship for us for we had long grown used to this type of amenities. The home was clean and sweet smelling with its new paint and hardwood floors. It did not take Mother long to make colorful rag rugs to place about on the floors. The back half of our new home, was a treasure trove to me. Stacked on shelves, all around the cavernous room, were old newspapers, magazines, and books galore. I was in hog heaven. I spent all my time in there, to the point Daddy complained to Mother. "Jane, that girl is going to put her eyes out if you don't make her stop reading in the dark. She stands by the window trying to get light enough to see by." "Well," drawled Mother with upraised eyebrow. "I would suppose the answer to that problem would be, I will give her a chair and you will put in a light." Two days later, I not only had a light and a soft chair. I also had a nice comfy rug and a window fan installed in the window compliments of Mr. Gully, the owner of the dairy farm. I made an extra effort to show my appreciation to Mother and Daddy. I decided to be fair, by not ignoring my regular chores and read only after they were finished. I think Daddy was grateful, when I stopped trying to help him with his own chores. I took a notion to help him round up his livestock for milking, one morning. I did not know the claves on the back forty were weaned and being raised for beef. I planned the escapade the night before, as a great surprise for

Daddy. I told Bo what we needed to do and solicited his help. We got up early and taking Joe the cow dog, we three headed for the back pastures. While Daddy set up the milking machines and put feed into the bins. The cows would dutifully wander up and inter into the outer holding pens, where they would wait their turn for the morning munchies in the milking stalls. This was a morning ritual unknown to me. While this daily happening was taking place; Bo, Joe, and I were in the back pastures gathering all the wild yearlings from the thickets and brambles. We did a good job of it too. Like professional cowboys, we hazed those rambunctious calves straight to their mamas. "You mind the gate Bo, while Joe and I herd em through," I hollered. "Don't let none of em git away." None of them tried to get away. The little devils were only too glad to skip through the gate. Mr. Gulley stepped out the door of the dairy barn and swore. His eyes bugged as he swallowed and choked on his chaw of tobacco. "Jasus Gentry, get the hell out here," he bellowed. Cows were milling and bawling. Calves were latching on teats from every direction, by the time Daddy got outside. "Grab em," Mr. Gulley yelled. "Get em the hell away from my damn cows." Daddy made a mad dash for one calf, which promptly eluded him, after he snatched it away from its mamma's bosom so to speak. The angry mamma knocked him cockeyed and face first into a cow paddy. Old crook, the cow with a crooked horn and just plain ornery by nature anyway, took a swipe at Mr. Gulley with that crooked horn. Trying to dodge her horn and get the calf loose from her tit, he slipped. Falling backwards, he sat on Daddy's head, driving his face deeper into the cow paddy. I was beginning to get a bad feeling about everything, by this time. All did not seem to be going as I had planned. Mr. Gully had finally made it back on his feet and shouted for Joe. Making a wide circle with his arm. He gave Joe the command to gather and put the yearlings back out the gate. "You girl, stand by the gate. Open it to let em out and close it, each time one goes through. You understand?" With a gulp, I answered, "Yes sir, I do and I will." As I headed for the gate. With Bo, Joe, Mr. Gully, and Daddy working together to separate cow from calf and put the young ones out the gate, order was restored before the cows were totally drained of their milk. Daddy made Bo and I wash cow udders, while he hooked up the milking machines.

It was a pitiful stinking entrance, when Daddy, Bo, and I came staggering in the back door of the house about mid-morning. Mother took one look, before she doubled over with her hand covering her nose and mouth, then made a beeline for the outhouse. We could hear her peals of laughter all the way to the back yard, where Daddy was hosing us down. As she served us a late breakfast, she said. "They were only trying to help, and I guess a little short help is better than no help a tall." Daddy glowered and grunted. "Let it be known from here on, I want no help a tall. I am grateful for one thing only. They drove those wild assed yearlings into the small pens, where there were only fifty of the newer cows to be milked." He shuddered and closed his eyes. "What if they had gotten into the pen where there were over a hundred and fifty?" Mother gave another whoop, as she went to the sink and began to wash dishes.

Daddy went to bed and slept, till afternoon milking time. I crept into my reading room and stayed there. Bo hid behind my chair for a while. I tried to ignore him, for I felt he was deliberately trying to antagonize me, when he began swatting the back of my chair and the floor with a magazine. Each time he would make a resounding smack, he would say ain't, over and over, till I could not ignore him any longer. "It's not ain't," I yelled. "It is, isn't." He became quiet momentarily, then in a sarcastic falsetto voice he replied. "Oh just look at the little isn't crawling into your chair." I threw my book down and leaned over to look. "Good gobble de wobbles!" I exclaimed. There were hundreds of sugar ants on the march. All headed for my chair and the syrupy biscuit crumbs Bo had deposited there. "Go get the bug sprayer, you little Machnock," I shrieked. Shoving out his lower jaw in that bulldog pugnacious way, he had when angry. He said as he went out the door, "I isn't ever gonna do anything you ever tells me to ever agin." It took making him a kite of newspaper, willow sticks, and my much horded ball of twine, to get back on my brothers good side once more.

I sat on the front porch steps and watched an inch worm measure a shroud, inching his slow way along a sweet olive branch.

Bowing his back as he brought tail to head then stretching forward with his head before repeating the process, he measured his way along. Each time he reached forward with his head, he wobbled and patted it around like a blind man tapping with his cane to find the way. I wondered if he feared to find a yawning crevice before him, in which he might find himself pitched head first into the great unknown. I was very familiar with that feeling myself. Where are you going, you silly worm? You will find nothing but the end of that limb and the wide open space, you seem to fear. Then you will either have to take the plunge or inch your tiresome way back. I was about to leave the inchworm to his tedious journey and go inside, when I heard the hysterical cries for help. I stood on the top step. Looking down the road, I saw a women running. Her hair and skirts flying in the wind and a small bundle clutched to her breast. I ran to the screen door and called to Mother. "Mother, come quick, someone is in trouble." Drying her hands on a tea towel, she stepped to the porch, her eyes following the direction I pointed. By this time, we could see a young women with a small child clasped in her arms, running full speed. She was screaming, "Help, my baby." Mother ran to meet her. "He can't breathe," she sobbed. "He is choking." Mother took the baby from the frantic women. I watched as she turned him upside down and slapped his back between his shoulder blades. He was so fragile. His tiny hands and arms hung limp past his head. His wizened little face was perfectly still and blue. Mother ran her finger into his mouth, while he was still upside down, then cradling him in the crook of her arm. She began to press on his chest as she breathed into his mouth. His body shuddered, as the small lungs began to pick up the breath of life she blew into him. One fist clenched then waved vigorously, as a high thin wail drifted on the air. As he indignantly waved those little fist and voiced his displeasure, at the shoddy treatment the world was dealing him, his face grew to a healthy pink. Then turned a startling red as his lung power revved to full potential. Laughing and crying, the woman took her baby into her arms. Mother led her to the house, where she gave her a pan of cool water to wash her and the baby's face. Then she served her a glass of iced tea. I went to my reading room. As I sat and read, I could hear the sounds of their laughter and gossip as they got acquainted. I could hear the exclamations of delight, as Mother showed her needle work to her new friend. I was glad Mother had found a friend, she could enjoy a visit with from time to time. This friend soon became two then three. It soon became a group of ladies, which gathered for a sewing circle once a week, bringing bags of quilt scraps and sewing implements. They were amazed at Mother's ability to take strings of nothing and make beautiful rugs and quilts from them. These were things of beauty as well as practical use. They were also made of memories. "You see," Mother explained as she displayed the cathedral window patterned quilt. "This piece was taken from my Mama's dress. This piece was from my little girl's baptismal gown. Here a piece from Louie's army uniform and pieces from each of my baby's first little apron's I made for them." On and on, a beautiful work of art made of loving memories. Mother thrived and grew in self-confidence. She was more outgoing and laughed often. She seemed boundless in her energy and hummed while she worked. I watched her blossom and my heart soared on wings of hope. Daddy stayed sober and industrious. He seemed to like his job and his boss liked him.

At the supper table one night, Daddy said, "Jane, you know you could pick yourself up a nice amount of change from what you are doing for free. You could set up regular sewing classes for the ladies from the surrounding communities." Mother paused with her fork halfway to her mouth, and then carefully laying it back in her plate, she clasped her hands in her lap. "Louie, are we having a financial problem?" He stared at her a long moment across the table. "No, no," he denied. "We are doing fine. I only wondered if you realized the service you are providing and what it is worth." Mother fidgeted nervously with her fork as she tried to explain. "I think I do," she said. "But darling, these women are my friends. I don't think I have had so much fun doing something I like in all my life. It would spoil it if I charged money. I will if you think it necessary although it will take away the spice and I will lose something nice if I do." I held my breath as I watched her and Daddy. Her hand trembled, as she reached for her tea glass and she tucked it back in her lap. Daddy sat with open mouth, seeming at a loss for words. Then he replied. "Jane honey, we are doing better than fine. You misunderstand me. I just wanted to make sure you knew what you could do if you wanted to." Giving him a smile she answered, "I am doing exactly what I want to do." He went back to eating his supper. "Well, then everything is fine." I gave a sigh of relief.

After finishing his supper, Daddy pushed back his plate and said with a grin, "I have good news. Gully has rearranged our work schedule. I have the weekend off. What do you have planned for tomorrow?" "I was going to churn tomorrow morning," she answered him. "I will do that now, while you clean the kitchen," he offered. "Then what cha say we go out and kill a couple ah them pullets you got shut up. I will help you clean em and you can fry em up in the morning and make us a bowl of tater salad. I smell that chocolate cake, you baked. Let's save it for tomorrow and we will get up in the morning and take these young'uns to gulf shores." We were all excited. Daddy had worked seven days a week and there had been no time to explore our environment beyond the parameters of the dairy and the local grocery store. There were times, when we could smell the tang of salt in the air but I was thrilled beyond words to think I would get to see it up close. Daddy said we could even swim in it.

"I wonder what made Mr. Gully decide to change the work schedule," Mother mused while they were plucking the chicken carcasses. Daddy chuckled, "Aside from wanting his boy's to take a more active interest in the business, he realized I needed a break once in a while. After the old son of a bitch was able to stop laughing at me over the snake and rat in my britches, he sat down in the feed room and told me how he wanted to organize things." Mother and I both began to laugh. "It wasn't funny, Magee," Daddy quipped. The last was said in reference to a radio comedy, Flibber Magee and Molly that Mother and Daddy never missed, if they could help it. I must tell you about the rat and the snake.

Daddy and Mr. Gully were cleaning the feed room. A large black rat ran from behind one of the feed bags. A long black snake was hot on his trail. Petrified with fear and seeking a hiding place, the rat ran up Daddy's pant leg and the snake intent on not losing his dinner followed. By the time the cussing and shouting had drawn Mother's and my attention to the barn yard, Daddy was trying to climb the fence with his britches and underwear around his knees. I don't know if Mr. Gully was trying to push him over or pull him back, but he was screaming, don't kill my snake! He eats rats! Don't kill my snake! Daddy g-deed the snake to a fare the well and tumbled the rest of the way over the fence. He landed on his butt. The rat vacated the seat of his pants and made a run for the feed room. The snake kept up his pursuit of the rat. Daddy screamed once more then flipped onto his back. With all his glory shining, he lay there and gasped for breathe. Mr. Gully anxiously leaning over Daddy asked, "Are all the family jewels still there, son." I will not repeat Daddy's answer. Mr. Gully left and was back shortly with a cat and her family of kittens. He deposited them in the feed room with these instructions to me. "Don't feed them, Boots Annie. They won't go hungry. They will take care of the feed room problem for poor ole Louie." Then he wiped his eyes and laughed some more.

We went to bed early that Friday night, so excited we could hardly sleep. The smell of frying chicken woke us early the next morning before Mother got our oatmeal on the table. We still had to go through our morning ritual of Fred sneezing. We all stood back and Daddy kept a napkin ready. He always sneezed on his first bite. Then he would pick out his raisins and feed them to Daddy one by one and say, "Here Daddy, you eat the bugs." He did the same when we had cinnamon rolls.

Bo, Fred, and I rode with the picnic basket on the back of the truck. I do not know which the worst angst was for me on that ride. The smell of the fried chicken and chocolate cake or waiting for my first glimpse of the gulf. I smelled the tang of the salt air first. Then I heard the mighty roar and pounding of the surf, and the swish of the receding waves. As the old truck trundled along to slow to suit me, my first sight of the white sands came into view. I saw high hills of sand that Daddy said were sand dunes. When the truck halted to a slow stop, I could hardly disembark fast enough. I skinned my knee coming over the tailgate and did not notice till in the water I felt the sting of the salt. I did not care. It was awesome. Roiling water as far as the eye could see till it meets the sky at its distant horizon. Far out dolphins played and leapt into the air. I ran willie nillie to the closest sand dune. I just had to climb it. At the top, I dropped to my knees and ran my hands through the warm sand, then lifting it up, I threw it into the air as high as it would go. I celebrated with a shout of joy, as I watched the sunbeams glitter through where it showered back to the earth and me. No matter where I may go, my heart my soul, will forever dwell with the white sands and blue green waters of the Gulf of Mexico. The spirit of that lowland girl still quietly walks the bayous, when I dream.

In the afternoons, Mother would sit and listen to the soap operas on the radio. These programs were sponsored solely by the soap making industries, thus the name soaps operas. On Ma Perkins advertised Oxadol washing powders. Stella Dallas touted Octagon soap, another, Rinse-So-White, a happy little washday song. I liked that one. It sounded like a Bob White call. Mother truly believed idle hands were the devil's workshop. Her hands were always busy, even when she was listening to her soaps. She would either be crocheting, embroidering or working on her quilts or rugs. I was usually content to carry whatever I was currently reading to the living room and read while I listened to her programs. We would laugh when she questioned my ability to read and listen to the radio at the same time.

It was one of those lazy afternoons, that I gathered my nerve and broached the subject of Mama. There had been a thunderstorm that morning. The electricity was off for a few hours. There were no soaps to listen to. Mother decided to make me a dress. As I watched her lay out her material and began to cut her pattern, I asked. "Mother, why did Mama give up Grandpa and go hide on the mountain?" She seemed flustered, as she glanced up at me and sharply exclaimed. "Betty June, you do ask the most outatious questions. Why do you want to know about that?" I watched her eyes closely as I answered. "Because she is your Mother, my Mama, and I want to know about her and understand. I love Mama." I saw her eyes soften. "Well," she said as she slowly laid down her scissors, pulled up a chair and sat down. "I suppose if you are old enough to ask, you are old enough to know and understand." I watched her marshal her thoughts and look inward. I patiently waited. I knew she was going back to another time and place and taking me with her. Then she told me the story of Bed Kelly, the half breed trapper, his daughter, my uncle Tommy, Kate, and Grandpa John Walden.

Chapter 14

THE WOODSMAN'S DAUGHTER

Adults left to right
John Walden, Dovie Kelley Walden
children.
Tommy Walden, Merty Walden

The Lamp sputtered and burned low, where it sat on a rough handmade table in the kitchen. The woman hurriedly threw the dish water out the back door and wiped her dishpan. She was rushing to finish the kitchen chores before the lamp went out. It was almost empty of the coal oil it burned. "John," she called to her husband. "Can you spare the mule and wagon tomorrow? I need to go to the trading store. We are out of lamp oil and I need a few more staples. I used the last of my flour tonight. Are you going to take the corn to the mill and have our meal ground?" "No Dovie, I ain't," he answered. "It's too damn molded and full of weevils. It ain't hardly fitten to feed the mule much less feed us. You will have to buy cornmeal for a while. Use the egg money. You kin take Tommy with you if you want help loading the wagon. I think I'll go fishing while ya'll gone. Bring the lamp in here if you through with it. I can't even see how to hit my spittoon." "Well go sit on the porch. I done told you the lamp was empty. There's a candle on the mantle, light it." She said as she stepped into the front room.

"Hey woman, what say we take our quilt out under the pines," he whispered as he put his arm around her shoulder. "Big purty moon out there. We don't need no light to see what I got on my mind." He snickered as he tried to cuddle her closer and nuzzle her ear. "Do what you want in the dark John Walden," she snapped. "I am going to bed. I got to git up early in the morning." She called to her oldest son as her husband went out to sit on the porch. "Tommy, lay out your clean shirt and overalls. You are going to town with me tomorrow." "Okay Mama, I hear you," he answered. As she slid her nightgown over her head, she thought sadly of the man on the front porch. She wondered if he would wait till she was asleep to slip off the porch and hie away into the night.

She noticed her neighbor Kate, did not come visiting as often as she used to. When she did there seemed to be an unusual tension about her and it would take a blind fool not to notice the flirtatious eye contact when John walked into the room. No one could ever accuse Dovie Walden of being a blind fool. She wondered how far it had gone. 'Lord knows I love John with all my heart,' she thought as she slid beneath the covers and pulled them over her head. 'But I just cannot lay under that man any more. I got eight children. Nine if a body counted, the little one that lived only a few hours. Look what happened to John L., my baby boy. I should have been watching him closer. Should not have left that bottle of lye water sitting on the window sill, but after scrubbing all these floors and walls I was so tired. Lord, I am so tired. Please give me strength,' she prayed as she drifted into a troubled sleep.

Before sunrise, Tommy filled the water jug and hitched the mule to the wagon while his Mama fried some fatback and wrapped it with the biscuits left from the night before. Going to town was almost an all day job. It was getting on past mid-morning when they reached their destination. Tommy guided the mule and wagon to the back of the store and put them in the shade. Dovie climbed from the wagon. "I will be in the back bagging my cornmeal and flour. Eat your dinner. Then you can come in and get us loaded up." She went through the back door and Tommy sat on the wagon while he ate his biscuit. He stepped down and was leaning against the wagon taking a last drink of water from the jug. He glanced at the back door of the store. He could see through the screen to the front. "Hell," he muttered as he put the top back on the jug. That looked like Kate coming in the front door. She was headed for the back where he knew his mama had gone. Tommy was sixteen years old. He knew what was going on with his daddy and Kate. He had seen her slipping through the corn field late in the evening just about the time his daddy bathed in the creek that ran behind the fields. He was sure his mama suspected as much. Would Kate have brass enough to brace Mama there in public in front of God and everybody? He sure hoped not but he headed that way, on the double. He could hear the angry voices of the women before he reached the back of the store. Kate's high and shrill as she demanded that Dovie step aside. His mama's low and firm. She was not backing down one iota. "He is my husband Kate, in the eyes of God and law. Who are you to say I don't love him? We have children to think of. He is the father of every one of my children." With a shrug of her shoulders, Kate dismissed this as no concern of hers. "Do you think you can use them to hold him? You can't. You don't love him like I do, never have. He told me all about you. You just married him to stay off the reservation," she snapped spitefully. Dovie lifted her finger and pointed in Kate's face. "Enough, shut your mouth. I am warning you Kate. You have brought this to me but I swear I will finish it." Kate did not heed the warning. "Don't act so shocked," she sneered. "Everybody knows what your daddy was." Tommy stood stock still. He knew better than to interfere with his mama. "Don't say it Kate," was his whispered plea. Lifting her nose in the air she blundered on. "The whole tribe of you would have been shipped off to the rez if Bed Kelly had not hid in the woods all his life and your mama hadn't been a white woman. They were fixing to send you anyway if you hadn't married John first. Why! Bed Kelly wasn't nothing but a half breed bas." That was as far as she got. Dovie come from beneath the back of her shirt with a long bladed knife. She made one slash, catching Kate in her left shoulder. Curving down and across the top of her breast, the blade left a long deep gash. Dovie had aimed for the throat but Kate had spun away to run as the angered woman had swung that wicked blade. Kate staggered sobbing and screaming to the front of the store. Tommy took the knife from his mama's nerveless fingers. He ushered her quickly to the back door of the trading store. On the way, he opened the lid of the flour barrel and thrust the knife as far down in the barrel as he could before replacing the lid.

Standing outside the store, he held his mama's trembling body in his arms and offered what comfort he could. He knew he had to think and encourage her to act swiftly. "Oh, I missed, I missed," she cried. He shook her. "Be glad you did," he said. Dovie clenched her fist. "That woman is a spoiler. She is worse than a wolverine. That what she can't have, honest, she spoils with her filth so no one else will want it. Now what is going to happen to my children?" Then she wept. "Shh Mama," Tommy soothed. "Your children will be alright. Most of us are grown and able to care for ourselves and take care of the two that aren't. It's you, we need to think of right now." Drawing a deep breath she wiped her eyes as she made an effort to collect herself. "What do you think I should do son," she asked. "Go to earth, Mama. You can do that. Bed taught you how to live of the land. It was the best the old feller knew how to do for you. Now for a while, you must use what he taught you. Go to the Collins first. Tell them what you need to get by. They will give you all they can spare. I will go tomorrow and get what they don't have and leave it with them. Lay low for now. You can slip back at night once things simmer down. If you need anything, leave word with them and I will see that you get it. Now go." With one last hug, he shoved her towards the trees then went back inside the store. There he perched on the flour barrel till the Sherriff gave up his search for the weapon.

Tommy listened to the sheriff question the store keeper and cleverly pieced his story together around this man's account of the things that happened that day. "Sheriff I would witness if I could but I didn't see anything to witness. Tha woman bled everywhere and alls I know is I'm the one gotta clean it up. What a mess," the store keeper grumbled. "Now Clayton," said the exasperated sheriff, "Come here. Put that mop and bucket down for now. You know this is serious business and you got to stand still and answer a few questions for me. You are the only witness I got, like it or not. Now, what I want to know is, who was in the store besides you and Kate when you realized Kate had been assaulted by the Walden woman?" Throwing the mop into the bucket in a fit of pique, the store keeper answered the sheriff. "I never realized any such thing. I never seen no Walden woman. Told you that." Turning a bit red in the face, the sheriff asked. "Well, what did you see?" "There were a man and a woman here. I was checking them out at the register when Kate came wobbling up the isle screaming and bleeding. Then she fainted. Dead away right there in front of the register." The sheriff nodded his head. "Now we are getting where I want to go. Who are the man and woman? I need to talk to them. Maybe they saw the Walden woman," he said. Giving a long suffering sigh, Clayton set his jaw at a stubborn angle. "I don't know who they were. They were in such a hurry to get gone, they didn't even get their change. I took it from the cash register, but as I looked up Kate was falling and them two was beaten it out the door like rabbits with the hounds after em. And I tell you agin sheriff there weren't no woman here. Walden or otherwise, cept that one that run out the door. Seems like it's plain enough to me who tried to do in Kate! I heard two women raising their voice's back there and they sounded a mite angry. Then them two comes up all nervous acting like they can't git out the door fast enough. Now what does that tell you? Why you so mind set it were Dovie Walden?" The sheriff put on his hat and hitched up his gun belt. "Because Kate named Dovie Walden as the person who attacked her, that's why. Now I need to find Dovie Walden." The clerk grabbed his mop bucket. "Talk to that boy back there. That's Tommy Walden, Dovie's boy. He oughta be able to tell you all you wanna know about his momma." "Clayton, you about as bothersome as the blond headed Swede's red headed child. Now why the hell didn't you tell me who that boy was to begin with? I gotta arrest somebody. I just might start with you. I bet you could remember things a little clearer from behind my bars." Clayton began to mop his floor. "Don't know why you so all fired off at me. You didn't ask who he was. You got a one track mind sheriff," he complained. Tommy was still sitting on the flour barrel when the sheriff ambled to the back of the store. "Hello son, you are Tommy Walden, Dovie's son?" He asked amicably. "Yes sir," replied Tommy. "I need to talk to your momma. Is she in town with you today?" "No sir, I dropped her at aunt Mae's in Guntersville about daylight this morning. Then come on here to pick up a few things we need ta home. I sure need to be getting on back there before it gets any later. The owls are going to be roosting on my coat tail as it is, and I sure don't want to be a fretting my daddy no more n what he's already gonna be. I was just kind ah waitin here till some of the ruckus died down, so Clayton could ring up my purchases. Then I gotta git on my way." The sheriff eased himself down on the cornmeal barrel. "Well first I want to know what you can tell me about this ruckus as you call it." Tommy looked the man straight in the eye. "I can't tell you much. When I first came in, I thought for sure the place had been robbed. I saw Kate on the floor and a man and woman running out the door, like scalded cats." "Did you think to block their exit? Slow them down? After all, you say you thought a crime had been committed." "Hell no sheriff, they were going out the front door, I was coming in the back. I see Kate laying on the floor. Two people running out the front door, and Clayton standing there with his hands on top of his head. Now what was I supposed to think or do? I sat down and stayed out of everybody's way. Then you come in and start tearing the place apart, so I am still here." The sheriff pondered on this a bit before he asked the next question. "Did your momma have a knife on her today?" "Not to my knowing," answered Tommy. "How do you know Kate?" "Everybody here ah bouts knows Kate," replied Tommy. "I need to talk to your momma as soon as possible. When will I find her at home?" Tommy showed a bit of embarrassment, which was not all together feigned for the sheriff's benefit. Tommy was by nature a very privet person. "Now that, I can't tell you cause I don't know. I have to tell you straight up, she left daddy this morning. That's why I took her to Aunt Mae's. Them two is close, you know. More like sisters then sister-in-law." "Tommy, I have at the most an attempted murder, at the least, an assault with a deadly weapon. Your momma's in deep trouble. Kate has named her as the guilty party. I got questions that need answers. Mrs. Walden must come in and address these charges that are being made against her or I got to go out and find her. It will look better for her if she comes in on her own." "Sheriff she ain't here and she ain't been here. I won't play cat at the mouse hole with you. I will tell you about this. It was Kate's doing that caused Mama to leave Daddy. I didn't want to tell it. Its family business, but here it is. Kate and Daddy have been hanging the harp on the old willow tree for a while now. I guess Kate got tired of waiting for Daddy to make up his mind, so she slipped up accidently on purpose and in her on sly way she let Mama wise up to what was going on. Daddy don't even know Mama has left him. He thinks she is in town with me. Where she might be by now, I can't tell you. She might not have even gone in at Aunt Mae's. When I dropped her off, it was still dark an I didn't see which way she went. She won't want Daddy to know where she is till she is ready to be found. That will happen once she gits over some of her mad and makes up her mind what she wants to do. You can't put much stock in what Kate tells you. She's got her own ax to grind. She would convince the devil hell needs ah ice cream parlor if it suited the purpose to git what she wanted. And she wants John Walden, by hook or by crook." The lawman gave Tommy a long level look before he rose from his seat atop the meal barrel. "Well," he said. "One thing is for sure, somebody took a knife to Kate and she says it was your momma. I am sorry for your family troubles son but I have a job to do sorting this all out. You go ahead and get on home. Tell your daddy I will be out to see him tomorrow." As the law man was leaving the store, Tommy began filling his cloth bags with cornmeal and flour. He quickly took the knife from the flour barrel and slipped it into his bag of flour. "I filled the twenty five pounds of flour and cornmeal Clayton," he called out to the cashier. "I'll put it on the wagon and fetch me two gallon of coal oil if you will put it on the tab for me." He did not have much choice in the matter seeing as Mama had vamoosed with all the money still in her pocket. "Sure thing Tommy," the clerk called back. "I wouldn't worry too much about what Kate claimed, if I were you. Hell, my wife done threatened to knock both her roving eyes into one herself. She had more enemies then one I can tell you." "Thanks Clayton, I'll see you soon," said Tommy as he hustled his bags to the wagon.

Dovie tarried at the foot of the mountain, as she gazed into the depths of the forest night then lifted her eyes to the stars high above the tree tops to get her bearings. What did she have to fear here? She was her father's daughter. Had not she followed him up these trails many time as a young maid? She had listened and learned, as he taught her the ways and wisdom of his people. As she walked, she softly chanted the song to draw strength from the four corners of the earth and firmaments he had taught her. On that walk, she became Cherokee. She was Wahya, daughter of the wolf clan. Her husband was no longer her man. The mountain offered safe sanctuary, as it had done for the ancient ones, since time out of mind.

She had laid the two blankets flat, placing the minimum of cooking utensils and light weight food goods in the center. Then rolled and folded it to make a long but narrow back pack that reached from the top of her right shoulder to her left hip. Light weight rope held it together and made shoulder straps to carry it on her back. This way if she needed to move fast she would not have to worry about it catching on tree limbs and hindering her movements.

The Collins family had been friends with Dovie's family as long as any of them could remember. Merriam had cried and cursed John Walden as she gathered what she thought her friend could use in her exile. Dovie had chosen candles over the lantern that had been offered her. She rolled these and safety matches along with a tender box and flint in oil cloth, which she put in the water proof leather pouch to buckle around her waist. Her canteen she carried over her shoulder for easy access. She knew the matches would not last long, so she was happy to have the flint and tender. Clifton offered her a gun but she rejected this and took a knife and slingshot instead. She wished she had her own knife rather than the Bowie Clifton gave her. Her knife was light weight and fit well in her hand. Her accuracy with it was deadly. She had named it on the list of the few items she asked Tommy to leave with the Collin's for her to pick up later. She warned her friends, it would be several weeks before she dared trek down the mountain to come into town. By then, they should know how the wind was blowing and how best to advise her. She planned to come in well after dark and leave before daylight. Dovie made her way deep into the woods, before she stopped and cut a stout limb. She rested, as she took the time to sharpen one end to a point. Now she had a staff to aid her walking, as well as a weapon to probe the thick under growth of the game trails, she would need to traverse. She was careful to leave as little sign of her passing as possible. She traveled on through the night. It was well after daybreak, before she found the high place on the mountain and a small cave, where she had camped those long years ago with her father. There was a runoff from a clear mountain spring close by for water. She blessed Miriam for the tin of coffee, she had insisted on putting in the pack. Dovie decided to rest here by the cave today. She knew from here on, she would sleep in the cave by night, only when she needed shelter from bad weather, but camp in different locations by day.

Moving about, she did not camp in the same place twice, being sure she left no trace of her being there. After using her campfire, she would put it out. Before moving on, she turned the earth over it, then covered the spot with detritus of the forest. Not good enough to fool a Cherokee tracker but plenty well hidden from any curious white eyes. There were dark places along the creek, where she could lay patiently on her stomach and tickle for fish. She would lay still till the fish would swim in and out between her fingers. Then flip them to the bank. She made snares and set them for small game. Daily while moving about; she gathered wild greens, nuts, and berries. The bounty of the mountain was plentiful and gave freely to its child.

Dovie soon learned, the worst thing she had to fight, was the loneliness. There were times when she wanted to shout to the heavens, I am here, I am here, do not forget me. At night by her campfire, she would stare through the flames. She thought she could see shadowy forms moving, just beyond the glow and hear soft whispers. "We are here, daughter. You are not alone." After she put out her fire and rolled into her blanket beneath the stars, a soft breeze would sigh through the trees. Like cool gentle fingers, a touch would brush the hair from her tear dampened face and she would sleep.

Dovie stayed on her mountain, through the spring and through the fall. Coming down only rarely, to replenish her supplies and ask for news of her family. Kate had ensconced herself firmly with my Grandpa and seemed content to let her accusations against Dovie lay fallow as long as Dovie stayed out of sight and did not fight the divorce proceedings. When the leaves began to turn and the nights grow cold, she ended her lonely exile but she did not return to Albertville. That is another story promised Mother.

Floating Isle

The willow bends her bough to sleep, the
morning dove coos long and sweet.
We listen for the call of the whippoorwill,
when shadows gather quite and still.
Honey suckle, that southern tease, flaunts
her fragrance upon the breeze.
It's at this time there comes to mind, a legend of Mobile Bay.
Of a southern bell's lonely vigil, at the closing of each day.
Her softly gliding footsteps, her sweet angelic smile.
So haunted native people, she was called the Floating Isle.
The ocean cruel and grasping, had took her navy man.
To leave her vainly waiting, stranded upon the land.
The sea is a jealous mistress, what she claims will not return.
Floating Isle could not accept it, so her heart would ever yearn.
Her beauty faded, old and bent, she still would make her way,
Down to the rolling waters to stare across the bay.
Once a fair young maiden, now the dock
hands laughed and mocked.
Till in sharp retaliation, she learned the dock hands talk.
Those who knew her understood, her mind had grown most fey.
They would nod their heads respectful, then look the other way.
Born a rich man's daughter, now she lays in a pauper's grave.
Her restless soul for her lover weeping waits there by the bay.
Come inside you naughty children, you will hear the mothers say.
Its supper time and late the evening,
Floating Isle might walk this way.
Aye, the sailors oft times see her, gliding quietly in the eve.
Her golden hair striking moon beams, blows softly in the breeze.
Floating Isle I hear you crying, or is it wind that I hear moan.
Did I see you stepping lightly, where the seawall greets the foam?

Betty June Gilliland

163

Chapter 15

FLOATING ISLE

School had started back in Baldwin County. I was in the fourth grade and I did not like anything about it. My teacher seemed to feel there were haves and have not's in this world and she had labeled me a have not. She also found me to be a rambunctious trouble maker to boot. I must say, I fear she was not too far from wrong about that. I did not know and furthermore did not want to know my multiplication tables. I still do not and still do not want to. My spelling ability was and still is atrocious. My dear teacher in Jemison thought because I could give the spelling words out to the class and read so well in reading class, I automatically knew how to spell. She was so wrong. After she found me sitting in a swing on the playground reading, what she said was fourth year collage material, she never asked me to take another spelling test. I was so absorbed in a book of ancient Egyptian and Greek mythology, that I had missed the bell. She seemed astounded, when upon quizzing me, she found that I understood what I was reading, enough to explain it. After that, I always stood before the class and called out their spelling words for her, while she graded papers.

My new teacher was so sour, she reminded me of mother's clabbered milk. Her facial expression even looked soured to me. I did not endear myself to her when I told her, she looked like someone had clobbered her with an ugly stick and she had stayed clobbered for the duration. Mother was sent for and I wore strips from the hickory stick for a week or better. I cannot say it was not well deserved but I am still of the mind, that teacher earned my enmity. My reading privileges were indefinitely suspended and I was forced to accept endless study and grilling of the multiplication tables and spelling words. Would anyone wonder why I would be overjoyed, when daddy got his letter calling him to work at Brookly Field? We were to leave Baldwin County and move to Mobile, Alabama immediately. Daddy went the next day and found us an apartment, in a place called Alabama village. The people that lived there were, for the most part, decent hard working people, trying to save toward a better day when they could buy a place of their own and live the great American dream.

My first impressions of downtown Mobile were dismal. We had crossed the bay and entered the city proper on lower Government Street, by way of Bankhead tunnel. It was named in honor of the actress, Tallulah Bankhead. I was of the opinion, they did not do her any honors. The tunnel was dark and scary. It stank of exhaust fumes, so heavy it gave me a headache. I was nauseous and dizzy before we were halfway through. It is no wonder, I disgraced myself over the side of the truck. My senses felt abused as they were assaulted by the first sights, sounds, and smells of a city so large and busy. As we travel closer to our new home, I noticed another disquieting aroma in the air. "A paper mill," Daddy explained. "You will get used to it after a while." "Never!" Then I heaved again.

In the passage of time, I grew to appreciate and love my city with its excitement and bustle on one street. Then finding one's self suddenly on a wide quiet boulevard, centered in the middle with ancient spreading oaks draped in Spanish moss. Its stately homes were surrounded with rolling lawns and azaleas. One can find buildings there so old, they still hold the square nails they were first built with.

I was especially gratified recently, to hear the powers that be have agreed to salvage and restore the beautiful old L&N train depot on Water Street.

It was the first time for us children to meet and come in daily contact with others, our own age. For the short time we lived there, we made fast friends with the other children of the neighborhood. There were Martha, Sara, and Ray, who loaned me their roller skates and taught me how to use them. Then there was Mrs. Robinson, the lady with no legs. She sat in her wheel chair alone, with only the companionship of her dog and bird. There was only one visit a week from her son, when he came to do the grocery shopping for his invalid mother. I never heard but one word of complaint from that lady. It was about the afternoon sun that came in her front window. It was too hot and it also blurred the screen of her television. She always welcomed Bo and me. We enjoyed watching her little Boston bull dog and parakeet do tricks together. We enjoyed watching her TV too. It was the first one we had ever seen. Bo and I found her a large mimosa tree, in an old abandoned cemetery just off Dunlap Circle. I say abandoned because the graves there were all caved in. The place was so over grow, that we children could swing from tree to tree on the heavy vines. One very small grave with the barely legible words inscribed 'The sunshine left our home', was dated from before the civil war. One I tried to restore, for it was the final resting place of a civil war soldier. I knew it to be so because I could make out enough of the epitaph, to read the year of his death and the words, Our Johnny Reb marched home. I asked him for permission to take the tree and explained why I needed it. I guess I was a romantic fanciful child, for I seemed to feel he gave his blessing on my endeavor. As a thank you, I struggled to straighten his blackened moss covered head stone but there was nothing I could do about the broken caved in slab. May he rest in peace, I have not forgotten him. We recruited some of the neighborhood friends to help dig up the big tree. We drug it to Mrs. Robinson's apartment and planted it in front of her living room window. Bo and I took turns watering it each day. Would you believe it survived and grew fast? For the one good deed I did, there were quite a few, well not so good. Like exploring the attic. I talked Sara into climbing up and walking across to see how far it went.

As she called out to me, her voice grew farther and fainter. I ran into the duplex apartment next door to mine. "Where are you, Sara?" I shouted, running to the far end of the apartment. "Right here," she called back, jumping up and down. Oops! I saw two short fat legs come through the ceiling. They were followed by a round eyed little girl, who found herself deposited amid a hail of plaster, in the middle of our neighbor's bed. There was no way I could blame it all on Sara but that did not stop me from trying. That also did not stop me from getting my jacket tanned either.

I had a nice fourth grade teacher at Ellicott Elementary. She gave me a card of multiplication tables and told me to use those to do my arithmetic. She advised Mother to lighten up and not push so hard. She was of the notion that, they would come to me automatically, as I used them in class and home work. So would the spelling. She was so wrong.

I wanted out of school early. I was eager to try out the new pair of skates Aunt Ester had bought me. An unwary dog had managed to find his way into the halls of the school house. I got him to follow me to the little girl's room, where I force feed him a bar of soap. Once I had him foaming at the mouth, I shoved him out the restroom door and ran down the hall screaming. "Mad dog, mad dog," at the top of my lungs. The janitress screamed and threw her mop at the frothing animal. Then leaving me to whatever fate awaited me, she ran from the building. It did not get me out of school early. The only thing it got me, was the unwanted attention of my irate teacher. I was made to sit under her desk the rest of the afternoon with her feet propped in my lap. Every so often, she would poke me with a ruler and asked, "Are you awake." At least she did not call my parents

Mother attended church services for a short interval, at a small Pentecostal Holiness church. We went to church every Wednesday night, Sunday morning, and Sunday night. Sometimes, they would have a revival going and we would attend every night, till the wee hours of the morning. I slumped on those hard pews, till I had first bruises and then calluses, all up and down my backbone. I would be so tired, I would fall asleep in the classroom.

Mother seemed to grow more despondent and apt to fly into those terrible rages, when she would strike out at others. I believe she missed the feeling of respectability, she felt among her friends in Baldwin County. She found something there she had always craved, which was acceptance and the respect of her peers. When we moved to Alabama Village she felt the loss greatly and this affected her feelings of her own self-worth. Daddy had started drinking heavy again. I do not know if her mental problems drove him to his weakness or vice versa. I just know it seemed to be a vicious cycle, which was destructive to both of them. She had to be placed in the Holcombe unit which was the mental ward at Mobile General Hospital, for short periods of times more than once. We were back to living on dry beans and cornbread.

It was at a revival meeting, she meet a man who called himself a self-ordained itinerate preacher. He drove a large white van with religious scripture, in big red letters painted on it. He played gospel music and preached over a PA system, he had installed in the van. Mother had become angered at some of the church members because they interfered with her when she was whipping me in the church yard. She quit going to church and began following the roving preacher man. He would pick us up in the van and take us wherever he was preaching at the time. Most often, he held his services in his garage. Just Mother, her children, his wife, and a six year old granddaughter, who lived with him would attend.

Mother asked the preacher if he thought it was a sin to celebrate Halloween. "Why no, Jane. I can't think the Lord would begrudge the children a little fun. What do you have in mind?" "The school is having a Halloween party and Betty has asked to go. I am a little worried about letting her walk that far alone after dark." "I can take care of that problem for you," he said. "I will drop her off at the school for you and pick her up later. I always drive around on Halloween night, to kind of keep a safe eye out for the trick-or-treating children."

He dropped Bo and me off at the school house, Halloween night. It was not long before he was back, telling me it was time to go. "I will have to find Bo," I said. "I have already talked to Jim," he said. "He will meet us outside." I followed him to the van. "Where is Bo?" I asked as I climbed in to the front seat. "I sent him down to the corner to get some ice cream. He will be here any time now. Come and help me pick out some records to play on the way home." I followed him to the back of the van. I had no idea or warning of what he was about to do. He put his hand over my mouth and pushed me down on a cot. He hurt me awful bad. I cried and was sick. He took me to the front of the van and sat beside me. "You had better not tell anybody what we did," he said. "I didn't do anything," I said and cried harder. "Yes you did. You tempted me, and if you tell, I will tell your mother you did. I will also tell her you asked me to do that and said Louie did it to you all the time, and she will have him sent to jail. You know she will believe what I tell her. Now stop crying before Jim gets here. When you get home, I will go in and talk to your Mother. While I talk to her, you go get in the bathtub. I will talk to her till you get out." He drove around the neighborhood for quite some time, playing his music before he took us home. Once there, he held my arm while Bo climbed from the van. He hissed in my ear, "Remember what I told you. Now you get a bath and go to bed." I nodded my agreement and went straight to the bathroom, then to bed. He told Mother I had an upset stomach, from all the party junk I had ate. She accepted his explanation with no questions asked of me. I avoided the man, like poison from then on. I pulled every trick in the book I could think of, to make sure I was never sent off alone with him. I became quiet the little expert at being sneaking and conniving. I learned to lie like a rug. I knew I could not avoid him forever without drawing Mother's attention to it. I sought and plotted a way of revenge that would not implicate me.

I hid on his street one day. I waited till he left to preach and play his music. Once the sound of the PA sounded far away, I went into his back yard and knocked on the door. His granddaughter came out to play with me. As we sat in her backyard swing, I questioned her. "Why do you live with your grandparents," I asked. "My mama went away to heaven. Daddy had to go away to the war so he left me here with grandma and grandpa, till he comes home." "Do you like living here?" She did not answer. After the silence grew long enough to make me wonder, she finally said. "Grandpa told me you let him do the same thing to you that he does to me. He said you were a big girl, you didn't cry." I choked and got spitting mad. "He lies, I didn't let him. He just did it. I did cry and I hate him." "Me too," she whispered. "Why don't you tell on him?" Her eyes grew very round

169

and tears fell. "Ooh noo," she said. "If I do, he will pray to God and God will let my daddy get shot and he will never come home." "Does your grandma know?" I was curious, so I asked. She wrinkled her nose. "Grandma sleeps real hard when she smells funny. She doesn't wake up at all. She is asleep now. Grandpa gave her some medicine before he left. I have a picture of my daddy, you want to see it?" "I don't want to go in the house," I answered her. I was not about to let myself get trapped in there. I wanted to make sure I had running room if I needed it. "I got a letter from Daddy this morning. If I bring it and the picture out, will you read my letter to me? Grandma went to sleep before the postman came." I agreed and she went into the house and came back with the picture and the letter. I felt so sad for her. She was just a baby. There just had to be something I could do to protect her and me. As I began to read the letter, I grew very excited. Oh my goodness, it was wrote to his mother as well as to his little girl. He said he would be home in a few days. The war was over. Then I remembered hearing the neighbors and my parents talking about it. Daddy had said. "Well Dwight D. Eisenhower did what he promised he would do if he became president. He is bringing our boys home." The neighbor answered him, "Yea, but I got mixed feelings. I am glad to see our men return, but it goes' against the grain to know we had to accept defeat for the first time in American history to the likes of Korea." When I looked up from the letter, I saw tears fall to the glass covering her daddy's picture. I picked her up in my arms and swung her round and round, as we both shouted for joy. "Nobody can shoot at my daddy no more?" She asked with trembling lips. "They can't blow him up now?" "No they can't. He is on his way home. When he gets here, you will tell him what your grandpa did, won't you? He can make him stop." "I will if you want me to," She answered. "Take the letter and lay it on the table," I told her. "When he comes in, he will read it. He will be afraid to put his hands on you. That should be enough to keep you safe until your daddy comes home." I prayed I was right as I walked home. Within a short few days, her daddy was home. Within two days from that, her grandpa was in jail. Her grandmother was sent away to a sanitarium. As the horrified neighbors discussed the headlines in the newspaper,

I heard my mother comment. I certainly am glad my little girl had sense enough to avoid that horrid man. I was never asked any questions about him what so ever.

Daddy grew tired of riding a bus to work, so he found us another place to live. He moved us to a government housing project called Birdville. All of the streets were named after birds. This housing complex was not, genteel shall we say, as Alabama Village. It was however, within walking distance of Brookly Field. Late on the afternoon of our first day there, Mother called us children together on the front porch. She pointed to a street light. "Do you see that," she asked. "Yes mam," we all answered. "When you see those lights come on, no matter where you are, it is time to come home right then. Do not tarry. If you are lost, or hurt, or afraid of anything, look for a man in a blue suit with a badge on his shirt and a gun on his hip. He is a policeman. He is always your friend. You can trust him. He will help you." We roamed where ever we pleased, as long as, we came home as soon as the streetlights came on. Most of our time was spent at the Thomas James recreational center, when we were not in school. Mother had gone to work at Albright & Wood drugstore. I had to be sure I was home in time to have the housework done, before she came home. Other than that, she was being fairly lenient with me. There was a small library at Thomas James. I read every book they had, from top to bottom and all the way around. It was there, I got my first taste of The Hardy boys, and Nancy Drew mysteries, and Nurse Amy. I cried as I read Concerning Mice and Men, and Slinky Jane. I loved to play ping pong too, when I could find someone to give me a match.

Mother would give me money for Sunday school collection and send me off to church. She had stopped going most of the time. She had to work on Sundays. I would take my Sunday school money and buy a candy bar, a coke, and Sheena of the Jungle comic book. Then hideaway someplace quiet to read. She made me a beautiful dress of navy blue Dotted Swiss with white dots. The morning I wore it, I decided to enjoy my ill-gotten goodies, perched in the top of a high oak tree that grew by the railroad track. When I come down from that tree, there was not a white dot to be seen on the now totally black dress. It was also ripped and holy in a few places. Mother had an old kitchen safe, in one end of it there was a flour bin. It could be pulled down and would hold twenty five pounds of flour. There was a sifter in the bottom of the bin. Standing on a chair, I pulled the bin and stuffed the dress in the top. It stayed for a long time. Imagine mother's consternation, when her sifter stopped up and upon examination, she found what was left of my dress in the flour bin. Thank goodness, she had other things on her mind that day and had no time to question me. By then, I had found a safer place to go while away on my Sunday mornings. I would go up to Michigan Avenue, just across a little wooded area and down under the viaduct. The cars ran over into Brookly field and the trains went under. I sure wish I had one or two of those comics, I secreted away under that bridge. I hear they are worth a small fortune today.

By nineteen fifty one, Mother and Daddy had split. He had lost his job at Brookly Field and they were fighting it out in divorce court. Mother had gone to work at Fryanoore's kitchen, at the State Docks, packing frozen fish. She bought herself a Studebaker and taught herself to drive. Her last trip to the court house, she got lucky. Trying to Parallel Park in front of the court house, she attempted to park between the vehicles' of two Judges. Pulling forward, she side swiped one. Backing up, she crunched the left front fender of the second one. The policeman escorted mother straight to the judge's chambers. This judge pushed the ticket back to the policeman with instructions to take it to the other judge and see what he wanted to do. "Tell him," he said. "The lady has no Insurance and her earnings are small. She supports five children." The second judge with ticket in hand, came in swearing at the first one. "What does the woman want?" With his head in his hands, he answered. "She wants child support!" "Well by damn, give it to her. Don't make her come back to town again," he roared. Then he tore the ticket up and threw it in the trash can. With one last glare at mother and his fellow judge, he stormed from the judge's chambers. Mother got her child support that day and did not have to go back to court anymore. The policeman was waiting for her when she exited the courthouse. He made her wait while he pulled her car out from between the two cars. He helped her into hers and closed the door for her. He winked and said, "Have a fun day, honey. I have had mine already." Then he laughed and waved her on her way.

I was taking on a few babysitting jobs and had a little money to call my own. Mother was working and drawing part of daddy's government check. She did not pay much attention to what I did, as long as I was home in time to have the house clean before she got home from work. It was close to Christmas and I planned to catch the bus down town and hang out. I wanted to see all the decorations and maybe go by the penny arcade for a while. I did not have enough to slip in a movie today but I could still have fun. I carried my skates so I could skate in Bienville square. After getting off the bus, I took one look and knew there would be no skating today. People were jostling for maneuvering room everywhere. If I was in luck, Uncle Raymond would be on his corner selling his newspapers and parched peanuts. Slipping up behind him, I put my hands across his eyes. "Hey daddy-oh. What's shaken," I giggled. I did not really like Uncle Raymond much. He was Daddy's brother but right now, he had something I wanted and I knew how to handle him. I wanted a safe place to ditch my skates for a while and I wanted some of his peanuts to feed the squirrels, in the park square. "I'll shake you," he said. "Does your Mother know where you are?" "Sure she does. She doesn't mind as long as I get home on time. Can I leave my skates with you? I will pick them up on the way home. Thanks Unck," I said as I grabbed a bag of his peanuts and danced away. "Hey, hey, you little thief! I'm gonna tell yo mama on you." "Tell my daddy too," I catcalled and kept skipping. The policeman on the corner fitted his cap back on his head and shook his finger at me, as I danced by him with a big wink and a wolf whistle, at the good looking yellow cab driver waiting by the curb. I did all I wanted to that day. Then decided I had just enough for bus fare home and still some change to go by the Planters Peanut place and pick me up a bag of salted cashews, to eat on the way home. I would sometimes stand in front of that shop and dream of the day when I was grown and had a good job. I intended to come back there and buy some of everything in the place. For right now, I had to fight every inch of my way just to get to it. The crush of people was unbelievable. I was within a few steps of my destination when the crowd got tighter. I heard a screech and felt a blow to the side of my head. Startled, I turned my head and looked. I was eyeball to eyeball with a little wrinkled faced old lady. Whap, she whacked me again with her umbrella. "Mam," I sputtered, throwing up my arm to block the next swing. "Miss please!" Then I got a good look at her. I gasped in disbelief. It was the women from Brice hospital I had seen when Daddy carried us to visit Mother. It was the lady everyone called floating Isle. She even had her extra bonnet and dress rolled up under her arm, and that infernal umbrella. While I stood there blinking, she got in another resounding smack. Then she shook the umbrella at me. "Masher," she shrieked. "You think just because you got a sausage in your pants, it gives you the right to do anything you want?" Whack, she got me again. I was embarrassed more than I was hurt. The crowd was so thick, the little old lady could not get enough swinging room to do me much physical harm. I crawfished my way backwards, until I could squeeze my way through the door of the Planters Peanut shop. Ruefully rubbing my head, I gazed out the shop window at her. She glared back at me through the window then disappeared in the crowd. I guessed I could be taken for a boy, with my short haircut and my collar turned up. Lord knew I was straight as a stick. Not a womanly curve showing anywhere yet. I bought my salted nuts then keeping a sharp look out headed back toward Uncle Raymond's corner and the bus stop. My exuberance a bit dampened now, I picked up my skates and made a wild dash for my bus just as the doors were closing. Well, I thought as I settled in my seat. It really is a very small world after all. Sorting thoughts of the likeness and differences of this sad old women and my sunny Miss May, I stared out the window and munched my cashews. Floating Isle has her own place in Mobile's history, but my memory of her is deeply woven in the fabric of my tapestry.

Our Family

We have so many memories of our days at Wilmer Hall.
Through the best and worst of them, there is one of sweet recall.
I remember children's laughter, happy voices calling me.
Their exuberance spilling over, it sparkled for all to see.
Thus I learned that love, is a caring nurturing thing.
And the children that came to Wilmer
Hall, had so much love to bring.
We bonded very quickly as we shared our lives together.
It has lasted all these years, and will be there forever.
Like waifs, we came from near and far, cast from a stormy sea.
Battles won and battles lost, survivors all were we.
We may have had deep anger, for what life had done to us.
But Wilmer Hall changed that, and taught us how to trust.
We learned about the kind of love when children are put first.
In this respect it made us, the richest kids on earth.
The bond we share is not by choice, nor accident of birth.
But it was so strong we realized just what each one was worth.
Woven together by the strongest threads of shared respect and love.
Those same threads still bind us, as if carried by one white dove.
Though sadly some have gone to rest, there's still a tender hold.
For in our hearts here or not, we are siblings of the soul.

Betty Gentry Lowery & Orene Carlisle Fennell

Chapter 16

CHILDREN OF THE STORM

"Hello, are you with me today Betty? I am looking forward to you and me getting acquainted." I had heard his pleas before, and told him to go away, to leave me in my safe place. I did not want to hear him, much less answer him. I yearned toward that gray place. Wanting, needing to stay there. The place that was safe, where I did not feel or hear. There was no pain there, only blessed silence. There was no need to make an effort to be loved or accepted. Why, oh why would this man not leave me alone and let me hide there? Why did he keep calling to me? I did not know what to say to him. I wanted out of this world. "Betty, I want to help you. Your time is almost up here. I can't keep you here much longer. I don't want to send you to a state mental facility, but unless you will respond to me soon, you leave me no choice." Buddy, that got my attention like a dose of ice water. I sat up straight, and then glared when I saw him smile. "I want to stay here," I said. Totally misunderstanding me, the psychiatrist answered. "You can't stay here, you are in the Holcombe unit at Mobile General Hospital. This is the mental ward. We evaluate you here and decide what is best for you. I need your help to do this." I knew what the Holcombe Unit was. Mother had been in and out of there a few times over the past three years. "I am not crazy," I replied. "I believe you," he answered. "But you made an attempt to take your life. That tells me you were being irrational in the way you think. It is my job to find out why. To enable me to help you understand why. Only then, can I feel assured you won't do such a thing again." I began to cry and sat mute and miserable.

What could I tell this kind man, who seemed to feel I was worthy of his help? "I want you to do this, Betty. Go to your room and think about what I have told you. Then you decide if you want my help or not. If you do, then I will see you again the day after tomorrow. That will give you some time to think about things we need to discuss. I promise you, things are going to get better."

I went to my room in a deep study. A nurse brought my lunch tray. "I hope you are feeling better today Betty." I bit my lip and cleared my throat. "How long have I been here?" "Two weeks," she answered. She came and sat on the side of my bed. Taking my hand in hers, she stroked and patted it while I sat with my head down. "Your Mother brought you a cherry pie this morning. Would you like to come into the dining area and eat with the rest of the people here? I can take your tray in there. There is enough pie for you to share with the others, if you would like. You can see your mother tomorrow if you feel like it." "I can carry my tray." I said as I slid from the bed. "No, I don't want to see Mother." She carried me to the dining area where she introduced me to all the people. Some smiled and thanked me for the pie. Some were silent and sat at the table with their heads down. They were where I wanted to be. Off in another world. I stayed in the sitting room that evening and watched the others there. One lady talked a lot but what she said did not make much sense. Others seemed perfectly normal. There was one lady who seemed okay to me. Her name was Mary. She spoke when spoken to and seemed to pay attention to what went on around her. Maybe a little sad, but hey I could dig that. Who would not be? Three attendants come into the sitting room. One of them placed a hand on Mary's shoulder. "Mary, it is time for your treatment," said the nurse. "Nooo," she screamed, and tried to run. Two attendants held her. One by each arm while the third one picked both feet off the floor. He said, "Oh Mary darling, now you don't want to be this way, do you." I guess she did. She kept screaming as they carried her down the hall. I heard the heavy double doors as they closed and locked. Then all became quiet. I heard the lady who spoke nonsense, softly sobbing as a nurse comforted her and took her to her room for a nap. Another patient assured us all, Mary would be much better tomorrow. Geez manetti! I could be sent to the fruit cake bonanza because I did not want to think or talk? I had to think of something to explain my actions. It had to be something the doctor would accept or I might end up like Mary. Tell the truth? Well maybe a little of it.

"How are you today," Doctor Fueks asked. I put my hands under me and sat on them to keep him from seeing how bad they were shaking. "I am worried about Mary," I said. He gave me a sharp look as if he had gone on alert. "Why would you be worried about her?" I gulped so hard, I thought I had swallowed my tongue. "She didn't get out of bed this morning," I said. "Betty, I assure you Mary's fine. As a matter of fact, we are having a group session this afternoon. Would you join us? You don't have to talk to anyone unless you want to. Just listen and hear how others cope with different problems." I agreed, but for the life of me, I cannot tell you a thing anyone said. I do remember Mary was bright and cheerful. The life of the party you might say. It was the next day, Doctor Fueks sent for me. "I have some good news for you, little lady." He said as he motioned me to a chair. "I have a place for you to live for a time. Will you agree to visit me for therapy for a while, if I let you go live at a place here in town called, The Protestant Home?" What could I say? "Yes sir," I agreed. "I want you to understand Betty, this is a trial period. You will keep all of your appointments. They will be set once a week for a while, then maybe once a month if you find you can talk to me about your problems. We will try this till I feel satisfied you have it all together. I have faith in you. I believe you will succeed. By that time, hopefully a place at Wilmer hall will come available. That is where I want you to be. I think you would be happy there. Now here is what I want you to do. Your mother is in the waiting room. Go there and visit with her. Then go pack your clothes. Do you remember your social worker, Miss. Holly?" "Yes sir." "She has come to drive you to Protestant. I have already talked to your mother. She understands this is the best for you. I believe if we give you time in an environment where you are not taking the responsibility of an adult, a place where you can be a normal kid, you will heal. Now go visit with her for a few minutes, while I get the paper work done. You are on your way, kiddo."

I cannot tell you much about the days at the Protestant Home. Most of it, I lived in my gray world where I was cushioned from thoughts that I did not want to deal with. I did come to enjoy and respond on my visits with my psychiatrist. Over a period of time, I began to emerge once again, from that place where I felt buffered from the thoughts that hurt. There was a visit that I think was the beginning of my recuperation. "Betty, I am curious about this safe place you spoke off. Can you tell me about it?" I sat silent as stone. He waited for a moment. Dr. Fueks was a quiet, watchful man. He seemed to bring a calm peacefulness with him, when he walked into a room. He did not miss the slightest expression or nuance when he asked a question, whether I answered it or not. "How do you feel about helping other people, if you could?" I shrugged my shoulders. "I guess I would, if I could," I answered. He held my eyes with his gaze as he explained to me. "Some things I learn from one person, may help me help someone else. It would help me a lot, if you could tell me about this safe place." I had never noticed how nice his eyes were before. They looked kind and safe. Like I could trust putting my secrets there. "It's Mama's place," I stammered. "Her name is Dovie. It means, a quiet peaceful place." I took a deep breath. There I had said it. "How do you get there," he asked. "I look for the clouds, and then I just slip through." "What's it like there?" I rubbed my hands together real hard and played with my fingers, while I thought about the question. This was truth. I could answer this. Would he believe me? Would he think I was a hopeless nut case? I would just die, if he laughed at me. "Have you ever been on a boat on the water, in a fog?" I asked him. "I have," he answered me. "See, it's kinda like that. You hear sounds but they don't reach you. They are far away. The gray clouds keep thoughts away that I don't want to think about. If I don't hear and I don't think, I don't have to fool around to talk to anybody either. I am safe there. I just don't see why I can't stay there, if I want to." "What if you slip into that other place and cannot find your way back? It has happened to others before." Giving an I do not care shrug of my shoulders,

I answered in a petulant tone. "Then I would stay there. I would rather be there than here." "Are you living when you are there?" "I breathe, so you must know I am alive." What a strange question to ask me, I thought. "I know you are alive, but are you living? Do you understand the difference? It is called a concept. To be or not to be. There are different ways to look at this idea. There is living. There is death. There is a living death, where you are alive but not living. Which category do you fit in? Which one do you think is the most fun and useful to live in? Will you take time to think about this and come back to me next week with an answer?" "Yes sir," I replied.

There was one constant in my new home. One memory that is with me till this day. A little girl named Ruby. In the morning, she would meet me at the foot of the stairs. I do not remember ever speaking to her for a long time, but she chattered at me nonstop while we were together. She would take me by the hand and lead me in to breakfast. Ruby encouraged me to eat everything on my plate. If the weather permitted, she would take me outside to a place out of the wind. She would place me where the warm sunlight was shining on my face and tell me to look up and close my eyes. Sometimes, she would just talk to me and brush my hair. Other times, she would bring her jacks or paper dolls and colors. I think she was about my age, around eleven years old. She went to school. I did not. I have never thought about that till just now! They must have held me out of school. That would mean, I lost a lot of schooling that year! I am not sure how long I was at Protestant Home.

Ruby bounced her ball and picked up her jacks. I watched her small hands move like lightning to snatch the jacks and catch the ball. "Ruby," I begin, unsure on how to frame my question. "Are you living when you play jacks?" She clutched her ball, her hand still up in the air while she stared at me. Then she pinched herself. "Yep, I have to say I am alive." "No, not alive, living." I emphasized the last word in two syllables. "What's the dif?" She asked as she reached over and pinched me. "Ouch, you are nuts Ruby." I exclaimed as I scrambled beyond her reach. "Well, well. You are alive too, I see. Excuse me, living I mean. If you are asking me if I am happy playing with my jacks, the answer is yes. I am having fun, so I am happy."

"Will you teach me," I asked. I was asking for so much more than learning a game. I believe Ruby understood this plea. With a lot of whooping and giggles, Ruby taught me how to play jacks. By my next session with Dr. Fueks, I had the right answer to his question. So began the slow process of learning to face and talk about the things, I wanted to hide from. Those last days at home had been horrible beyond words. I spoke of them in slow painful increments, over a period of sessions with Doctor Fueks. I have never told another, till now. The thoughts of those days, still bring tears. It is not self-pity. It is just the sadness for the mother I love, and the way things were.

Doctor Fueks helped me understand. Divorce is a traumatic thing to overcome for anyone, even though the love that nurtured the marriage has died. I heard Mother, the night she lay across her bed, weeping like her heart was breaking, while she cried out to God. "No more Lord, No more. Take the love for this man from my heart." I guess he did, because shortly after that, she began to date. She had lots of boyfriends. Some of them were nice. A few seemed downright skuzzy. There was one who came in and ate everything in sight. "Sis," Bo said. "That son of a gun eat all the cookies, and drunk all the milk last time he wuz here. He used all the toilet paper too. Now he's coming back tonight. Can we hide the candy?" "Ye know Bo. They may be somethin we ken do about this one. Let's fix him a special batch of brownies for tonight." He grinned and asked. "What cha gonna do?" I smiled as I took a box of brownie mix from the cabinet. "Go look in mother's bathroom and bring me that box of X-lax." "Yea, yea," he chortled as he raced to the bathroom and back. "How much should we use," I wondered. "I don't know," answered my shrewd little brother. "All of it I think," he said as he dumped it under the mixer blades. That evening, the man ate till the brownie plate was empty. Bo hid the toilet paper. We worked slowly, cleaning the kitchen. We wanted to keep our eye on the unfortunate recipient of our chicanery. We did not have to wait long. With a bewildered look, he rubbed his belly. We could hear the rumbling sound, all the way across the room. His facial expression changed to consternation as he hurriedly excused himself and made a bee line for the bathroom. When he reappeared, he was sweating profusely and washing his face with one of Mother's washcloths. "Jane, I seem to be having a digestive problem. I will try to see you later. My god," he said as his stomach rumbled again and he beat a hasty exit out the door. "Or not," snickered Bo. We never saw Jimmy, the cookie monster, again.

I do not know what brought about the last break between Mother and me. I believe she felt some of her men friends paid too much attention to me. I do not know why they did. I tried to stay out of the way as much as possible. I did not like having to dodge grabbing hands when she wasn't looking. I do not feel it was my fault. It was more the type of men, she seemed to choose to associate with. I believe she was searching for a life mate and saw me as a threat. She had found a good job working at a fish packing plant at the State Docks. With her earnings and the child support checks, her financial burdens had lightened. I had taken on all the house work except cooking and laundry. My brothers pretty much took care of themselves, but I was there for them, if they needed me.

I had prepared her bath water for her that afternoon. I even filled it full of bubble bath. I stood on the porch and watched her coming down the street. "I smell something fishy," I sang out. She laughed as she climbed the steps to the porch. "I am ready for that tub. They say when you can smell yourself, everybody else has been able to smell you for two hours." "I have your bath ready and your robe and house shoes in the bathroom for you. Go on in while I make you a fresh cup of coffee." I heard the shriek all the way to the kitchen. I ran to the bathroom door with my heart in my mouth. She was standing with her hands over her face peeping through her fingers, while she looked down into the tub. I ran to her side and looked down. I almost fainted. All of her nice bath water was gone. The bottom of the tub was squirming alive with crawfish. "Oh Mother, I will clean it up. Those boys must have done this while I was in my room doing homework, or one boy. Most like Fred. He's the fisherman around here. I have your coffee making. Why don't you sit down and I will get it cleaned up for you. I did have your bathwater ready. I am so sorry." Then I giggled. Mother lowered herself to the commode. She wiped her face then broke out

in a fit of laughter herself. "Go get me a trash bag, and dust pan."
She gasped, "I will help." Once she was settled in the bath, I went
to look for the rest of my homework assignment. Aww geez. It was
not there. Going to the bathroom door, I rapped on it and called to
Mother. "I need to go next door and get the rest of my homework
assignment. I will finish it up there with Meredith cause I'm bout
out of notebook paper." She answered but I did not understand what
she said. Thinking it was okay, I went across the street. We were
almost finished with it, when I heard Mother on the front porch.
I could tell by her tone of voice, I was in deep trouble. I gathered
my homework and apologized to my neighbor, then made haste to
get out the door. Mother caught me by my shirt collar and yanked
me down the steps. Once I was on the ground, she put me in front
of her and beat my back and head all the way across the street and
into the house. "I am tired of watching you priss your tail around
like you, think you're grown." I tried between slaps to explain. "I just
went to do my homework. I had already cleaned the house." This
seemed to infuriate her more. "Oh yes, miss nasty nice. You seem
to think you are better than the rest of us. The home I provide is
not good enough for the high and mighty Miss Gilliland. Well, you
are going to mind me. I don't intend to chase you up and down the
street, when I come in from work. You get more like your daddy
every day. Sorry and trifling. You are supposed to be here taking
care of your brothers." She then began to rain blows down on me
with her fist, till she beat me down to the floor. Then she used her
feet. The last thing I heard before I fainted was, "I brought you into
this world and I can take you out of it." Mother was cooking supper,
by the time I came to my senses. I picked myself up from the floor
and went into the bathroom to clean myself up. My brothers were
still out playing. I was glad of that. I needed the time to pull myself
together. My shirt was ripped to pieces and I was bruised and bloody
from one end to the other. After I cleaned myself up and changed
clothes, I went to the living room and sat on the couch. I was not
crying any more but I was still holding a tissue to my nose to staunch
the blood "I am going out," Mother informed me. "I will leave dinner
on the table. Clean up the kitchen after everybody eats." It was not

long before a horn blew and she took of her apron. "I will be home by midnight." She never so much as looked my way as she went out the door. I surmised this must have been the cause of her anger. She was anxious about going out and thought I was about to leave her stranded with no baby sitter. I also think she felt guilty about going out dancing in the first place. Unreasonable I know, but are not most guilt trips?

My friend Meredith knocked on the door. "My mom is worried about you. She wants you to come over. She wants to talk to you. Will you come?" "I mustn't stay long," I said. "My brothers will be home soon. They'll tear the house down, if I'm not here to stop them." She put her arm around me. "It won't take long. Come on." Her dad was in the kitchen, drying dishes when we come in. I thought this a strange sight. I had never seen a man do women's work. "My God," he said as he threw down his towel and called for his wife to come there. "Dot, something has to be done for this kid. This can't be allowed to go on." She pulled me down to the couch beside her and held me close. Her husband gave her a wash cloth. Making soothing sounds and clucks like a little mother hen, she washed my tears away. Once I had quieted down, she spoke to me. "You don't have to stay where you are abused. If I tell you how to help yourself, will you do what I tell you to do?" "I will try," I said. "There is a place on Government Street. It is three blocks down from the bus station on the right. It has a big sign with a red feather on it. It is called Child and Family Service. I will give you five dollars for bus fare and to get you something to eat. Will you go there and tell these people what is happening to you? It's got to stop honey, before she makes a miss lick and hurts you worse than she already has." I did not see how it could get any worse. I hurt all over now, but I took the money and gave the promise.

As soon as Mother left for work, I dressed and ran to the bus stop on Michigan Avenue. There, I caught the bus going downtown. I arrived at the Child and Family Welfare Red Feather Center before they opened the door. I sat at the top of the steps, till a lady came walking up them with keys in her hand. I heard her take a sharp breath as she paused on the step below me. "What is your name, sweetheart?" I stood up as I introduced myself. "I am Betty Gentry." I was so terrified by what I felt I must do, I could hardly get the words out. She cupped my face in her hand and gently lifted my face. "Who did this to you, child?" I cried as I answered, "My Mother." She told me her name was Miss Holly. She unlocked the door and took me to a sitting room. She asked me to wait there, till her supervisor come. She assured me it would not be long. Within minutes, Mrs. Taylor arrived. Miss Holly introduced me to her and we went into her office. Mrs. Taylor examined my bruises and split lip. She made sure I had no broken ribs, then sat down to question me about my home life. She then turned me over to Miss Holly. I sat in her office, while she made phone calls. She asked me if I thought I could hold out at home, long enough to give her time to find a place, to place me. "It will take no longer then three days," She promised. "Go home but don't tell your mother you have been here. It would not be wise at this time. Just try not to do anything that will anger her. Be very careful."

I took the bus back home. Then I cleaned the house, as best as I could. When Mother arrived home, I spoke to her. "Your bath water is ready, Mother, and the coffee is fresh. If you want me for anything, I will be on the front porch." I tried to be as quiet and submissive as I knew how.

I had not seen my Uncle J.D., since he came to visit that night in Jemison, so many years ago. Imagine my surprise, when he walked onto my front porch that afternoon. After all these years, I knew him instantly. "Pat?" He questioned, as he knelt beside me "Uncle Josephine," I whispered, as I sighed and nestled my head on his shoulder. I rested there for just a moment. It was pure heaven. He stood up and looked down at me. "You wait here." Then without another word, he stormed through the front door. I could hear the rage in his voice, as he bellowed for Mother. They went to the back bed room and closed the door. I could hear a lot of yelling and screaming, but I could not hear what was said. When they come back into the living room, I heard my uncle say, "I could not believe Inez, when she called and told me what was going on down here. Jane, you were the one sister, I held the most regard for. I believed in and expected the best from you. How in the name of God, did you fall to this low? Hanging out with trash down on lower Government Street," he accused with such contempt even I shivered. "And abusing Pat. Damn Jane, an egg sucking dog doesn't deserve the kind of beating you put on her. Don't you know the law can put you behind bars for such as that?" Mother began to cry in earnest. "You just don't know what it's been like J.D.," she cried. "I put up with a drunk and worried about her for years. Now I have a chance to live my own life. Don't you think I have a right to do that? I work hard to support and give them the things they need. I don't think it's too much to expect her to help take care of her brother's." I heard the sound of a dining room chair scraping the floor. I left the porch and went through the other door that led into the kitchen and set up the coffee pot to brew. From there, I could see Uncle J.D. sitting at the end of the table. He was holding Mother's hand. "Look Jane, I didn't come here to make things harder on you. I came to see what I could do to help. It's just that when I saw Pat, I lost it. I brought Mama down with me. I left her with Inez. We brought all her belongings. What about I go bring her here? You need her, Jane. Will you try this?" "I suppose it wouldn't hurt," Mother answered him. He left but soon returned and unloaded Mama with all her clothes. She and Mother shut themselves in the bed room and talked, till long after bed time. The next day, Mama would not talk to me. I hugged her and told her, I was so glad she was there. She looked at me strangely. No warmth about her at all. "Go to school," she said. "You don't need to be late." I did not go to school that day. I went down and hid under the bridge. I did not want anyone to see my face. That would have been to humiliating to bear. When I come home, Mama was waiting for me. Hands on hips, she confronted me. "Where have you been? Don't bother lying. The school called. You have not been in two days. I am not going to cover for you. I have to tell your mother, when she comes in from work." I took my bicycle and went back to the bridge. This bridge ran from the end of Michigan Avenue for traffic into Brookly Field. The cars went over and the trains went under. My friend Carl and a few others, from our neighborhood, came to play under there too. It was kind of a neighborhood hangout, when we were not at the Thomas James Recreation Center. When it began to grow dark, they all went home except Carl. "It's getting dark," he said. "Come on and I'll walk you home." "I am not going home, till Mother goes to bed and is sound asleep. Then, I can get up in the morning and leave before she gets up." That should buy me one more day and I would hear from Miss Holly by then, surely. I thought I might as well get out, while the getting was good. It was for sure, things were not going to get any better for me at home, even with Mama there. I did not know what Mother had told her about me, but it did not seem like any of it was good. Maybe I was bad to the bone. I sure as hell, could get myself into some awful twists. "Have you eaten?" "Not since breakfast this morning." "Let me use your bike, so I can hurry. I don't like you here by yourself. I am going home and pack us some sandwiches and cokes. Is there anything else you need?" "Yea, a flashlight. So I can read my Sheena of the Jungle comic book." I grinned up at him. Carl was such a nice boy. He could make me smile, with the world coming to an end. "I'll bring two flashlights. I like Sheena too." I sighed as I questioned him. "What's your mom going to say about you being out so late, you gotta take your supper with you?" He grinned back at me. "Mom won't say anything. Haven't you noticed, I'm a big boy now?" I snickered at him and said. "Well, be glad it's dark, big boy. You look a bit ridiculous on that little girl's bike." Then I mumbled, "Wish, I was a big girl." "I will wait," I heard him say into the night, as he rode away. He came back with sandwiches and cokes. We talked about a lot of things, while we ate. He told me of his plans for the future. As soon as he graduated, he intended to make a branch of the military, his career. He had not made up his mind which branch. He even asked my opinion about that. Of course, I did not have one, but it still made me feel good for him to ask. He only brought one flashlight. "We will have to share," he said as he pulled me down next to him and put his wind breaker around me. Sitting on a folded blanket he had brought, we leaned against the cement wall. He snuggled me under one arm and held the flashlight, while I held the book and turned the pages. Carl kept time with his watch, till midnight. "Think it's safe to go home?" I stood up and began gathering our trash and loading it into the basket of my bicycle. "I think so. She should be well asleep by now." He pushed the bike and we ambled toward my house. Carl lived two streets over from me. "Take my bike," I urged him. "You can unload the basket. I have to be quiet." He squeezed my hand. "Okay, you take care," he said as he rode away. It was to be a long time before I saw Carl again.

I went to the front door of the house. It was locked. I slipped around to my bedroom window and removed the screen and raised the window. I was about half way through, when the light came on. There was Mama. Arms akimbo and her eyes blazing like the fires of hell. "Git in here girl." She reached across the narrow bed and helped me the rest of the way in, none to gently. "Shush Mama. Please don't wake Mother up," I begged. "She ain't here. She went out. I expect she'll have plenty to say to you, when she gets home. She already said, she was going to beat the tar out of you, when she catches up with you for skipping school. Then you go running off this evening, before she could get home from work. If this is the kind of trifling she has been putting up with, I don't wonder at her cracking up and whipping you, like she did." I covered my head with my arms and began to cry. "Mama, you just don't know." I tried to explain. "I know what I am seeing. You drove her to it. What you trying to do, drive her to another nervous breakdown? For shame, I can see you are as out of control as she claims. Go to bed. She will tend to you when she gets home." She slammed the bed room door and went back to bed. While I crawled under the covers, I thought of what was to come, when Mother got home. To make matters worse, it seemed I had lost the love of the person, I had most believed in. I had put Mama on a pedestal. She believed Mother. The feeling of betrayal was more than I could sustain. I cannot take another beating, I thought. Moaning, I covered my head. What to do? Should I get up and slip out. Where could I go where she could not find me? As I lay there, my fright and anguish turned to anger. This was not fair. I had not done anything to deserve this. The anger turned to rage and burned hot, till in a red haze, I threw the covers off and got out of bed. There was a way to escape, I thought.

Oh yes there is and I am going to take it. No one but no one, will ever beat me again. I cursed the world and every one in it. I took the ottoman to the medicine cabinet and climbed up. There on the top shelf behind all the other medicine, I struck gold. There was a full bottle of sleeping pills. I got a glass of water and took the whole bottle. I went back to bed and daydreamed of Carl, till I fell into a deep sleep, wishing with my last thought, I could have said goodbye. I vaguely remember someone crying. I think it was mother, while she and Mama were trying to pour hot coffee down my throat and walking me back and forth, in a long spooky hallway. I remember a man sitting by me and asking me questions. Then I found my clouds and made my get away. "You know more than I do about the rest, Doctor Fukes." He laid down the paper weight, he had been playing with, while he listened to me. "Yes, I am the man who sat beside you, asking all the questions. The doctor in the emergency room, pumped out your stomach and had your mother giving you coffee and trying to walk you up and down the hall, in the emergency room. I had asked him to help me hang on to you till morning, to give me a chance to reach Child Welfare. I knew something had happened and I did not feel it safe to let go of you, without someone to investigate your circumstances. I reached Miss Holly and found out an investigation was already under way. With Miss Holly's assistance, I had you court ordered into the Holcomb Unit. It's been a long hard battle, but we won. Now, Miss Holly is waiting for you. What say we three go celebrate with an ice cream soda and a big ole hamburger?

By the time I had begun to respond to Ruby's friendship, Miss Holly came and took me to Wilmer Hall. Ruby hugged me bye and told me, what a great home I was going to. I could tell she really wanted to cry but she did not. I did though. I wanted to take her with me.

It took only a short time, before I felt I belonged with my fellow brothers and sisters, in my new home. We squabbled, forgave transgressions, and loved like siblings, in any home would do. We were the survivors of life's storms. None of our stories were the same, but there was a sharing and bonding that last between us, till this day. At certain times, I think it would be on holidays like Valentine's Day or Christmas, Wilmer Hall and the other orphanage homes would give parties and invite each other to attend. This was not only a welcome fun diversion, but was an added pleasure to me, because I would get to spend time with my friend Ruby.

Before I close this chapter, I wish to say. Writing this has been the hardest thing, I ever attempted to do. I fear, others will feel I have condemned my Mother. This is not the case. I know my Mother had been a sick person for a long time. As she grew older, the times when she would lose control and grow violent came less frequent. Once I was grown and on my own, I never called for her assistance but she did not hesitate to hasten to my aid. She would do anything for me if I asked. I knew she loved me. Her doctor told me, she had early dementia. I placed her in a nursing home. I was already taking care of an elderly mother-in-law and a very sick husband. They died with less than a year between their demise. After David died, I took a four week sabbatical, then came back to take up the remnants of my life and walk on alone. Mother's doctor had placed her on Hospice Care. They only do this when it is believed, a person cannot last beyond six months. My youngest daughter, Connie and I went to visit Mother and tell her my David had gone to heaven. She asked, "Will you take me home with you? I don't want you to be alone. If you can't, I will understand." "Mother, I really don't see how I can. I have to keep working." She took my hand and kissed it. "It's okay baby, I do know how hard it has been on you. You need to rest." I went to the car and sat in the parking lot. I did not want to drive yet. "Do you want to do this, Mom," Connie asked. "Oh Lord yes. I do but I just don't see how." "Just do it, Mom. Just do it. You can. I will help you." I felt like a hundred pounds had been lifted from my shoulders and I had wings on my feet, as I went back inside to tell Mother the good news. I took her home with me and she bloomed like a little rose bud. She lived about two more years before she finally gave up. She told me, she was just so tired and felt so sick. She did not want to live like that. Even then, I tried to take care of her but my back and knee joints were gone. I could not help myself or her any more. She only lived a few months after I placed her back in the nursing home. How I missed her and grieved every day that she was not with me and I could not take care of her. Mother did an exceptional job raising five children to become decent adults. She did it under the harshest of conditions and much abuse to her own person, at times. Mental as well as physical. The things she did to us when we were children, were things she never remembered later. I am thankful she could not. I thank God her mind received peace in the last years of her life. It was a blessing from above, for both of us. I adore and yes, respect my Mother.

Chapter 17

WILMER HALL

Miss Holly delivered me to Wilmer Hall and introduced me to Mr. Whitt, who was the administrator. He was a pleasant man. He made me welcome before he took me into his office, where he told me what to expect from those who would be responsible for my care and what was expected from me in return. Everyone had their chores to do. The chores were rotated so no one had to do the same ones over and over. At the end of the day, I would join the rest of my sisters and brothers of my age group in study hall to do my homework. I would be in the seventh grade and attend Sidney C. Phillips high school. Mr. Whitt did not lay down a lot of rules. He made everything simple and easy when he said, "this is your new home. We want you to be happy here. It is my job to make sure you are. It is yours to do unto your brothers and sisters, as you would like them to do unto you." Then he introduced me to Miss. Fullford, my house mother. She was a short gray haired little old lady with a peppery personality. I did not think I would like her much. However, after getting to know her better, I came to realize she loved all her charges and wanted only the best for us all. Supervising the kitchen was a little bitty man, Mr. Burbage, and his assistant, Mom Ford. Mom Ford was exactly what she sounds like. A large built woman, by no means fat, just a big built person. She seemed to be forever on a diet. I thought this unnecessary because I found her to be just right. She was comfortable and motherly appearing. Mr. Burbage may have been small in stature but believe you me, there was nothing else about him small. He loved the children with all his heart and it was a big one. He made sure we were all well fed and taught us how to cook. His kitchen and dining area was spotless. He made sure we kids knew how to keep it that way. He had a rather high squeaky voice when exasperated. He squeaked at me on a daily basis. I regularly pilfered his food pantry and robbed his refrigerator. He loved me anyway. He said I grew on him, sort of like a wart. Then there was Mrs. Harris. She was supervisor over the little boy's dorm, but she had plenty of say-sos on what went on anywhere else. The upstairs girl's dorm was remodeled the first year I was there. The big girls were separated from the little ones and given their own room, two girls to each room. They were celebrating the occasion by jumping up and down on the beds while singing hail, hail the gangs all here. As Mrs. Harris stormed the stairs like a one man platoon set on quelling a national revolution, she was heard to say, "Yes and it's going to be hell when I get there too." She was a nice but very smart lady. No one pulled the wool over her eyes and got away with it. I was very shy at first but it was not many days past till I felt part of this family and carried on with my life and the pure joy of being a child.

On Father's Day, a group of air force men come from Brookly Field. They volunteered to be dads for the day. They carried us back to Brookly, where all kinds of fun things had been set up to entertain us. We did everything dads and their kids would do on a fun outing. The first thing I wanted to do was see my dad's airplane. Like any dad would do, mine never said no to plenty of hot dogs, Cotton candy, and cold drinks. When time to return home, he turned his sick little piggy over to my house mother with his rueful apologies.

Our school homework was over and done on Friday nights. This left the week end free for home visitation for those who wanted it. The staff members would usually gather the ones of us left into the station wagons and off we would go to the drive in movies. We attended church on Sundays at Saint Paul's Episcopal Church. I liked this. The services were quiet and orderly and so beautiful. I liked dressing up and wearing a hat too.

The older children attended Murphy high School. Murphy High and Vigor High were football rivals. We attended all the games. Two of my sisters; I think it was Sharon and Ann, and myself decided it would be great fun to sit on the Vigor side of the stands and cheer for Murphy. It did not take long for Degie, who was one of our house mothers, to round us up. I must say she got there a little too late. We three Murphy musketeers rode home with popcorn down our collars, orange crush, and mustard in our hair. Those Vigor fans could get really nasty when stirred up! They did not appreciate us one little bit.

During the summer months, there were plenty of outside activities planned for all of us. Trips for the girls to the beauty salon at Creighton Towers, Movies, summer camp, swimming trips to Gulf Shores, the Creighton pumping station or Johnson's Lake. All of this along with our everyday chores, T.V. and lots of play time, made for full happy days.

I had lived at Wilmer Hall only a few months. Ann and I walked home from church together. Ann was a very pretty girl with long wavy blond hair. Mine had morphed from blond to a light brown as I grew older. It had been almost white, the last time my birth father had seen me. Ann and I walked arm in arm into the living room and found a man waiting there. He seemed hesitant, as if unsure of himself. After making several attempts to speak; starting and stopping each time he looked directly at Ann and questioned, "Betty." Pointing at me, Ann answered him. "This is Betty. I am Ann." Taking a step toward me, he still seemed to find it hard to find the words to express himself. "I'm Thomas, your daddy," he finally was able to get the words out. I saw tears run down his face as he held out his arms. I ran to him then. As he lifted me in his arms, I heard him whisper with awe in his voice, "Oh so beautiful. I never dreamed, my little girl all grown up." He was trembling as he sat me back on my feet and wiped at his eyes with his hands. We visited together for the rest of the afternoon. He gave me a package to open. "Do you remember the last time I saw you? You were only four years old." "I remember Daddy. You taught me how to spell my real name, Gilliland." I spelled for him. "That's right, and you asked me for something. Do you remember?" "I do," I giggled. "Well open that package and let's see how close I come." Tearing open the package, I pulled out a stuffed sock monkey. "I couldn't bring a real one. Didn't think it would be allowed you know," he grinned. There was also a pair of boots and a pink bathing suit that fit perfect. "You remembered. How did you know the size?" I wondered. "Mama Dovey told me," he said. He did visit once more and asked me if I would leave Wilmer Hall and go to him. We discussed my Grandmother, his mother whom he said he wanted to take me to meet. "She wants very much to get to know you," he said. "Daddy, I don't even know her name. Mother always referred to her as my Grandma Willet, the witch. Mother told me she was an evil woman. It would hurt Mother to much if I did this. I am happy at Wilmer Hall. They are good to me and I don't want to leave." He left and I never saw him again. Mother let him take Jimmy Ray with him supposedly for a visit but he did not bring him back. Mother went to the law about it and was told no custody had ever been settled over Bo and I. Mother said, "Well enough of this noise." She went to friends of hers who could help. She traced Daddy to Starkville, Mississippi. Then she hired six of the biggest burly longshoremen she could find and not only went after my brother, she brought him home. Bo told me to be glad daddy never got his hands on me. He said daddy was a bad man.

A trip to gulf shores was in the planning for the coming up week end. I was all excited as I tried on my new bathing suit. I was also excited because I had turned thirteen and was moved from the little girl's dorm to the big girls. My excitement dissolved to a full blown pout, as I scrutinized myself in the full length mirror. Not fair, all the other girls were developing boobs. While I was not fulfilling my idea of what I felt a woman should look like. I removed the offending garment and threw it on the bed. "I am not going," I wailed. "What?" Asked Sharron, peeping over the dividing partition between our rooms. "Not going? You most certainly are. What is wrong with you?" "My suit don't fit," I sniffed. "It's flat on top." "Put it on. Let me see. From what I saw it looked down right sexy when you tried it on." Grumbling about her deprived eyesight, I advised her to eat more carrots. Never the less, I did as she bid me, and put the suit back on. "See," I said. "It's all flat and wrinkled." Sharron began to pluck and tug on the material. "You know there is something we can do. How much money do you have?" "I got a dollar and fifty cents." "That's enough I think. I will pay the bus fair and loan you what you need if you don't have enough. Get dressed, hurry. Go tell Miss Fullford we want to go shop for some things we need for our swimming trip." Miss Fullford gave permission and away we went. All the way down town to Kress's five and dime. I am sure the unsuspecting lady thought we were going only as far as Creighton. She would have never let us gone to town alone. It was there I purchased my first pair of genuine falsies. I was so proud on the day of our swimming trip. Once on the beach, I removed the strap that hooked around my neck and put it in my beach bag. My, oh my, did I feel cool. I did till I began to play in the water. Jerry, one of the big brothers I most admired, bounced me up and down in the waves. About the third bounce my suit came down to my waist. Dear brother's mouth fell open. His eyes bugged. He dropped me like a hot potato and ran. My pretty lacey boobs escaped from my swimsuit, caught a wave and gleefully headed for shore. Snatching up my suit I went after them as hard as I could go. Alas, I stopped in the water and watched them as they made shore ahead of me. The boys found them before I could get there and began a rousing game of keep away. I sat on the beach and cried. My sisters, upon learning the cause of my distress, joined in the game. With snarled insults and jeers, they captured my false boobs and returned them to me. Gathering around with comforting comments about boys, who were really just baboons and not to be sanctioned with a girl's attention any way, they stuffed my bathing suit front and put my strap back where I should have left it in the first place. Upon returning home, Miss Fullford summoned me to her room. There she commandeered my falsies' and threw them in the trash. Good riddance, I thought. I was glad to see the last of them.

Mr. Burbage made the best sesame cookies ever. We called them bird seed cookies. I could never seem to get enough. No one was about in the kitchen that day and the pantry was unlocked.

The cookie barrel was full of fresh baked birdseed cookies. I only intended to eat just one or two. I locked the door from the inside and sat on one of the barrels. I ate cookies till I heard Mr. Burbage pounding on the door and screamed. "Who's is in there? Come out right now. Right this minute, come out," he demanded. I quickly stuffed my pockets and mouth, before strolling out. "What were you doing," he screeched as he sprang through the door. I slammed it shut and locked it from the outside. I let him holler till I had finished all my cookies. Err, his cookies. Then I unlocked the pantry door. I ran out the back door while he banged around the kitchen, heaping dark wishes upon me and any little monstrous progeny, I may ever have in the future. Heck, I did not do him near as bad as Ann did. She locked him in the cooler and went away and left him there. She did remember to come back later and let him out.

I was filled with joy. I was a big girl now. I was finally to be allowed to work in the kitchen to do more than washing dining tables or mopping the floor. Mr. Burbage had promised I could make cornbread muffins. He gave me a recipe, set out bowls, measuring spoons and cups. With a gimlet eyed look he quipped, "I feel sure you know where everything is to be found in the pantry." I innocently assured him I did. While I measured and mixed according to the recipe Raeford prepared and preheated my muffin pans for me. I thanked him for this because the pans where so huge and I was a very small person. They would have been entirely too much for me to handle. He took them from the oven and I proceeded to fill each muffin hole with the mix. I waited anxiously during the baking time. Raeford and Mr. Burbage removed them from the large ovens and placed them on the counter top. They were golden brown and oh so beautiful. "My, my," said Mr. Burbage, as he smiled and reached to touch one with his finger tip. Plop! A big bubble drifted up. Frowning he reached to touch another one. Plop, it caved in and another bubble drifted up. He began to prod and sniff in earnest. "Why that's, that's washing powder," he stammered incredulously. We all three ran for the pantry. The lids on the barrels told the sad tale. They had been switched. The lid marked cornmeal was on the washing powder barrel and the washing powder on the cornmeal. I had not thought to check the contents to tell the difference. We all ate light bread for supper. Mr. Burbage gave me a second chance. The following night, we had excellent cornbread muffins for supper.

Looking back I have to say, the year of nineteen fifty three was my last year as a true innocent child. In one hour of a day; one might find me building a play house for my dolls, balancing a broom stick on my nose, or participating in a wrestling match, or football game with the boys. In the next instant, I would be sprit zing perfume and trying a new shade of lipstick. I was outraged when Degi said to me, "Betty, you must not play football with the boys any more. You are becoming a young lady now. Those rough games are unbecoming and there is a good possibility you could get hurt." "I love my boys," I protested. "They are more fun than girls and they would not hurt me for anything. They are very careful of me, Degi. They always play two hands touch instead of tackle, so I will be safe." Raising her eyebrows and taking a deep breath Degi sputtered, "Betty, understand me. Those boys are not playing two hands touch out of consideration for your delicate gender. You will not play football with the boys anymore." Disgruntled and my temper all out of sorts, I stomped into the playroom to watch Mousekateers on the TV. Henry was there ahead of me watching a western movie. Giving him an evil eyed stare, I switched the channel. He switched it back. "Go to your dorm and watch your own TV," I screeched as I smacked him up side his head. I tried to get him in a head lock to take him down but he shoved me backwards to the couch. I was wearing a flared tail skirt with three full crinolines underneath. Landing backwards on the couch, the crinolines flew over my head. I must have looked like a full blown pink and white rose with two legs and a pair of pink panties at the center, thrashing wildly before Henry's amazed eyes. Batting my skirts from my face, I reared up to bring the fight to him until I saw the expression on his face. He appeared as though he had been bonked on his noggin with a hot air balloon, his eyes and mouth forming three large zeroes. With nary a word, he switched the channel back to the Mousekateers and sat down beside me. I watched it a few minutes and thought, it is a rather childish program. Then I went to the TV. Looking over my shoulder, I smiled at Henry as I changed the channel back to the western. I settled beside him on the couch. Henry took a big Baby Ruth candy bar from his shirt pocket. "Pac?" He asked. With a shy smile, he halved it with me. Maybe Degi was right, I thought. I guess I am too old to play football and fight with the boys. Eating their candy and enjoying their consideration is much more fun than fighting, and I was not really that good at football anyway.

When the teen hormones began to beat on the front door, I do believe all my good sense and human decency fled out the back. I was a terrible monster. I became jealous of any girl I thought was prettier than I. I coveted Ann's beautiful hair. She had a record collection with all of our favorite rock stars in it. I wanted one of her Elvis records but she would not give it up. We fought and I do not know why the others girls took up the quarrel but they held her down and I cut off her hair. It was a horrible thing to do. Ann was so hurt and angry. She took her whole record collection and threw them down the stairs one at a time. Records were flying everywhere. I went to bed and covered my head. Why had I committed such an unforgivable act against my sister and best friend? I did not know. Ann was as loyal as could be. She had always backed me up with everything I choose to do. We did make up and she forgave me. I do not know how she could have but she found it in her sweet heart to do so. Once more my dear sister, I give a public apology and ask forgiveness.

I was home for a week end visit with my mother and brothers. We had all sat down at the dinner table. I noticed Chester was eating with a spoon. "Use your fork, Chester." I admonished him. "Babies eat with spoons. Are you a big baby?" He did not say a word. He just looked at me with the biggest blue eyes I had ever seen. I saw tears begin to form. He lay his spoon down and left the table to go outdoors. "Well for goodness sake," I said. "What is wrong with him?" Placing her hands in her lap, Mother leaned toward me. "Betty June," she said. "Your little brother can't eat with a fork. He shakes and jerks to bad. The doctor says he has a disease called Saint Vides Dance." With fear in my heart I asked, "What is this? What caused it?" She shook her head as she replied, "I don't know. It has something to do with his nerves." I sat still while I absorbed this information. "Please excuse me, Mother. I have a fence to mend," I said as I went out the door. Chester was sitting on the ground with his back against a tree. He was crying quietly. I felt my throat constrict and my heart melt as I walked towards him. He was such a beautiful child. A feeling of protective love welled inside me. I sat beside him for a while and just held him. I told him I was sorry I hurt his feelings. I promised never to do so again. A new bond formed that day between Chester and I, which extended beyond the two of us, to all of my brothers. I think it is the purest form of love that can exist with human kind. The love that can be found between brothers and sisters is a caring love, totally unselfish and forever.

My brothers do not have very many memories of our child hood. I can only suppose they chose to block them out. Maybe they had to in order to survive. This book is written for them as much as for me. I think they can take great pride that we all grew to be God loving honorable human beings. I know I am proud of them.

Wilmer Hall was located within walking distance of Springhill Collage. In the nineteen fifties, the collage was an all-male Catholic institution. There was a large lake belonging to the collage. It sat in the middle of a heavily wooded area, called Rag swamp. The boys from our home were allowed to go to the lake to swim. No girls were allowed. No un-uh, not allowed, none ever. That in itself was like waving a red flag under my nose.

I had already had my first run in with one of the good fathers of the collage. I was bike riding, an English made bike, on one of the cobbled streets of the campus. I was on a steep downhill grade when my brakes went out. The only thing to stop me was the brick wall at the bottom of the hill. At least it was, until a priest walked into the intersection. I tried to dodge him. I swear I did. Did you know some priest sometimes say ugly words?

The girls and I all agreed to be the first people to go swimming in the New Year. On the first day of the New Year, we all headed for Rag Swamp. We felt safe enough to skinny dip because no one would come to the lake at this time of year. How could we have guessed my one time abused priest would bring his little flock to the lake to meditate? He surely had his hands full that day, ordering his charges not to look and screaming at the girls to come out of the water. Naked girls were scrambling from the lake and grabbing clothes from the bushes. I was not a fast swimmer and I had been in the middle of the lake, so all the girls had scattered into the woods, by the time I got out. I was hastily grabbing my clothes from the bush and trying to run at the same time. "I know you," he bellowed pointing his finger at me. I made a hasty retreat and put my clothes on before leaving the woods. Damn, I had left my bra on the bush. It had my name plus my current boyfriend's embroidered on it. Nothing was said till supper time. When someone lost an item and it was found, the finder would present the lost item and the owner would have to sing at the supper table to get it back. All was unusually quiet in the dining room that evening. The girls were very subdued for good reason, but why were the boys being so silent? Then I knew. I heard the snickering start. I raised my head and looked toward the other side of the room. There sat Jerry with my bra swinging back and forth from the end of his finger. With my face burning, I marched across the dining room. "Sing, sing!" The boys chanted, as they beat on the tables. "I got a feeling, bird brain has already sang," I snarled as I snatched my bra from his hand. "I got a feeling someone needs to learn how to keep her clothes on," he snarled back. After supper, all the big girls were read a riot act. We were grounded for two weeks and made to sit on the stairs two hours in the afternoon. Poor Lucy had a date that week end. Her boyfriend came only to find his date grounded and sitting on the stairs. He sat in the living room. Making obnoxious comments, he teased her through the banisters unmercifully.

I had fallen in love. As usual, like most of the choices I made, the boy of my choice was not acceptable. He ran with a wild bunch. He had dropped out of school, had no job and was on probation. Jeremy's story was and I stuck to it. His cousin stole a car. Then come to Buddy to show off his new wheels. He took Buddy for a ride and offered to let him drive. Ergo, the police caught Buddy behind the wheel of a stolen vehicle.

We had lost Mr. Whitt to a heart attack the year before and Mrs. Harris had taken his place as administrator. Degi and Ma Fitt had become two new house mothers that past year. Looking back on those days, especially after raising daughters of my own, I can only imagine the anguish they felt at my hard headed actions. "What do you want your life to be?" Degi asked me. I tried to explain. "I want a home of my own. I want a husband and babies. I want someone to love, that will love me back without telling me I got to do this or that before they can love me. That's all I want." She put her arms around me. "Honey, you can have all of that and so much more. Think about what you are asking for. Who do you think is going to pay for that house? Who is going to buy food and clothes, for those children you want? Who will pay the electric bill and the water bill? There will be doctor bills. All of these things you want, you can have some day. First, you must grow up and train yourself for a job. You must finish school. Then, you can have anything you want." "But Degi," I wept. "I don't need school. I know how to keep a house clean and take care of children. Jeremy will pay the bills. He will get a job, if everybody will just give him a fair chance. What you say I must do will take years. I don't want to wait. I don't want to go to school. I hate school, and besides it is wasted time. I don't need school." With those words, I left the shelter of Degi's arms and bounded up the stairs. My mind was made up. I went to the phone and called Jeremy. We made our plans to run away and get married. We would go to Mississippi. I would get my daddy to sign the papers. Then we could live with my daddy, till Jeremy found a job. "I will call Jake," Jeremy said. "He has a car. He will take us to Starkville. If I give him gas money, I bet. I will call you back soon, to let you know." Jeremy called me back right away. "It's all set. Meet me on the little dirt road, an hour after dark." I packed my bag and hid it under the bed. After the sun set, I slipped down the stairs and ran to the road that bordered the grounds of the home. True to his word, Jeremy picked me up. Jake was driving. Two other of our friends, Rhythm and Lester were in the car. Excited and laughing, we headed to Mississippi. Just across the state line, Jake pulled into a service station. "Hey daddy-oh," he said to Jeremy. "We gotta have some more gas and some snacks. All our tanks are about empty." Jeremy pulled out a twenty dollar bill and handed it to Rhythm. "Ya'll go get what you want and gas up. Me and my baby gonna sit here and schronch. Bring us back some chips and a drink. We will share." For those of you who may wonder, schornching means kissing. When we left the station, Jake was driving fast. "Slow down man, we going to a wedding, not a fire. Why the speed?" "I didn't have enough money to pay for the gas, man. I needed a full tank. I ain't staying in Mississippi, ya know. I gotta come back home." It was then we heard the sirens. "What ya want me to do," asked Jake. "Now's a fine time to ask asshole, you know you can't outrun em in this bucket of bolts. Pull over." When the policeman saw how many of us there were, he called backup. Two more cars came. They loaded us all up and took us to jail. I do not know where they put Jeremy and the boys. They took me to a different place and locked me in a cell. I looked around me and thought, 'My God, do they expect a human to stay in this pigsty.' There were metal plates with molded food stuck to them. A mattress on a metal cot bolted to the wall, appeared as if it had been used by hibernating bears for many winters. There was a rusted sink that I am sure someone had used for a piss pot by the smell of it, with a blackened metal cup sitting on the side. No commode, just a bucket that stank to the high heavens. I stared around in horror and dismay. The final straw to break the camel's back was the deputy. He came into the cell. He looked like a cocky little runt to me. "Let me have your belt." He said with a grin. "What you want with my belt?" "Why, little girl I want to make sure you don't hang yourself." I was beginning to feel a wee bit put upon by then. "Fool," I snarled. "I ain't fixing to hang myself and you ain't getting my belt, and what's more, I refuse to stay in this filthy place." While the deputy thought things over, he leaned against the bars and chewed some on his tobacco. "Well now," he drawled. "You here and here you gonna stay." He jangled the keys at me. "Now let's have that belt. Then you can crawl on that cot and go to sleep, like a nice young'un and don't give me no more trouble." He held out his hand and wiggled his fingers in a gemmy motion. "Daddy-oh, you ain't seen no trouble yet." I purred as I backed into a corner. "You ain't getting my belt, and I ain't

sleeping in this filth." He came after me. That was his first mistake.
I aimed a kick at his straddle. I missed and caught him in his knee
cap. Glaring at me, he bent to rub where I had kicked. That was his
second mistake. I reached and got him by the hair with one hand
and slugged his nose with the other. Play fighting with my Wilmer
Hall brothers had taught me how to pack a punch. He came in for a
close grapple and I began to scratch, bite, and slug for all I was
worth. All the cussing and screeching brought the sheriff from the
front office. "Bob, what the hell are you doing? Get your hands off
that child." The deputy turned me loose and backed away, while
trying to wipe his bloody nose. "You said get her belt, and she ain't
no child. She's a little hell cat, is what she is. You need to be finding
out who she belongs to quick. We will probably have to pay them to
take er back. She don't like our accommodations much either." He
pulled out a handkerchief and wiped his face, as he stared at me like
I had horns. Picking his hair loose from my hands, I said. "You keep
him away from me or I will make his balls ring like the bells of saint
Mary's next time." The sheriff's mouth fell open and his face turned
red. Turning on his deputy, he barked. "I didn't tell you to come in
here and start a young war. You just ruffled her little feathers the
wrong way is what you did. Now come on and leave her alone." They
locked the cell and went back down the hall. "I can't believe you
couldn't handle her without roughing her up that way," the Sheriff
grumbled. "For Christ sake, she ain't no bigger than a bar of soap
after an all days washing." "Hey," I yelled down the hall at their
retreating backs. "I want some hot water with lots of soap and a mop
and broom. Some rags would help to." I muttered as I looked
around. They laughed long and loud as they slammed the door, at
the end of the hall. I did not wait long. I lifted the mattress, dragging
it to the bars, I turned it sideways and threaded it through. Then I
picked up the metal plates and stacked them beside the bars. One at
the time, I reached through and sailed them down the hall toward
the door. Moldy food flew against the walls and on the floor. They
made a very satisfying clanking sound as they struck the door. Then
I picked up the tin cup and played jingle bells up and down the bars.
"Now what the Sam hill is this?" I heard the sheriff's voice boom, as

he opened the door. "I told you, Dan. See, I told you. Don't you let them pretty blue eyes fool you. That one is the devils daughter." "AWW shut up, Bob. Go see what she wants," he said kicking the tin plates. "And whatever it is give it to her. Whatta mess, but for God's sake don't open that cell till you do." Here comes Deputy Bob. His face all scowling and scratched. "Now what do you want. Ain't you created enough hell to suit you tonight." I told him what I needed and with an angelic smile requested a clean mattress and blanket to boot. After delivering the things I requested, he asked. "I don't suppose you want to clean up the hall to?" "Not hardly," I said as I handed him the stinking pot to dispose of. "I didn't think so," he sighed as he took his long suffering self, down the hall.

Mrs. Harris came and picked me up the next morning. She drove us home without a word, till we arrived there. She faced me in the living room. "You will go upstairs and get a shower. Then come down to the kitchen, I will talk to you while you eat." I did as I was told. I found her and Degi waiting for me along with my food on the table. I sat at the table and said grace. Then I waited. "Eat," said Mrs. Harris. "I have brought you home in the hopes you have learned a lesson. We love you but you must learn. Rules are made for a good reason. They keep order. Without them, our homes and communities would be complete chaos. I have other children here to consider besides you. I will not let you destroy the reputation of our home, nor the hard work of people, who have only yours and the other children's best interest at heart. You cannot stay here and see Jeremy. You have a choice. Stay here, attend school and obey the rules of this household. Forget about Jeremy till you finish school. Then you may be wise enough to go wherever and do whatever you wish. If you continue to see this boy, you are no longer welcome here." With that ultimatum, she left the table. Degi took my hand and squeezed. "Everything is going to be okay, Betty. Just try to do like she asks for a little while. Show her you are trying. I am not saying you don't love this boy. But if you will try for just six months to do your best, I believe you will see a difference in the way you feel. If Jeremy really loves you, he will go back to school or at least get a job and prove himself. If he did that, I believe Mrs. Harris would agree to let the two of you date till you finish school. Just six months. Will you try?" I agreed to try. As it turned out, Jeremy was no longer a bone of contention. He was charged with taking a minor across the state line for immoral purposes and sent to prison.

Things did not get better. I really did not give them a chance to. I was resentful and surly. I did not do my best at school. All of my grades were down. I just could not seem to find the wherewithal to study or care about anything. I had a mad on at the whole world. My bad attitude had lasted for a few weeks when finally, Degi tried to talk to me again. "Betty, there is a special school in Mississippi, I wonder if you would be interested in looking into." "What kind of school?" She sat down beside me. "It is a school for special people. You once told me you wanted to be a nurse. This school would teach you all of the things your regular one does but teach you all the other things you need, in order to fulfill your long term goals for whatever you wish to accomplish later on." I closed my mind to her right then. "I will think about it," I said. I got up and walked away. Fuming to myself as I went up the stairs, I thought. Special all right, yah sure, it's special. They want to stick me on a funny farm with a bunch of drooling idiots because my grades are not good. Well I will not go. I did not slip away in the night that time. I just packed up and walked out. Everything good that had been offered me, I destroyed and threw away out of spite and misunderstanding. Not wanting to hear the wisdom of my elders. Not willing to learn the art of compromise. Not trusting the advice of those who loved me. Is there any way to understand a troubled teenage mind? They only want to love and be loved. They do not comprehend the responsibility that must go with loving and being loved in return. There are some, who want to belong to the group so they follow and find trouble they do not know how to handle. Given time and firm guidance, these will come aright. But there are some who walk to the beat of their own drum, rebellious to the point of self-destruction. More than a firm rein is needed. Loving but strict discipline, where one is force fed the instruction of wise adults, can and should be applied. It took more than a few hard knocks and some years, before I was willing to look back to what I had been taught at Wilmer Hall and let those teachings help me find the way to become the kind of person, I wanted to be. I had a long hard road to walk ahead of me. As Aunt Pearl once said to me, "um um chile, you sho do picks the long row to hoe, you does. Maybe you learn someday if you live long enuf." She recognized my rebel heart before anyone did.

Chapter 18

BEND OR BREAK

I went to Aunt Burma begging sanctuary. We agreed that I would help with the house work and baby sit my two cousins, Charles and Milton, to earn my way while Aunt Burma worked. I did not mind this. Aunt Burma made no demands on me that I could not deal with, and Uncle Roy was a prince, as far as I was concerned. My little cousins loved me and I loved them. Sometimes, I pretended they were mine. As long as I kept my ten o'clock curfew, I was free to do as I pleased. If I came in late, Uncle Roy would slip to the door and unlock it for me, scold me in whispers and threaten to cut out my allowance or ground me. I would just laugh, kiss his face and go to bed. Word soon spread through the neighborhood that I was back. Carl hunted me down and we began to see each other a lot. Not official dates, just meeting at the rec. center and hanging out. Late one afternoon, Carl came to the house. Rule was no boys in the house unless the adults were present. We sat on the porch and talked, while we watched the children play and waited for Aunt Burma to come home. "I graduated this year, you know," he told me. "I heard," I said. "Congratulations. What do you want to do now?" "I told you what I was going to do. I joined the army. I leave for boot camp in three days. Will you be here when I get back?" My heart skipped a beat. "I don't plan on going anywhere." "Will you wait for me? Will you be my girl," he asked as he slid his arm around me. "I have waited for you a long time. I wanted you to grow up." He took a small box from his pocket and opened it. I was breathless at the sight of the tiny ring with two hearts entwined. "Will you wear my promise ring?" Tears filled my eyes and I trembled all over as I said, "yes." He was so shy and sweet as he slid the ring on my finger and kissed me so gently. "Wear it till you are ready, then I will have another much more important question to ask you. Will you think about going back to school while I am gone? I believe you will be happier with yourself if you do." "Maybe I could go to night classes. I will think about it." Late that evening, we walked down to the vie dock to hang out with some of our friends and give me a chance to show off my ring. After every one left, Carl and I stayed and played around on the train tracks skipping rocks. I felt restless and unsettled. I wished Carl would kiss me but he was treating me like I was still no more than his playmate. I liked Carl's kisses. They were different from any kiss I had ever had. The others were nice and fun but when Carl kissed, something wild happened. They made me want something but I did not know what. But damn, he sure was stingy with them. We heard a train whistle. "Come on," Carl said as he reached for me. "It is getting dark anyway. I need to walk you home." I dodged his hands and pointed up the track. "See that white post beside the track? I bet you a kiss, I can get to it before the train does." "No, it's to close." I sprinted down the tracks. I heard Carl's running footsteps, pounding behind me as we both raced down the tracks. I heard him scream once. "Get off." Then I heard nothing more but the frantic blowing of the train whistle and the wild blood pounding through me. I evened up with the white post, split seconds ahead of the train. I baled of the tracks as it went screaming by. I hit the ground, rolling downhill till I came to rest in the brush and wild Yaupon at the edge of the woods. I heard Carl sobbing a curse as he tried to pick himself up, some distance from me. He ran stumbling toward me and fell beside me on his knees. He began to run his hands over my arms and legs, asking if I was alright. When I answered him that I was, he grabbed me by my shoulders and shook me hard, then leaned back against a tree and pulled me onto his lap. "Why did you do that? Why, tell me why?" "To prove I could." Was the only answer I could give. "My wild child, how I love you. I always have, I always will," he said as he held me close and begin to kiss me, like he never had before. The frogs and crickets had stopped their singing. The rustling in the woods had gone quiet. What was this great blundering commotion that had disturbed their nocturnal peace? Then as he unbuttoned my blouse, murmuring broken words, "I've got to, lord I can't help it, you belong to me." He laid me back on the fallen leaves. The earth children renewed their chorus and went back to their nightly rambles. The wild child grew quiet and pliant. There was no danger here. Everything was as it should be. It was just Mother Nature glorifying the sweetness of life, the way only she knew how.

He walked me home and sang, Love Is a Many Splendored Thing. At my door, he pulled me down in the swing. While he held me, I felt the tears come from his eyes and wet my face. I touched his face and kissed each eye. "Why are you crying?" I asked. "Don't you believe I will wait for you? Six weeks is not a long time." He wiped his eyes on the shoulder of my blouse. "It's not that so much honey, well maybe some. I fear for you and these wild hairs, you get sometimes. That was a dumb thing you did tonight. I did something that I know is wrong too. I wanted to wait. We should have and I am sorry, but God, I was so scared and I wanted you to be mine so much." Wrapping my arms tight around him, I tried to ease his anxieties. "I am not sorry for what we did. I am yours now for sure, for all time." We were together on the next day, again pledging our vows to one another. I promised to think before I acted and never again, risk myself with childish pranks. Then to soon he was gone. My Carl never returned. There was a terrible tragic accident while he was in boot camp. I never understood how it could happen but his gun jammed. It must have been a heavy piece of equipment. It discharged its ammo back into Carl's face. I did not go to the funeral. I just could not intrude on his mother's grief with my own. I never cried. I put the ring on a chain around my neck and tucked it beneath my blouse. I pulled my pain inward and held it hard inside, next to my heart, so no one could see until it became a part of me.

Dixie was a girl who lived down the street. I did not know her well. She seemed okay when she came to the house and sat on the porch with me. One afternoon, she asked if I would like to go out with her and some of her friends. I accepted the invite. When she came back, she was with a carload of boys and girls I did not know, but I climbed in with them and away we went. It was agreed we would go to the Sea Breeze for the dance that night. Meantime, we would just cruise around the neighborhood and have burgers at Johnnies. Someone pulled out a bottle of Gin and begin to pass it around. The stuff tasted like pine resin to me. I pretended to sip, wet my lips and passed it on. They stopped at a gas station to gas up before we headed to the Sea Breeze. Everybody was loud and rowdy by then. Some of the things they were shouting and the language they were using, would have made a sailor blush. I saw a boy, whom I vaguely remembered as a friend of Carl's, leaning against the building. The look of disgust he gave, as he looked me in the eye, almost brought me to my knees. My face flamed hot and the shame I felt, made me sick. I turned from him and reached into the car for my purse. Slinging the strap across my shoulder, I walked away into the night and went back home.

From then on, I spent most of my time alone. I haunted the library at the rec. center and found friends in the pages of the books. I loved the historical books of famous men and women. Nancy Drew, the Hardy Boys, Concerning Mice and Men, and Cherry Aims Nurse. These were the kind of people I wanted to be, if I could just figure out how.

Sylvie was a pretty girl, I had seen at the rec. hall on a regular basis. Like me, she was another one who kept to herself most of the time. Once in a while, she would play me a game of cards or ping pong. She was tall and slender, with short black curly hair and the strangest golden eyes, I had ever seen. Sylvie never had much to say, so I was surprised when she sat down at the table with me in the library. "What cha find in these ole moldy books?" She asked popping her gum and giving a lopsided grin. "Nice friends," I said. "Hey goose, I can be a nice friend," she laughed. Laying my book down, I leaned back in my chair. "Ya think?" "Yea I think. Come and go with me and some of my friends tonight. Live a little. We don't cause no trouble, we just have fun, ya know? Besides, I got this hip guy that wants to meet cha." "Do ya'll drink," I asked. "Some of us drink a few beers but its cowboy's car. He drives an ya know, he don't drink at all." I was hesitant but I asked, "Ya'll going to the Sea Breeze?" She shook her head. "Naw, not safe there tonight, shipload of sailors have come in. The place will be crawling with them. Bikers will be there. Bikers and sailors don't mix." "Yea I got caught in that once. Once was enough. We had a hot set of wheels under us to get away in. We still counted six bullet holes in the trunk. So where do we go tonight?" "There's a place over in Prichard. You got ID?" When I did not answer, she said. "Here, I'll loan you some. See, when you go in the door, keep your thumb on the picture and flash the card quick. The door keep will let you through. No problem, he knows what cooks." I took the ID. "You know where I live?" She nodded yes. "Pick you up around seven," she said. By seven o'clock, we were headed for Prichard. The place was jumping. The music was good and the beer cold. I danced some with the new guy I meet. He was good looking but he just was not making it with me. He only wanted to dance the slow dances and hold me too tight. I always liked the fast dances. I danced for the pure joy of it. No other reason. We had not been there but maybe two hours at the most, when all hell broke loose. I do not know who shot John or why, but everybody was mad. There was a whole lot of slugging going on. I grabbed my full bottle of Little Gobel and a long necked empty, side stepped one lumberjack, going down like a felled redwood and dove under the booth. With my back against the wall, I sipped from my beer in my left hand and clutched the empty in my right. Woe to the man who tried to stick his head under that booth. Chairs were swinging, tables crashing all around and a lot of screaming and stomping but I was safe I thought, till I heard a curse and someone yelled cops. Oooh Nooo, I thought. Now I am in it deep. Yes Sir, I surly was. They cleaned that joint out, faster than a drunken duck can switch ends. I sat tight and quiet and hoped. A pair of black shoes below blue pants legs stopped by the booth. "Come on out," he said. "Don't make me come in and get you." I turned my bottle up and drained it, then rolled both bottles out into the open. "I ain't armed and I wasn't fighting. Can't you let me stay?" A big hand reached under the table. Grabbing my shirt, he dragged me out and hauled me to my feet. "Well, if this don't beat all," he said. "What cha got there,

Charley?" Someone asked. "I think I caught me an imp. Put her in the car. I will be there shortly," he sighed in consternation. "Come on, bobby sox. What's yer name kid?" He pushed me along in front of him. "Trouble, with a big T. If I don't come to it, it comes to me," I mumbled. Charley grumbled to his partner, all the way to the station. He did not want to do the paper work. His vacation started at midnight. "Just lock her up and let someone else take care of it in the morning. Go on home," his partner told him. They turned me over to a nasty looking man, they called the turnkey. He put me in a cell with six other women. "What's this," one yelled at the man. "You robbing the cradle for clients now?" I spent two weeks in that cell. I listened to their life stories. I was surprised to learn none of them grew up and decided to become prostitutes. They were raised to it. "It's just a way of life," said one. "I got used to it early on. My dear daddy sold me to the highest bidder." Another told me her husband bought her when she was twelve years old. "I decided I rather get paid for it, so I ran away from the mean bastard. Now I got me a man that's good to me. He makes sure the Johns treat me right. You want a phone number to call, when you get out of here? He would put you in his stable, he treat you nice." Another yelled across the cell. "Jean don't be putting that kind of shit in that girl's head. She don't wanna be no damn whore. That's a nice kid." With a loud huff, Jean replied. "Well somebody got to teach this baby some way to take care of herself. Where she gonna be? Always sitting in the slammer?" Laughing, another woman answered her. "What you gonna teach? Your black ass is sitting in the slammer." Jean swayed across the cell, with one hand on her hip. "Let's don't be callin no names here. You know, yo white ass is turned as many tricks as my black one." To my amazement, everyone roared with laughter. Then someone called out, "Betty, they say among thieves, there is honor. Among whores there is nothing, but I say. It's no disgrace to lose your drawer's, you can still hang tight to your honor."

Who knows how long I would have languished there, if not for a happening with a crazy drunk. The turnkey threw her in with us, in the middle of the night. I was sitting on my cot, smoking a cigarette someone had gave me. The new comer looked like she had not eaten a decent meal in months. She was a real bony Maroni. She had sores on her arms. Jean leaned from her top bunk. "Watch that one, kid. She's got a monkey on her back, stay clear," she whispered. I backed up on the cot and stayed quiet and still, but I kept smoking my cig. The woman lay in the floor where the turnkey had thrown her. After a while, she raised her head and looked straight at me. With a scream, she was off the floor and on me, fast as a lightning bolt. She grabbed me by my hair and ripped my ring chain from around my neck. She still had my hair as she fell back to the floor and I could do nothing but follow her. I put my cigarette out in her face but she still did not turn lose. I was trying to get my hands around her scrawny neck. I would break it if I could. All the women were screaming; fight, fight. Jean came from the top bunk and landed on her head with both feet. She turned me lose then. Jean grabbed me up and hustled me to the front of the cell and pressed me to the bars with her body. She was screaming for the turnkey. I was fighting to get lose but Jean was a strong woman. "She has my ring," I kept crying. The crazy woman came at Jean from behind but Jean turned enough to backhand her across the face. "Sit on the hopped up bitch before I have to kill her." Two other women held her down, till the turnkey got there and while he called for help. As more police arrived, Jean was raging at the turnkey. "Why you put that crazy bitch in here with us. She would have killed this kid if I had let her. You crazy mean son of a bitch. You just trying to have a little fun. You know, she should have been put in the tank." One of the men trying to help restore order, was a plainclothesman. He asked the turnkey, "What's that kid doing in here herself, is what I want to know?" The turnkey shrugged. "Ask Charlie. He brought her in and said find a place to put her. This was the only cell with an empty bed." Angry now, the detective asked me. "How long you been in here kid?" I shrugged my shoulders. "Twelve days Sir," someone answered for me. "Christ almighty. What's your name girl and how old are you?" "My name is Betty Gentry and I am almost sixteen." The poor man turned so red and choked, I thought he had swallowed his tongue. Rounding on the turnkey and stabbing at him with his finger, he roared. "While I check this out, you get her into a cell by herself. If my memory serves there is a missing persons report on her and we have been searching high and low for her for over a week." When the detective returned, he found me in a cell as he had ordered. "Your papers got lost in the shuffle kid. Seems you fell through a crack. It's all straight now. You will have to stay here till you see the judge. But that will be tomorrow, so no need taking you to juvie. Are you hungry? I brought you something." He pushed a bag through the bars. I backed away and just stared at him. "What's the matter? Come on, I don't bite." I eased toward him and snatched the bag from his hands, before I made haste to get away from the bars again. He studied me through narrowed eyes. "Has anybody, you know?" He stumbled awkwardly over the words. "Bothered you in here?" I eyed the turnkey. The detective slowly turned his head and lowered a smoldering gaze on him. "I ain't touched the little bitch. And if she says I did, she is lying." I stepped up to the bars and spit at him. "No he hasn't, but it wasn't for the lack of trying. He tried to buy me off with food. Ask the sisterhood. They heard him. It's them that's kept me safe." "You listen to me, you piece of filth. If you lay one hand on this child, I will tear you to strips and serve you to the judge in pieces. Now get away from here and don't let me find you in this section tonight." The nasty man shuffled down the hall. "Eat your burger kid. I will be back to check on you off and on till you are out of here."

The detective brought me a good breakfast, and the necessary's needed to bath and wash my hair. He gave me a clean change of clothes, from the skin out. "Your Mother brought these in," he said. "Do you want to see her before you go to the judge?" "No," I answered. I did not go into a court room. The judge saw me in his chambers. Mother and Mrs. Harris were there. The judge asked me, "What do you want to do with your life? Do you have any idea?" "I just want to live it. I just want everybody to leave me alone and let me do what everybody in this world wants to do. Be free to do as they please. I don't hurt anybody. I just want to be left alone." Everyone in the room stayed silent, till the judge leaned forward in his chair. "You are a child. You have no more idea of what you need then a baby chick, and as witless I might add. Here is what I am going to do. You will as of today become a ward of the state. I am sending you to the State Training School for girls. There you will remain until such time as they deem you fitting to leave. It is in hopes, you can be reformed and come back to this community and take your place as a responsible citizen. Wait outside for someone to come and take you back to your cell, while arrangements are made." Bang, went the gavel. Clang, went the doors.

I stood in that cell and gripped the bars. In a red rage, I shook them as hard as I could. I wanted to rip and tear something up. I wished I could tear down the stone walls, brick by brick. Mortar and iron bars do not rip to well. "You won't beat me," I raged. "I won't give. I won't bow. You will never beat me, never." I mouthed the last word as I sank down on the cot and cried myself to sleep. I thought I was dreaming, when I woke to the smell of fried chicken and a gruff voice calling me. "Hey kid, thought you might be tired of hamburgers by now. Come and get it." I sat on the cot and tried to get myself orientated, before I got up and walked to the front of the cell. The detective slid a plate in to me. "Sorry about it being so late. I got called away for a while." I held the plate and leaned my shoulder against the bars. "Why are you being nice to me?" I asked. "I have a daughter. She went through a bad patch there for a while, when she was about your age. I would like to think no one mistreated my little girl back then. She spent some time where you are going. It's not a bad place. It is what you make it. You only get out of anything what you are willing to put in. Capice? Learn to bend a little before you break. Let them help you there." I did not answer him. "I will bring you you're breakfast in the morning. Then you get ready and we are out of here." "We? You got a mouse in your pocket?" I smiled and took a bite of my chicken. "Cheeky brat, yea, me. My wife and I are going to take you to Birmingham. You're going to arrive in style kid."

I was dressed and ready when my benefactor showed up with my breakfast. Instead of waiting while I ate in the cell, he took me to his office. I made myself at home at his desk and wolfed down the bacon and eggs he had provided. Then he escorted me to his car. He put me in the back seat before he got in the front and turned to me. "Wife will be here in a little bit. I thought you might rather wait out here, than in side. Now listen up. I am supposed to shackle and hand cuff you. I won't if you will give me your promise, you won't try to run. How about it, will you give me your word?" I sat there, while I wondered if there might be some way I could run. "Well, is it that hard to make up your mind?" "If I give my word, I have to keep it." "Sure you do, else it's not worth a penny with a hole punched in it. So come on, give." He waved his hand at me. "Okay," I said, "I promise." Breakfast gave me a bad stomach ache. I stayed curled up on the back seat most of the trip. I did not want any lunch when we stopped. His wife escorted me to the ladies room and let me walk outside while they ate. I kept my word. I did not take advantage of their kindness and try to run. I sure did curse myself for a dozen different kinds of fool, for giving my word though.

I was released from S.T.S. three months before reaching my eighteenth birthday. My detective friend had been right. It was not a bad place at all. The grounds were beautiful and well kept. Miss Emma and her group of girls did the yard work. Everybody loved Miss Emma. She was goodness itself. Each cottage was named after an Indian tribe. I was in Cherokee Cottage. The chores in the cottages were rotated among the ones who lived there. I do not remember how many rooms there were per cottage but it was situated almost like a real home. With laundry room, large shared bathroom with multiple facilities. Privacy was curtains hung in front of the stalls and showers doors. There were living room, dining room and kitchen. Each girl had her own private bedroom and no one was allowed in the other person's room at any time. We all got along well with each other for the most part. If there was trouble, the perpetrator of said trouble was locked in her room and kept there till such a time as her counselor deemed the problem was resolved, with the understanding that the behavior of the offender would in no circumstances be tolerated. We did chores half a day and went to school the other half. Everything worked on a merit system. Each one had a chart. You break a rule, you get a demerit. Three demerits in a week and come Friday night, you got no candy bar and no movie. You stayed locked in your room, while everyone else got a candy bar and went to the gym to watch the movie. Then on Saturday, you would be locked in while everyone else went to the gym to skate. I think the less privileges one gets, the more appreciated they are and one will try harder to be deserving of them. I must admit, I did spend a few times locked in my room the first six months or so. I know something made a change in my bad attitude. The counselors were strict but fair.

Miss Helen led our Sunday services and taught the singing lessons. I was never able to carry a tune in a water bucket. When I try to sing, everybody leaves the building. Miss Helen was a kind dear lady. When she had to ask me to drop out of the Christmas chorus, I could see it hurt her as bad as it did me. I felt sorry for her and accepted her edit graciously, but my feelings were hurt. This was not the old Betty. Why, a year ago, I would have thrown a stomp down fit! Then she comes to me and asked a favor. "Betty, I need a story for young children for our Christmas special at church. I have here, Amyl and the Night Visitors. Do you think you might do something with it to make it interesting, to small children? I thought maybe use animal characters." I looked at the story and promised I would try for her. The story turned out so well, Miss Helen put me on television. I sat with a group of children by a Christmas tree and read to the children. That went so well, she asked me to do the same to Dickens's Christmas Carroll. I thought I would have a heart attack, the day she carried me to her church. There was a huge auditorium with hundreds of people in it. When she asked me to tell the story, I thought she meant a little village church. I had never seen a place this big. I trembled so hard I tap danced right out of my sling pumps. But you know? After I got into the characters of scrooge Mc Duck, Tiny Tim and his poor church mouse family, I forgot all about the hundreds of faces out there looking up at me. It was just me and my story. Miss Helen was well pleased.

I wrote a piece of creative art that I loved. The only problem being, it was not my own work. I was a very patriotic person. I loved my country. This writing spoke to my heart, so I copied it from memory and passed it around as my own. The piece was so good, it drew the attention of one of the counselors, who decided to see if she could have it published for me. That was when the truth came out. My counselor called me to the living room and closed the door. She laid the article in front of me and asked. "Do you know what plagiarism is?" I looked down at the sheet of paper. I did not know the word but I knew what I had done. "No ma'am," I answered. She laid the dictionary before me. "Look It up." She instructed me. "I can't, I don't know how to spell it." She wrote the word down for me and I found it in the dictionary. I read aloud, "To steal some else's work." Oh my God, I had always prided myself on being truthful and never being a thief. This was terrible. What had I done? I scrambled for a way out. "No one thought it was bad when I rewrote the Christmas stories," I cried. "No, but then you did not put your name on them and pass them off as your own either. You know the difference Betty. You are not that naive. Can you tell me why you did this?" "I love the work. It says what I feel for my country. It spoke to me, right here." With those words, I patted my heart. Smiling she said, "I feel sure the real author would appreciate that. Have you ever done anything like this before?" "No Ma'am." Then I remembered, "Well yes, I took the Sunday school money Mother gave me and bought comic books. Oh lord. I stole from Jesus. Didn't I." She appeared astonished. Then she laughed. Wiping her eyes, she asked. "Do you understand what you have done wrong here?" Crying in earnest, I could only nod my head yes. I was horribly mortified. "I am not going to punish you for this. I think you have committed an offense more against yourself than anyone else. I do want you to think about what you tried to do. It was a very dishonest thing. Had you succeeded, you would have been taken to court and sued. You would have had to pay a large amount of money in restitution. You harm someone else when you do this kind of thing. I want you to think about this for a few days and then we will discuss it again." She was right. I beat myself over and over, in the next three days. I could not sleep or eat. I cried to myself as I went about my daily routine. I felt lower than a snake's belly. I knew I would never overcome the shame and disgrace I felt. Three days later, my counselor took me to the living room once more. "What's going on with you Betty? Mrs. Heart tells me you have been very depressed." I began to cry. "I can't undo what I did wrong. There is no way to fix it." "Are you truly that sorry for your actions?" "I am very sorry," I said. "But that don't undo it." "Of course it does. All you have to do is forgive yourself. You didn't hurt anyone else. You know goodness comes from inside. That's where you need to start. God dwells within each of us. He cannot forgive us unless we have faith enough in him to forgive ourselves. Just remember one thing. If you will, you will never go wrong. Anything you feel you must hide to do is wrong. If it can't be done out in the open, it is wrong. It is only Gods right to plumb and ponder the depth of each person's soul. Only his to judge."

I left State Training School with the desire to make a better life for myself. I wanted to go back to school. I still wanted to become a nurse. I still wanted a husband and a home and children of my own, more then I wanted anything else. Surely, I could be a better person then I had been in the past. Live and let live, was my motto. Remember the golden rule, and hold fast to honesty. Surely, that was enough. Ah, the best laid plans Of Mice and Men.

Chapter 19

CROSS ROADS

My time at State Training School was up. Like the proverbial bird from its cage, I flew to my freedom. I was giddy with it. I was of age. Grown up at last and I could do as I pleased without breaking the law. I still had the burning desire for a husband, a house with a white picket fence and children to love. I did not think of those other laws. The ones placed by society to prevent chaos in our midst. Self-destruction, bitter tears, and wasted years are our punishment when we rebel against these laws of society. I thought I was so smart. I was so not ready for total unsupervised freedom. I moved in with Aunt Burma and Uncle Roy. I found a job as a cashier in a laundry mat, and I signed up for night classes to finish my schooling. I began dating. I was searching for that special one and so afraid I would never find him, or if I did he would not want me. I did not contact my old friends at all. Alas, some of them found me. Three of Andy's old buddies showed up to visit me at my place of employment. They asked me to let them rob me. This totally came at me from left field. I had never known these boys to do such things. I guess they graduated from small miscreants to bigger things. At first, I was mortified and ashamed as I argued with them about the plans they were making. Then I got angry. "I tell you what," I sputtered. "You leave here and never come around where I am again. Forget you ever knew me and I will forget you asked such a thing of me. Otherwise, I drop a dime right now and report this to the police." "Well, just listen to miss goodie two shoes." Sneered one of the hoodlum's, shoving his way into my space. "Someone may teach you what happens to little girls, who think they are too good for old friends. What happened to you in that place? They took away your grit?" I drew myself up to my full height. I was every bit of five foot two and weighted ninety pounds, but I stood my ground and looked him in the eye. They looked like what they had become, with their hair combed in duck tails and their collars turned up, white suede penny loafers and to tight black jeans. "I'm not scared of you punk, and If you believe that, you never knew me. I would never have agreed to help you steal then, and I won't agree to it now." I spat as I reached for the phone. Finally convinced, they left. I never saw or heard of them again. Good riddance to bad rubbish.

I dated several different men off and on. One of them, Frank, was an oilfield worker. He seemed to have his life in order, but he was gone a lot of the time. He asked me to marry him. I asked for time to think about it and promised to give him an answer, when he returned. Before his return, I meet Bill and forgot all about anyone else. I thought I could win and hold him. He made me no promises, but I loved him and I believed he was going to love me. How foolish is a young girl's heart? I knew he was divorced and had a son by his first wife. I should have read the signs. He still loved her. By the time he accepted this and made up his mind to return to her and remarry, I found myself left behind in his dust and very pregnant. I never tried to contact him and never told him about his child.

I was at work when Frank returned home and called. Aunt Burma took the call. She took it upon herself to tell Frank I was in trouble. He was waiting for me when I came in from work. He asked me to walk out to the car with him, so we could speak privately. Holding my hand, he said. "You and I have some decisions to make. I only have three weeks before I have to be in South America. That's time enough to get married and you can go with me. What do you say?" "I say, you are moving too fast. Have you had time to consider the responsibility of taking on a wife and child?" He stared silently, and then answered. "No child. I will pay for the abortion. I have a friend who knows a doctor. I can take you to him. Betty, I can forgive a lot but I won't raise another man's kid. I want my own someday but not any time soon. You are a hot blooded woman child.

I understand how this could happen to you while I was gone for so long." He put his arms around me. "I will never give you cause for regrets. I will be so good to you. I will make you love me as much as I love you." I pushed his arms from around me. "No Frank, I don't love you enough to marry you, and I never will. If I did, I wouldn't be in this condition. You don't love me either or you wouldn't ask me to do such a monstrous thing. I won't kill my baby before it even draws its first breath. It has more right to life than I do. It's never done wrong. I would say the same thing, if I knew I was going to die giving it birth." By this time, I was in a shrieking rage. "Think about what you're doing, Betty. You are too young to take on raising a child. It will need so much, you can't give it. You know how the rest of society looks down on those kinds of children. You know what they will call it?" "Go away. I never want to see you again." I gave the car door an extra hard slam on my exit and a swift hard kick to boot. Frank left the drive, slinging gravel behind him. He passed Uncle Roy coming in as he went out. Uncle Roy put his arms around me and asked. "What happened baby, you two have a tiff?" "No, Uncle Roy." Then burying my face in his shirt front, I wept as I told him I was pregnant. "I will kill him," he said. "Honey, I promise you when I get through with him, he will be glad to do right by you." "Ah, you don't understand Unck," I sniffed as I wiped my face on his shirt. "It's not Frank's baby. It's Bills. I can't tell Bill. He is remarrying his ex. I don't want to cause problems there. I messed up big time, Uncle Roy. I am on my own. I did this all by my own lonesome." "No you're not baby. You got me and your Aunt Burma. We will figure something out." The something was an unwed mother's home in New Orleans. I left before the month was out.

I spent seven long months there, continuously, refusing the counsel to sign papers that would give consent to allow adoption for my baby. I was gave all the reasons why I should. "I would pin a rose on the mother who puts her child's best interest first," said my counselor. "Betty, I can't urge you strong enough to think of what you are doing. You have nothing to offer the child but a life of hardship. First, he is being born without the benefit of a father. That's the first strike against him. Second, you have no job skills.

How can you support him? You do not begin to realize the enormity of the problems, you are trying to take on. You are not equipped for this." I cried and refused to sign. "Let me get these job skills," I begged. "I have found a school close by. They are offering to teach me typing and filing. With this schooling, I could find a good job to support my baby and myself. Let me do this and keep my baby." She refused. "We are honor bound to protect the girls who live here. They are in seclusion, till they leave. We cannot let any information about our home, go public. We cannot allow you to stay here and go to school." I could not understand. Here was another door to mine and my baby's future, slammed in my face. I tried to make plans, but thoughts ran round and round in my head, like mice on a tread wheel. Mother called to check on me. In tears, I asked. "What do I do, Mother?" Mother cried with me. "Betty, if you are determined to keep this baby, I will help you. I called to tell you, Thomas called me. I am just assuming Mama called him. He always seems to know when you need help. He has offered to help. He says he has a good job. Betty, I don't want you to go to him. Let me come and get you, after the baby comes. You and the baby can stay with me, till you find work. Your aunts and uncles and Mama work on a flower nursery now. They even furnish housing for some of their employees. Jimmie Ray works there. Maybe you and he together, can get a place to live. Lillie and Bud live in a nursery house. If Thomas wants to help you financially, accept it but stay with me, till you get a place of your own." At last, a gleam of light in a dark future. "Mother," I asked hesitantly. "Why are you so determined to keep me away from my daddy?" "You know I don't like to discuss this," she answered. "I know you don't, but I need to know. I am trying hard to make the best decisions. Not just for myself anymore, but for my baby too." She was quiet for a moment, and then she answered me. "Betty June, you are going to think me a fool, but I know what I heard, and what I saw back then on the mountain. He doesn't want you for himself. He wants you for his mother. Your grandmother has always wanted to train you to carry on her work. You were her first born granddaughter." I became a bit exasperated. "Oh Mother, surely you don't believe this kind of stuff. It's not real. There is no way what she does, can have any effect on my life." Mother became very agitated. "Believe me, Betty June. It is your immortal soul, I have tried to save all these years. I have told you, that woman is a witch. Please stay away from her. Please stay away from Thomas. Promise me, Betty. They are bad. I will do anything to help you, if you will just stay away from them," she plead. "Alright Mother. If you are going to help me, that's all I can ask of you. I promise not to go against your wish. Do you really think I could get a job and a place to live at this nursery?" "The work is hard, but you are young and strong. I believe you can do it, if you are a mind to." My plans were laid, and I held fast to my hope and dreams of a better day. With Bo and myself working together and a little help on the side from my daddy, there was no reason I could not make do. I would stay away from the mountain and my grandmother. If that was his only reason for offering his assistance, I would know it soon enough. I thought about the pull the mountain still had on my heart strings from time to time. Foolishness, I muttered and mentally shook of the sad feeling.

After so many years, I cannot remember the exact date, but only a few nights after I had talked to mother, a bright flash of light and a loud bang woke me from a sound sleep. My breast emptied milk all over the front of my night gown, and as I sat bolt upright in my bed, I screamed, "Daddy!" At the top of my lungs. The girl in bed next to me, got up. Placing her hand on my shoulder, she asked. "Are you okay? Is the baby coming?" I could not control the tremble in my voice. I did not understand the terror I felt. "No, the baby is okay. I guess the flash of lightning and thunder boom scared me when it woke me. It flashed so bright and loud." She patted and rubbed my back. "Betty, you must have dreamed it. There was no lightning. The sky is clear and the stars are shinning." I could not seem to stop trembling. "Well, I am a mess," I answered her. "I will go take a shower and put on a clean night gown. Sorry I disturbed your sleep." "I wasn't asleep." I heard her say, as I scurried to the showers.

Two nights later, my baby was born. I picked a name for him, that I thought would be so distinctive no one else would ever have it. I named him David Jonathan. Now I thought, with that name, if we were ever parted, I would know him. Surely no one else would have that name. Silly me, I did not think of the fact, if someone else adopted him, they would have the right too, and most likely would change his name. I did not even go back to the home. Mother picked me and the baby up from the hospital. We went directly back to Mobile. I was still recuperating when she received a letter from Margaret, Thomas's wife. The letter sent news of the death of Thomas Gilliland, my birth father. The boiler of the barge he worked on, at the Pascagoula ship yard, had blown. Daddy was in the hold of the barge, when it blew. Margaret wanted to let mother know, that Jimmie Ray and I might have some claim on part of the money, the ship yard would pay Thomas's children. "We want nothing from him" Mother said as she ripped up the letter, while I lay in the bed and watched. Without another word, she walked away. I held my little boy and wept silently for my father.

Bo and I now were working at Flowerwood Nursery, but we were still living at home with mother. A mutual friend introduced me to a man named Bert. He was a fireman and a good deal older than me, but he was nice looking and very well mannered. He dropped by the house unannounced one afternoon, to ask me for a date. He apologized so sweetly, for asking at the last minute with the explanation, he had just found he could leave the firehouse for the night. I accepted his offer for dinner and a movie, for later that evening. Earlier in the day, I had made an attempt to bake an egg custard. It was a miserable failure. The crust was tough and the custard ran all over the plate. It tasted worse than it looked, like yellow glue! I think I forgot the sugar. In spite of all my cut throat gestures behind Bert's back, my dear Mother offered him a piece of pie. Like the gentleman he was, he sat down and ate every bite, but guess what? He stood me up. All dressed up with no place to go and no one to go with, I stuck my tongue out at mother." It's all your fault," I grouched. "You just had to feed the man that horrible pie. The least you could have done, was told him you baked it." Mother laughed and said. "Seeing as you are all dolled up with no date, come and go with me. I will take you out." I did not have to be asked twice. She carried me to a club, where all the people from the state docks gathered. She was acquainted with most of them, so I had plenty of dance partners. I was having a good time but I noticed a man, who each time I glanced up, would be staring at me. He had the most intense blue eyes. The lighting in the club was dim, but his eyes seemed to glow. I punched mother and whispered. "Is that one of your friends, I hope." Looking at him, she whispered back, "Ooh la la, ain't he too fine. But no I don't know him. Why?" "If you did, I could be properly introduced," I answered. "Is proper so important?" "Yes it is. I don't want to be a pickup." She took me by the hand and tugged me from the table. "Come and let's go to the ladies room." I tagged along with her, wondering what she had in mind. As she passed the security guard, she stopped and chatted with him a bit. He worked at the docks weekdays and moonlighted on these types of jobs on weekends, so he and Mother knew each other well. "I would like to introduce you to my sister," My mouth fell open but she pinched me, so I closed it without utterance. "I also want to know, do you happen to know the two gentlemen at the third table." "I know one of them." She gently pushed me toward the ladies room door. "Go on Honey. I will meet you back at the table. That's good enough," I heard her say to the security man, as the door closed behind me. I returned to my table to find the two men from table three firmly ensconced and the waitress taking orders. The security man seated me then taking my hand in one of his and the hand of the blue eyed wonder in the other, he introduced me to David Lowery. "Right and proper," he said with a smile as he joined our hands together. "And what I bring together no man's got a right to discount." Giving me a kiss on the cheek and slapping David on the back, he swaggered back to his post. "Let me buy you a drink," my new friend offered. "What are you having?" I picked up my glass and took a sip. "I have a full one. I don't need another. See, it still has lots of ice yet. It is only orange juice. That's all I drink." He tasted it to make sure I was telling the truth. "See," I grinned at him. "If I tell you a chicken dips snuff, look under her wing and you will find her snuff box." He thought this to be a confounding situation. So, it went. I gave him my address never believing he would remember it. He surprised me. He not only remembered, he showed up at my door the next day. We dated for a few months before he asked me to marry and I accepted. We agreed to not set a date right then but to wait till such a time in the future, when he felt better established on the job. By this time he was working at the flower nursery too.

He only worked a few days, before his daddy come to the nursery looking for him. "I have to go back to Evergreen, Honey," he said to me. "There are some family problems there, I have to take care of." "What kind of problems? How long will you be gone?" I asked fearfully. "I will be back this weekend. We will talk about it then. I will be back, and no matter what, you remember one thing. I love you." That firm declaration kept me going till the weekend. By the end of the week, Bo and I had moved into a nursery house. The lady next door would watch little David while I worked. She took him to the doctor for me. That's when I learned, he had asthma. I would need special medication for him.

This is where David found me upon his return. What he had to tell me broke my heart. He sat at the dining table and held my hands. "Betty, I don't know any other way to say this. I have a wife and two children." I felt my body go cold as ice. I tried to jerk my hands from his grasp, but he wouldn't let go. "Why did you do this to me," I cried. "I would never have let you anywhere near me, had I known." Still holding my hands and shaking himself, he answered me. "I know this, Honey. That's why I couldn't bring myself to tell you. Please Betty, hear me out before you throw me out. When we first meet, I thought we would date awhile and then go our separate ways. It didn't work that way. The more I got to know you, the more I realized you were someone I want to spend my life with." "Idiot," I screeched. "You can't spend your life with me when you already got a wife and two children." Finally getting my hands free, I picked up my coffee cup and popped him with it. He snatched the cup away and threw it out the door. He stayed on the other side of the room, well away from me and close to the door, till I sat back down in my chair. While I cradled my head on my arms, I cried my heart out. Pulling his chair around closer to me, he sat down and began to wipe my face with a wet cloth. "Please listen to me baby. Please?" "David," I sniffed, "there is nothing on earth you can say to make right, what you have done. I will not be responsible for breaking up a home. Especially one with children involved." I took the washcloth from him and covered my face. "You had nothing to do with it. I left her well before you came into my life. I married her before I left for the Philippines. Our son was born while I was over there. We were expecting our second almost immediately after I returned to the states. I wasn't nothing but a kid myself then. She was a lot older then I was. I sent money home to support her and money to be put in savings, to give us a start when I got back. It didn't happen. When I got home, she was totally broke and living with her mom and dad. With no explanation for which way my savings went, except she bought her dad a big fine car. Even then I stayed with her and tried to make a go of it. She refused to move out of her mom and dad's home. After our daughter was born, I finally got her to come to Evergreen with me. I thought she might like the south. Well, she didn't. When she left and went back to Denver, I went with her. I spent the most miserable two years of my life with a controlling woman and in-laws, I ever spent." He neglected to tell me about his controlling mother. He only vowed, "I will never go back to her, whether you are in my life or not. I had left her for good, before I meet you. We both are in agreement, to getting a divorce. I want you for my wife, as soon as I am free." I felt to upset right then to make any kind of decision, so I sent him away. He kept coming back every weekend and pleading with me, till I agreed to let him back in my life.

He worked in Evergreen with his dad and visited me each weekend. On one of these visits, he asked me to go away with him. "I want us to go someplace where we can be together. This house you have to live in, needs too much fixing up, for me to do for you. I can't do it, coming down two days a week. I can do better for you, than this. Besides, I miss you honey. I worry about you all week." I was scared to give up what I had. I knew it was not much, but it was a start toward the goals, I had fixed in my mind. I still had hopes and dreams. "We can go to Birmingham," he said. "It's a big city. It shouldn't be too hard to find work there." I listened to him spin his dreams and agreed to go with him. He would come to take us away the next week end.

I worked all that week, knowing by Friday, I would draw my last paycheck and tell them I was leaving. As I was packing on Thursday afternoon, a shadow filled my doorway, blocking all of the sunlight. I glanced behind me, to see the biggest man I thought, I had ever laid eyes on. He seemed as tall as the door height, and the width of his shoulders filled it from side to side. His sudden appearance in my door startled me at first but his beautiful smile set me at ease as he introduced himself. "Hello," he said. "I am Sidney Meadows. I am the manager of Flowerwood Nursery. My wife Mary has sent you some things for the baby. I also want to welcome you to Flowerwood and see if there is anything you need." I was to tongue tied with shyness to say much to him. I could only stutter a thank you. I did not even tell him, I was leaving. He looked around, at the shabby two room dwelling and frowned. "Things will improve here in time," He said. "I am told you are a good worker and a deserving person. That's good enough for me." He picked up a box of assorted baby paraphernalia and clothes, and sat it inside the door. I did not know then but one day, I would come full circle, and Mr. Meadows would reenter my life as the father figure and mentor, I so desperately needed. When I went to pick up my pay check and turn in my notice, the secretary said. "What a shame, Betty. You just received a nice raise." I should have listened to my inner voice. I was home. Everything I wanted was right there, waiting at my fingertips.

We all come to cross roads from time to time in our life. Had I been following the path of light, I would have listened to my heavenly father. I would have automatically chosen the right road, because it was the way of his statutes and commandments. I would have stayed where I was and asked David to wait, till the time was right for him and me. I did not. I lead with my left foot, instead of my right as usual. I hitched my wagon to a shooting star and away I went.

Upon arriving in Birmingham, we went to a friend of my family's. I had always called him Uncle Warren, though he was no blood kin. He owned a rooming house. We rented a small two room apartment from him. Before David could even think of finding a job, his dad called. David's Mother had a car wreck. It was a bad one and she was in a hospital in Florida. David left Birmingham the same day. I ran out of money after the first week. Little David was out of medicine and getting sicker by the day. I knew I had to make a move soon, or he would be out of formula before David returned. If he returned at all. I talked to Uncle Warren. "Betty June, I am too old to handle the responsibility of caring for a small baby, even if you could go to work. I doubt if you can find work close enough to home, to walk to. You know, lack of transportation is a drawback when you apply for a job. There is another problem you don't recognize either," He said. "I got more then I know what to do with now, Uncle Warren. What is the other problem?" He thought about it then explained. "I was in the process of turning this place over to a realtor when you and David showed up. I held off, giving you two a chance, before I went on with what I must do. This place has grown to be a problem for me, I can't cope with any more. It's falling apart and running in the red. I am tired and sick. I want to sell out and go to an assisted living home." "Why can't I stay here and take care of you and run the boarding house for you?" I asked. "Who has the doe-ray-me to sink into this place, to make it rentable?" He asked. "I don't. I am not willing to risk what I have. At any rate, I wouldn't have enough to get the job done. No, I am sorry, it won't work honey. I have called your Aunt Ester. Let's see what she can come up with." Aunt Ester came but I sure did not like what she had to say. "Sit down Betty and let me talk to you, and for once in your life, you have got to listen. You have no other choice." Feeling beat and all out of ideas, I sat and listened. "I have called the child and family welfare services. They have offered to take the baby for a time to give you a chance to get your own life in order. Once you do that, they will give him back." I felt sick all over. "Aunt Ester, how could you? They will take him," I said. "They will take him for good, if you don't make a move to try to help yourself. If you have not brought him in before four O'clock this afternoon, the welfare worker will be here before sundown with a court order to take him. Now let me take him to them. He is sick, Betty. He needs his medicine. Listen to his breathing. He struggles for every breath he draws. This is the only way you can give him a fighting chance." I loaded my sweet baby and his belongings in her car. We carried him to the welfare office. One would think I might have felt some relief, but I did not. How can I tell you? I felt like my heart had been ripped out and stomped. I went back to Uncle Warren and went to bed. I could not eat or sleep. I was beat at last, so broken I wanted to die. Uncle Warren became so worried, he called my Aunt Burma and Uncle Roy. They were living in Hattiesburg, Mississippi. They came to Birmingham and took me home with them. The welfare worker would not let me take little David with me. She advised me to get a job and establish a home of my own first. Then come back for him. I knew it would take schooling and years, to do what she was telling me I must do. I had made a lot of bad turns and decisions, but coming to Birmingham had been the worst one I ever made.

I put in applications everywhere I could, the first week I was in Hattiesburg. By the end of the second week there, I got a phone call from Birmingham. David had returned there only to find me gone. "Woman, do I have to chase you all over the forty eight states," He asked. "I didn't think you were coming back. I held out as long as I could." "I know honey. Warren told me how things went. I can only tell you, I am so sorry. I stayed with Mother till I felt sure she would pull through, before I headed back this way." I asked him about his Mother's health. "She is doing better, but it was touch and go for the first two weeks. Her chest was crushed. Most of her ribs and one hip broke, but I couldn't wait there any longer. I was too worried about you. Something told me, to get back as fast as I could. If my old car will make it, I will be where you are in about six hours. We will talk then. You just stay put, till I get there," he growled. Aunt Burma was fit to be tied. "He has some kind of nerve," she ranted. "I don't know why you would even speak to him, after he abandoned you to the mercy of the world. Have you lost what little sense you were born with?" On and on she raved, till Uncle Roy told her to shut her mouth. Having the last word, she shook her finger in my face. "When he gets here, I forbid you to let him in my house, and if you go out that door to go to him, don't you dare to darken it to ever come back in again." In a temper she went to bed, slamming her bedroom door for emphasis. I cleaned the kitchen and bathroom, then went and sat on the porch. I waited in the swing, till David got there. He ran onto the porch and without a word, he picked me up and sat on the swing. Placing me on his lap, he buried his head on my shoulder and held me tight, till he stopped trembling. Raising his head, he brushed my hair back from my face and kissed me. "Dear God, I thought I had lost you forever, I thought my old ford wasn't going to get me here," he said. "Aunt Burma said if I come out to you, I couldn't come back in. What are we to do," I asked? David seemed to collect himself "I see," He said. "Do you want to stay in Hattiesburg?" "No, I want to go back to Birmingham and try to get little David back." "You know, they won't let you have him till we are married, and we can't do that till my divorce is final. I have signed all the papers Dell sent me and sent them back. I don't know how long it will take. I burned my old car up trying to get to Mother and then back to you. It won't make it back to Birmingham. It's got a rod knocking and smoking like crazy. I can baby it along maybe and get us to New Orleans. I know I can go to work there, as a mechanic. I have a friend I was in service with over in the Philippines. He told me, if I ever came his way, to look him up and he would put me to work. He will let me rebuild my car in his shop and work there. I called him before I headed this way. Will you go with me? I promise, I will never leave you again. I promise, I will marry you and get David back for you." "I will go," I told him. Uncle Roy walked out the front door and sat down in a chair. David sat me on the swing beside him. Putting out his hand, he asked. "You are Betty's Uncle Roy?" "I am," my Uncle answered, as he shook hands. "Pleased to meet you sir, I am David Lowery." "I should hope so," chuckled Uncle Roy. "Have you come to take my girl away? Her Aunt won't even let you in the door here. She is mad as a hornet, and all set to sting. It's mostly because of the baby." "I understand," said David. "I know it looks bad, but I have not known which way to jump, in the last three weeks. I was needed in two different places. I tried to fill both needs and failed Betty in the doing." Uncle Roy lit a cigarette and leaned back in his chair. "You have a plan, I take it?" "Of sorts,"

David answered. "How much did you overhear?" "Overhear hell. I eves dropped son, plain and simple. I want to get you two on the move, before that dragon gets up and runs us all off. I think it best you go out to the car and wait. I will go in and pack Betty's stuff, and bring it out to you." We did as he said. Uncle Roy brought my suitcase and put it in the trunk. He gave me a hundred dollars and kissed me bye. Shaking David's hand, he said. "Son, please take care of her. That little girl deserves better then what she's had so far." David gave his word and we were on our way.

New Orleans is a varied and colorful city. Where else can you walk down the street and exchange a good morning with a clown in passing, or sit on your front porch in the cool of the day and listen to the melodious song of the crayfish, and watermelon vendors sing their wares. I will never forget my first sight and sound of a New Orleans' funeral procession. I thought Bill Haley and his Comets had come to town! With the brass horns and drums belting out when The Saints go marching in, people were running and dancing along the street. They laughed and clapped their hands to the music. No funeral dirge and sad faces, for these people. I could only gaze in wonder, when I saw the long black hearse following the band. There was no extra money for entertainments, but we did not mind. All we had to do was sit on the front parch and watch the world go by. Sometimes, we would walk to town and have coffee with beignets at café Du monde. We would stroll through Jackson square or down Bourbon Street. I did enjoy the street shows. It was free entertainment, at its best. One could find guitar pickers playing and singing the blues. Magicians, dancers, musicians of every kind were to be found. Everywhere I looked, there was color and happy fun loving people. David seemed to derive great pleasure in showing me the sights.

Our first six weeks there, were hard to get through. We found an apartment in a rooming house ran by an elderly Cajun lady, named Fifi. David only got to work one week before he got very sick. Fifi called a friend of hers, who was a retired doctor. He came to the apartment immediately. Doctor Sallatich spoke with a definite Cajun accent. He was such a caring old gentleman. He sent me to the drugstore, with a prescription. The druggist said, "No one makes these anymore. It's for a mustard plaster, but if Doc Sallatich wants it, we will have to find one." I left David's wallet lying on the counter, while the druggist made his enquiries over the phone. When he found what I needed and told me it would be the next day before he could have it for me, I reached for the wallet, only to find it and all our money gone. Fifi meet me at the door. When I told her my sad tale, she went into her apartment and returned with my rent money. She gave it all back to me. I had never known such unselfish kindness from a virtual stranger. Fifi went up the stairs with me and talked to the doctor. He told us David had La Grippe. He stayed by David's bedside the rest of the day and all night. He slept in a chair by the bed and checked his temperature and his lungs often. Once during the night, he put him in the shower and held him up, till the fever dropped. He applied the mustard plaster himself, the next day before he left. There were times during those first weeks, I did not even know where our next meal would come from. I picked up coca cola bottles and sold them, to get money for food. Dear Fifi waited on her rent, till David was back at work.

I found a job myself, once David was back on his feet. I went to work as a surveyor, for American home insurance. I was not supposed to sell the insurance. It was my job, to tell the potential customer what it was all about, and ask them to fill out the questionnaire and mail it in to the company. Most people were very nice. They listened to my pitch, took the paperwork with the promise to look over it and mail it in. Sometimes, I was not so lucky. Once, I was called a communist and had the brochure thrown at me. More than once, I was set upon and forced to outrun big dogs with big teeth. I quit the day I refer to as, the day of the geese.

I approached a neat little house on a quiet street. I checked the fence out to make sure there were no beware the dog sign, then entered the premises and rang the doorbell. The door was opened by a large smiling man wearing a robe. A smaller man wearing nothing but a timid look on his face and a towel peeped from behind the first man. Almost tongue tied, I began to give them my oft repeated spiel. "Who is it, who is it," asked the small man. "Hush dear, so I can hear. I think it is a sales person." "What's she selling? Invite her in. It's hot out there. Here, I will pour her a glass of wine." "No, no," I stuttered. "I am not allowed to come inside, and thank you, but I wouldn't care for a glass of wine." I did not get to protest more, nor tell them anything at all. With honks and hissing, two large white geese, actually a goose and her gander, bombarded their way past the two men and out the door. Fast behind their web footed friends, came two ferocious gray fur balls. I was on the run from two French poodles, two enraged geese and two party loving gay guys. As I trotted down the street, I heard one man bellow, "Gertrude, Brutus," and a high voice squeaking cried, "oh bad Fifi, bad Mime. Oh you naughty girls." I looked back just in time to see the towel drop, before I booked on down the street, at warp speed.

I was pregnant and showing big time, before I had enough money to buy maternity clothes. I stayed indoors and wore my big night gowns. I needed to cross the street to the store and nothing I had, would go around my waist. I decided to improvise. My David had the shoulders of a linebacker, with flat stomach and lean hips. I put on a pair of his pants. I tied them across my tummy, with a shoe string and rolled the legs up. Then I put on one of his shirts that come down to my knees, to cover the front of the tied together pants. As I crossed the street, two men in a car went by. The driver did a double take and ran up on the curb, coming within an inch of hitting a large oak tree. "My God, what was that," the driver shouted. "I don't know," answered the smart alack passenger. "If you can tell me what it is, I will tell you what to feed it." I was still wearing my put together outfit, when David came home. He took one look at me and said. "You better come and go with me." Then he paused. "On second thought, you stay here. I will be back soon." He returned within the hour with three new maternity outfits. "I am glad today was payday," he said as he kissed me. "Lord, I thought Halloween had come." I never mentioned the two men in the car.

I do recall another happenstance, which I think was one of the most embarrassing days of my life. David called to tell me he was working late that night. He would take a side job from time to time at the shipyard, cleaning the holds in the ships, to get them ready for new cargo. I hated those jobs. He had to make like a fly on the wall, to do them. The holds in the bottom of the ships were deep, and covered with spikes to help hold the cargo in place. On those nights, I would walk to down town New Orleans, cutting through the French Quarter's and occupy myself by taking in a movie. This night, I passed a small barroom. I noticed a car parked in front the same color, make, and model of our car. I paused and looked inside. There on the driver's side was a straw cushion, just like the one in our car. I stared at the car. I looked at the barroom. My blood boiled. Here I am, worrying myself to death about him, and he is cooling it in a barroom? I cannot go in there, I thought. It is too dark. I will wait for him in the car. Boy, has he got a surprise in store for him. The car was locked, but the window on the driver's side was cracked somewhat. I forced my arm through to reach the latch, but could only barely touch it with the tip of my middle finger. I struggled with it for a little time, then giving up, I tried to withdraw my hand. Oh geez, my arm was stuck! I hung there by one arm till a strange man walked out of the bar, jingling his keys in his hand and whistling a jaunty little tune. He stopped short and stared at me in surprise. "Young lady, what are you doing," he asked. "I am trying to get in this car," I answered. "Why do you want in my car?" "Your car," I gulped, and wished the sidewalk would open and swallow me whole. "My car," he replied succinctly. "But it looks like my husband's car. Even to the straw cushion in the seat. I was going to wait for him to come out of the bar," I babbled. Laughing, he unlocked the car and turned me loose. With the best apology I could muster, I waddled on down the street. I would like to say that was the end of my bad day, but no, I could not stop with one foolish incident. I had to compound it before my day could be complete. I walked on to the movie theater. I was still smarting over the incident with the car and paid no mind to what was playing on the matinee. I hurriedly paid for my ticket and bought a bag of popcorn, went in and found a seat. I was late and had missed a large part of the movie. For which, I am grateful. Once settled, I glanced at the big screen and dropped my popcorn. It was an X rated film called Isle of the Nudes. I wanted to get up and leave but I was afraid to call attention to myself, so I slid down in my seat and shut my eyes. Too soon but not soon enough, the screen went blank and all the lights came on. There was nothing to do but stand and walk out. There was no one there but men. I gritted my teeth as I heard a snicker, then chuckles began, as a ripple all around me and spread outward into loud guffaws. "Well," I heard one male voice quip. "It's easy to see how she got that way." Some days just ain't worth getting up for.

Our daughter was born February fifteenth, nineteen sixty at Turo Infirmary. The day after her birth, David came to the hospital all smiles. "Look who came to help us out, while you are recuperating." Bo stepped in the door. What a wonderful surprise. "I called your mother yesterday, to let her know she had a new granddaughter. She insisted I come and get Bo to help out. I drove all night to get him here for you. That's not the best of the news though. Look what I have." He laid papers on the bed. I picked them up and began to read. They were his divorce papers. "Now as soon as you are able, we are going to get married." Long years later, when Sandra found her birth certificate and my marriage license, I had some accounting to do over the discrepancy in the dates of the two documents.

Second Sight

A dull gray moth, I see flutter by,
Is never to be a bright butterfly.
No magic metamorphous,
To struggle no need, she is what she is,
That is all she can be.
Magic then happened, the moth spiraled high.
Gossamer silver dazzled my eye.
A delicate beauty reflecting the light,
In a moment of challenge brought truth to my sight.
I am what I am, no more no less.
Yet of that which I am I can be the best.
Spin and weave oh destiny,
Place me so in your tapestry.
My symbols not in colors bold,
But a gray winged thing whose truth I hold.
I am what I am, no more no less.
Yet of that which I am, I will be the best.

Betty Lowery

Chapter 20

GREEN CATHEDRALS

The tenants were in and out of our apartment bringing food and gifts, so regular it looked like a working beehive and our Sandra was the queen bee. We laughingly called her the naughty lady of Esplanade. Even dear Fifi with her bad knee came up the stairs at least once a day. The retired lawyer downstairs bought a bassinet. Doctor Sallatich come bringing bottles and bottle warmer. "Fifi say, you tried to breast feed and got in big trouble. Yes? Let me see what I can do for you." He fussed at me in that beautiful Cajun accent, like an old mother hen. He bound my breast and put ice packs on. "Now you gonna be brave little mother an do what I say now, you hear. You got milk fever. Can't feed the babe, no. Don't feel bad che're. Sometimes it happens so. I give you something to dry you up and ease some pain. Tisk, tisk, poor babe. No Fifi is not nothing wrong with the babe. Is the poor mama' I am trying to treat. If you will move aside dear lady, I assure you, I am not going to give shot to little baby. She is fine healthy baby. Muy petite Mama', she needs the vitamins. She is anemic." Dr. Salatich came to me every day until I was on my feet and healthy. When I tried to pay him, he would pat my hand and said, "Wait, don you worry. Not now." I supposed he would give a finale bill when he felt I was well, and did not need his service anymore. He never did. God rest his and Fifi's souls, two more indelible footprints in my tapestry.

I would hold my Sandra and feel so at peace. She was beautiful. I would tell her all about her big brother and promise her we would have him with us soon. She would take a deep breath then kick her little feet, wave her arms, and smile. Almost like she understood and could hardly wait.

Once more, I was all packed and ready to go. David's mother and Daddy wanted us to move to Evergreen. I felt so much joy. I was accepted and would soon be part of a good family. Surely, once they got to know me and realized I wanted to be a loving daughter to them. They would love me in return. We were to go to Mobile first and visit Mother, then on to Evergreen.

That first night at Mother's, she damped my sprits somewhat and set me to thinking. I began to worry a little bit over the reception I might get from my new in-laws. "Be careful Betty," she warned. "It just seems strange to me they never wanted a thing to do with you, until you and David had a child. Something about this sudden turn around doesn't feel right to me." I questioned David about it on our way to Evergreen. "Betty, Mother will want to do things for the baby and you. When she does, don't say no. I know she is going to love both of you, but you will get along better if you let her have her way." "How long will we have to live in her house," I asked. "Not long, Daddy says I can work at the Ellrod plant. They pay pretty well, so it shouldn't take long." "Then we can go to Birmingham and get little David," I asked. "Let's don't push issues. Okay? Let it rest. Don't nag me. I got enough on my mind right now." He had never spoken so sharp to me before. I wondered at this, but I let it go and played with Sandra the rest of the trip. David went in the house ahead of me with Sandra in his arms. Standing close behind him, I saw his mother's face light with joy when she looked up to see him standing before her. Then her gaze left him and focused on me. All the light faded from her eyes and her face closed. I hoped I could change her mind.

We lived with David's parents for six month. I felt like a nun in a monastery doing penance. Nothing I did was right or pleasing to her. She would come home from work and mop the floors I had just cleaned. She would strip down my bed and make it over again, while muttering under her breath and bitching the whole time. I did not try to cook supper for her anymore. I tried that a few times and it was a disaster. I baked sweet potatoes for us once and one of them exploded in the oven. She came home from work to find me with my head in the oven trying to clean it. I tried to explain what happened. She refused to listen. "You think, you can insult my intelligence with a tale like that. Don't open your mouth to lie to me again. If you do, I will slap your jaws." From then on, I just made sure the dishes were washed and all the water buckets were full and ready for her. Her daddy visited her once for a week. He was old and decrepit, so I did all for the elderly gentleman I could. One day, he had an accident. I helped him change his clothes and washed them for him and scrubbed the outhouse down. This made Mrs. Lowery furious. She called me an old washer woman. "I was only trying to help," I said, and tried to smile at her. "I don't need your help. If I do, I will ask for it. You just leave my Daddy to me and tend to your own business. Do I make myself clear?" "Yes Mrs. Lowery, I understand." She grew more and more possessive of Sandra and critical of me, as time went by. I didn't go to the kitchen and help with breakfast any more. The last time I did, was enough to let me know, I wasn't needed or appreciated. I cooked David's eggs the way he liked them, but his mother said they weren't "Fitten for a dog to eat" and threw them out the back door. She cooked more eggs for him. He hollered at me. Shoving his plate across the table, he said. "You know I don't eat runny eggs." I didn't answer him. I thought his Mother would speak up. She never said a word, just ate her breakfast with a malicious smile on her face. That was why I started staying in my room until they all left for work. David would leave first. Then Mrs. Lowery would sit at the table with Granddaddy and talk about me like I was not in the other room, hearing all the venom she was pouring fourth. Now these may sound like trivial little things that I should have overlooked but when they go on each day of one's life, they eventually take a toll on the mind. Now I fully understood what had happened to my poor mother all those years ago. Maybe I had to live this in order to understand her circumstances better.

While I was still living there, I received a letter from Mother. She asked if she could come to see Sandra and me. She wanted to know how we were faring. I laid the letter on my dresser and went to the front porch to sit in the swing. I intended waiting until David returned from work to ask what he wanted me to say to Mother. Mrs. Lowery called me to come to the kitchen. She wanted to talk to me. I went in to find her leaning against the sink counter, with my letter in her hand. "What are you going to do about this," she asked. "I was going to ask David what to do about it when he got home," I answered. "Well, this isn't Alfred's home. It is mine. I am the one you need to be asking." I kept silent and waited her out. I be damned if I ask her for anything. She braced her hands on the sink behind her and leaned back, she crossed one foot over the other. "I can't be hard hearted enough to tell you, your mother can't come to see you," she said. "But I want you to hear me and make no mistake about it. I won't have her anywhere near Sandra. She can come to see you while I am at work. I will drop Sandra off at Miss Annie's. You can even cook dinner for them if you want to. Just make sure they are gone before I get home." I was stymied. What in the world had David told his mother to cause this kind of reaction from her? "What has my mother done to make you feel this harsh," I asked. "She hasn't done anything to me personally, but I know what kind of woman she is. U.D. told me how he had to go to a whorehouse, to get directions to where you all worked. That's where you were when you meet Alfred. There with your mother." "You are misinformed," I answered. "David met me in a night club and we were introduced by a mutual acquaintance." I did wince a little over that one but I was not about to admit that I had practically been a pick up. "It may not be the best place in the world to be but it is a far cry from a whorehouse. I have never been in one of those. Nor my mother either. Granddaddy found her at work at the State Docks." "I know what it is," she answered me. "I'm not stupid. It's where sorry women go to pick up men. Why some sorry woman tried to pick up my husband while he was there." Well fry my pancake and call me fatty, I thought. My Mother-in-Law was not only a controlling bigot, she's a raving lunatic to boot. I knew better than to try to explain to her that his Brother-in Law had tipped the waitress an extra big tip to put the move on Granddaddy as a joke. "I just want you to know," she finished up. "Your mother and her kind live on one side of the tracks and I live on the other and it's gonna stay that way. You came from nothing and you will always be nothing." With her black eyes flashing and her lip curled, she turned her back and began to scrub the sink. I grabbed my pencil and writing pad from the table and ran out the back door to the woods. I gathered a pile of pine straw and lay it under a large oak tree. Sitting on it, I leaned back against the old tree. I loved the woods. They were my get away when I needed peace. I gazed up through the tree limbs toward the heavens. The green leaves made lacy patterns against the blue sky and clouds as the breeze moved them in gentle swirls. This was my church. God's own cathedral created by him. I felt closer to him here than I did in any man made church of wood and stone. I had walked through the beautiful Saint Louis Cathedral in New Orleans and felt like a tourist. I found no spirit there. Here in his own quit green cathedral, I felt God. Not the God the preacher hollered and screamed about who would put me in a fire where I would burn forever for being an unsaved human but a gentle loving being who bent to kiss me with warm sunlight and a soft breeze. "Why Lord," I asked. "I am being a good wife and mother. Why does she say I am nothing? What more can I do? Lord, surely you don't want me to give up my Mother and family. I love them. My Mother gave up hers for her husband's people, and I could see it was the wrong thing to do. Lord, I don't think it would change anything here anyway. So if you don't mind, I am going to hold on to my family. The one I have tried to belong to sure don't want me. For some reason, I am just not good enough for them." Ending my talk with God, I leaned back against the tree and listened to the quiet. You can hear quiet, you know. It moves softly around you and permeates the soul and mind to bring inner peace. Laying and resting there, I saw a moth circle slowly around. Just a simple gray moth I sighed like me. I watched as she began to move higher in the trees. Circling lazily on the air she caught the sunlight. The transformation took my breath away. What a lovely creature she was and she was made by God too. I took that lesson to heart. I went back to the house more determined to make others see me in a different light. When Mrs. Lowery sat me down after supper and cut off most of my hair and put in a tight kinky perm that made me look like a scared Mohawk, I made no complaint. I wore the heavy knit pant suits one size to large with elastic in the waist she choose for me to wear to church and followed her dutifully there most Sundays. It was many years before she changed her opinion of me. She never told me so. She told others and it was repeated back to me. Even then it was a back handed compliment. She said, "Betty changed and finally grew into a fine woman." I did not change. I hold the same values and love for God and others now I did then. The only difference in now and then is I had not released my life fully to God. I was still trying to do everything on my own. Still stumbling and searching. It took some long hard praying for God to help me remove the hatred my heart harbored for her. I did care about her and tried to do the best for her in her last years. I understand it this way. If I can forgive those who despitefully use me, I know that God who is so much greater then I will forgive them also. If I withhold forgiveness the burden of their wrong rest as heavy on my shoulders as it does on theirs. That is what it means to surrender all.

Mrs. Lowery had a coffee klatch gathering with some of her friends. They talked and laughed as they sat around the dining table. Then the subject changed and they began to discuss, I would say gossip, about a lady who was not with us. "She wasn't invited," my Mother-in-Law replied with a sniff to one inquiry. "Oh she wouldn't have come anyway," said another lady. "She is too ashamed of her daughter to show her face much. She didn't even come to church last Sunday." "They have sent her away and claim she is visiting relatives out west somewhere." "Well I wouldn't lie for mine like that. If she were to get herself caught, I would make her stay and face it. There would be no giving it away and then returning home. She would darn well pay by having to raise it and look her sin in the face every day." There were mummers of agreement all around the table. I had not said a word until one of them asked me what I thought about it. I don't know what got into me but I stood and set my tea glass down to keep my hand from shaking. "You want an opinion from the other side of the tracks?" I asked firmly. "Well here it is. Yes I would lie for my daughter. I would lie through my teeth for her. Why would I want her and an innocent baby I might add, to face vicious gossips and scandal mongers for one mistake for the rest of their life." I stared them all down until they dropped their eyes before I walked away. It was a quiet room I left behind.

David finally moved us into our own place three houses down the road from his mother's house. He promised me we would go to Birmingham as soon as he got his car in good working condition. Before this could take place, I received a letter from the courts in Birmingham. The letter requested that I either sigh the papers allowing little David to be adopted or appear in court to protest the adoption proceedings. I showed the letter to David when he come in from work and asked him to take me. "Go to your Mother and see if she will loan us her car to make the trip." He was gone a long time. Upon his return, he would not look me in the eye. "Sit down," he said. "We have to talk." I didn't like the sound of that. It was the tone others used when they were about to take a scalpel to a piece of my heart. I wasn't far from wrong. "Mother won't let us use her car. She says we can't bring the baby here." "The baby has a name." I corrected him. "Call him David. He is a person. Not a thing of inconvenience to you and your mother." "Now you shut up and sit down and listen to me," He shouted. There is no need for you to get on your high horse about this. Mother is right. That baby has no father and don't have my name. We and Mother have to live in this community. He would suffer here and so would we. He would never be accepted." "Your mother does not own the town of Evergreen," I screamed at him. I don't believe everyone thinks like she does." "No but she has a lot of influence in this town. I am not going to let you create a scandal here. Now sign the damn papers. She can set the KKK on us, you know." I began to cry. "Please David, you promised me. I have waited for you to be able to do what you told me you would do. Don't do this to me," I plead. "I am not God," he said. "I can't fix the mess you made of your life. We have our children." He was speaking of Sandra of course and the one I was pregnant with at the time. "Think of them instead of yourself and what you want for a change. You are just like Mother says, not only stupid, but hard headed to go with it. That's you, you got no common sense and no back bone but you are too stubborn to let anyone else advise you." Those words burned into my brain. I can never forget them. I hated right then. It was a terrible thing to feel, I could viciously kill with my bare hands. I ran out the back door to my woods. There was no peace there for me that day. I felt a storm inside me and wished I had the power to use it to destroy everything in sight. I screamed and cursed my wrath to the tree tops and beyond. My beloved husband, this man I had placed on a pedestal had played me false. When I went back to the house he was gone. I guessed he had gone to his mother's. I did not care if he ever came back. I sat down and wrote my mother a letter telling her all. I do not remember what all I did say but I do know I said, "Mother, I can't and will not sign these papers. If the welfare services have a good loving home for my child, let them put him there. I now know it's not fair for me to try to hold on to hope any longer. He is the one I am hurting the most. But for a mother to sign these papers is like she is saying I don't want him. I can't do that. Will you take this letter to Birmingham and give it to the judge? Let them make the decision." I let go and the courts took him. For reasons I don't understand that letter was saved and placed in his adoption records. Once he was a grown man and asked that they be turned over to him, he read the letter and come searching for me. I got to meet with him and see him twice. I talked with him on the phone a lot. Usually late at night when he couldn't sleep. His real Mother was refusing to speak with him as long as he was in contact with me. He was torn and very upset. I have tried to understand why she took this stance with her son. The situation was causing him much anguish but I don't understand till this day. Couldn't she see this fine young man she raised had enough room in his heart to love both of us? I think he needed me. My husband didn't approve either but he knew better than to forbid me access to my birth child. I think he feared I would tell my son the part of him and his Mother's thoughts and actions all those years ago. I would not do such a thing. I glossed over the truth and gave him a version he could believe without going into the whole disgraceful affair.

Three months after I buried my David, the adopted father of my first born child called. He wanted me to know my David Jonathan had died of a massive heart attack at the age of forty five, one year prior to his calling me. Even then his wife didn't want him to call and tell me. The man said he was doing what he thought was right. I don't even know what I said to the man. I felt so sad. I am sure I babbled on and made no sense at all. What I should have said and mean from the heart was I feel so sorry for his wife. She has a lot to learn about unselfish love before she can move on. For her sake, I hope she can.

Life seemed to go on in a kind of vacuum after the courts took little David from me. I turned a cold unforgiving shoulder toward David and his Mother. My baby was never mentioned. I grieved alone. I felt as far as they were concerned he had never existed. I knew I had to go on with life the best I could for the sake of the child I now had and the one I was expecting, so I struggled along to the best of my ability to act normal. The war with my Mother-in-law over Sandra was surely taking a heavy toll on me. I had begun to hear voices when no one was there. I knew things were very wrong and she was surely breaking my will and mental outlook. My David had started to stray. He would come in late at night. I could smell another's perfume. When I confronted him about it he didn't deny it. He said, "What do you care? It's for sure you don't want me anymore. I don't think you ever did." I gave him no answer. I was sad and tired and I thought I really don't care enough to fight over it. Let him do what pleases him. Maybe he has found someone who can make his Mother happy. When his Mother came harping at me about the things he was doing that she didn't approve of and wanted to know what I was going to do about it I told her just that.

It was Christmas, nineteen sixty. I had two children by David now, Sandra and Butch. Mother had promised to come and see me so often but not been able to make it. I wrote and asked her to come for Christmas. I told her I had put the old red rooster under the wash pot so many times to fatten him for her dumplings, only to turn him lose again. Now he runs to the wash pot every time I go out to feed him. She wrote back and said she would definitely come for Christmas. I was so happy. I missed my brothers and Mother. I cooked and baked ahead of time. It was to be my first Christmas in my own home. I vowed to put my grief aside and start a new year of happiness with my family. I spent Christmas Eve with my Mother,

her husband Jake Bodiford, and my brothers. I waited until late in the afternoon before sending David to bring Sandra home. I let her spend most of Christmas Eve with her Grandma. "David, will you go get Sandra? Tell your mother I want her to stay here tonight so she can open her presents with us in the morning. Then I will send her back to them for the day." He brought her to me and her Grandmother Bodiford and her uncle's played with her until bed time. I put Sandra to bed with David and I. Late in the night my front room lights flashed on. Mrs. Lowery came roaring into my bedroom. She was incoherent in the things she was screaming. She leaned across the bed reaching across David and me, trying to get to Sandra. I held on to Sandra. She had waked the entire household. Everyone was jumping up and grabbing for their clothes. David managed to scramble from the bed but I was trapped. She fell across me and sunk her teeth into my shoulder and hung on like a rabid bull dog. David tore her loose from me, tearing my flesh from me, and pushed her against the wall. He had raised his hand to strike but I had enough presence of mind to scream at him. "No David, don't hit your mother." He turned his head and looked at me with a dazed look on his face. "No, no," I said, shaking my head. "Never, ever hit your mother." He released her and stepped back. "Get out of my house," he said. "I am ashamed of you. Never come back again. Get out now." My mother cried as she gathered her belongings and they all left. David took me to town to the sheriff's office where he launched a complaint against his mother and filed for a restraining order. The sheriff informed us that Mrs. Lowery had already been there and made her own complaint. "I will tell you the same thing I told her. You should all get together and solve your differences. Legally there is nothing I can do. Most parents I know are glad to have the assistance of the grandparents to help with children." "Most parents don't have to worry about the grandparent outright stealing their child from them." I answered him. "She has a frustrated mother instinct. She doesn't want to be a grandmother. She wants to be the mother. She was too squeamish to have another one of her own. She would rather someone else had it for her." I knew this because I heard her say once, "That if Alfred had any sense he would have held out till Dell gave up and went back to Denver, leaving Rick behind, and she would have had him for herself." If that had taken place I am sure she would never have tried to take Sandra. She seemed only capable of loving one child at the time. "Were I you," advised the sheriff. "I would move a bit farther away. Maybe that would help."

I moved a lot farther away. I talked David into moving us back to Mobile. We rented a house across the street from mother. She had moved to shore acres after she and Jake married. I don't know an easy way to say this. David was a very unhappy man. He kept changing jobs. Each time he was out of work, we got farther and farther behind on our bills. He stayed out late at night and drank heavy. One night, he didn't come home. I called his place of work. "Mrs. Lowery," his boss said in response to my query, "your husband quit working here two days ago. I am sorry but I can't tell you more than that. Four days later he still hadn't come home. My electricity had been turned off. Jake came and took out my heater, said David had reneged on paying for it. It was freezing cold. Sandra cried for a bottle all day long and I was using the last of Butch's formula. The baby food was gone. Actually, I was hungry too. There was no food in the house. I put the babies in bed with me to try to keep them warm. Sandra cried and would not be comforted. I held her and cried with her. I knew she was hungry. When Mother come in from work, I went across the street and begged for milk for Sandra. She gave me the milk and said. "Jake is not going to let me help you. You have got to quit having babies you can't take care off. You see David is irresponsible. You should leave him and go to work and stand on your own two feet." "Mother, I can't go to work now. Sandra and Butch need me at home. Besides, I am pregnant again." "Betty June, you are without a doubt the dumbest and most outrageous character I have ever heard of. I will do this. Here is a dime. I will take you up to the corner to use the phone. You can call David's mother. It's her son that's causing your difficulties. Let her deal with it." I sure did not want to ask David's mother for anything but knew I did not have much choice. Gathering all the courage I could, I dropped that dime and made a collect call. After telling Mrs. Lowery the situation I was in, this is the answer I got. "I will come and pay all of your utilities and rent. I will buy groceries for you and buy you a heater, on one condition. You let Sandra come home with me. You never ask for her back. You give me your word. You promise me this and I will get you through this till you can go to work." "I can't give Sandra away like that, Mrs. Lowery. How can you ask me to do this? Sandra needs a mother and I need my child. I will go out and steal food for her if that is what it takes." "Don't be stupid, and then you would go to jail. What purpose would that serve? I am not saying you have to give her to me and never see her again. You can come and see her any time you want. She will know you are her mother. You can never seem to do anything right but this one time, you need to do what is best for the children. If I have to come down there and go to Child Welfare they will take both of them. Don't you think I won't do it. I will not let Sandra sit there and do without." I gave my promise. She came and took my Sandra. As she was leaving David drove up. She didn't speak to him. She threw Sandra in the car and peeled rubber down the driveway. David came into the house. With his hands on his hips he looked around and asked, "What have you done?" "What you have made me do," I screamed. "You left me here in the dark with no heat, no food. The Land lord was threatening to evict us. Your generous mother bailed us out for a high price. She took our daughter as payment." He went wild. He threw things and punched a hole in the wall with his fist. "If you would have waited a few more hours, dammit, I would have had everything took care of. I have been in New Orleans. I have been crawling around in the hold of those ships all week working day and night to catch us up. If you had just a little faith in me, I would have made everything work out." Then he sat down and cried. "David why didn't you tell me what you were going to do?" "You wouldn't have let me go without raising a lot of hell," he said. "You would have insisted I stay at that service station and slave for pennies. I wanted enough money to catch us up and hold us over till I could find a job worth having. I am sick and tired of living like this. We never have enough to go around and you are pregnant again. There has got to be better than this. Now we have lost Sandra. I guess you will blame me for that for the rest of our lives too. It's a no win situation with you. As soon as the rent comes due here we are going to move. I want to get as far from your mother and that son of bitch she is married to as I can get. If I never lay eyes on them it will be too soon for me." It was many years before the two of them were able to reconcile their hard feelings for one another. We moved several times after that. Each time he changed jobs we moved closer to where he worked. We seemed to get along better now. I guess both of us was growing up some and learning how to deal with each other and life. He still would go to the night clubs once in a while but not like he used to. During those years, we had three more children; Connie, Robert and Jerry.

I liked the neighbor hoods we lived in and made friends with my neighbors. One of those friends was Ester. Her husband was Bobby. I remember David and I having a loud disagreement. I don't remember what it was about. The next morning Ester came over for coffee. "So give," she said as she settled down with her cup. "What?" I asked her. "I have been sent to find out what the fight was about," she said with a grin. "Why would anybody want to know that?" "Because all the guys have bet on it, Bobby has got five in the pool. One says he cursed your aunt Lillie. Another says naw, he told her she was just like her mother. Bobby said you are all wrong, David would have to kick her cat to make her that mad. So who wins the pot?" She asked me. I began to laugh. "They all win and they all loose," I said as I dried my eyes and poured my coffee. "He called my aunt a fat assed witch. When I strongly objected to that he accused me of being as crazy as my mother. Then he kicked my cat.

Bobby's boss was a man called Shine. He was nicknamed this because he first made his money making moonshine out by Big creek lake. He offered Bobby a big house out there where his dairy used to be. It was rent free. Bobby got David a job as a meat cutter in the same store where he worked. We all moved into the big house together. They took the front half and we took the back. We shared the kitchen. I loved the place. I could go to the lake or wander in the woods at my leisure. Ester would watch my children and give me free time. I did the same for her. Shine kept a lot of cattle there for beef sales. One old Holstein found a way to get through the fence. She would come to my bed room window every morning. Pushing her head through the screen, she would wake me licking my face.

There was a small cemetery at the edge of my yard. I would guess about eight or so graves there. One day, I saw Shine's Cadillac drive up and park beside the grave yard, and digging equipment on the back of a big truck right behind him. I sat on the porch and watched as they sat about digging the graves up and loading the contents onto another truck. Curiosity finally getting the best of me. I walked to the digging site. They were loading up and getting ready to move out. "Shine, what on earth are you doing?" "I am moving my people," he answered. "I gathered that much," I said. "Well, you see little lady. My time on this planet is up. I have worked hard and built all this. I am a rich man. Now I have to go and leave it all. You know we can't take it with us. I got nobody to leave it to but my wife and that damn nephew she thinks so much of. The first thing she will do is sell all of this side of the lake to those bastards down at city hall. I been fighting them all my life it seems. I hate all the crooked sum bitches. This Lake is a reservoir. Now they gonna take my land and flood it. All this is going to be under water. That's why I am getting my people out." I pointed at three remaining graves. "What about those," I asked. "Them I don't care about. Let city hall have em. Where they going they gonna need all the water they can get." He spit toward them. Then his chauffer helped him into the car. Poor old rich man, I thought. Sure wish I was his daughter. I would be glad to help him kick city hall in the pants from now on for this beautiful piece of land.

Late that afternoon a perfect double rainbow appeared in the sky. One end of it dipped and ended right in the middle of Big Creek Lake. I heard the sound of car engines. I looked toward the dirt road that comes from Snow Road to the lake. It was four miles long. There were cars almost bumper to bumper following the rainbow. They couldn't get any farther than my house without walking. The lake was fenced off and gated at the edge of my yard. All of those people got out of their cars and stood or sat in my yard watching the rainbow. Sure did wish I had a hotdog concession stand. Oh well, money didn't make Shine happy, I thought. Got to be more to life than that too, sure wished I knew what it was and where to get it.

We went to Evergreen to visit Sandra. Granddaddy told David the Ellrod plant had shut down. They had lost all of his retirement money. He was going back to logging and wanted to know if David would come back to Evergreen and help him. "Oh no David," I protested when he tried to talk to me. "I don't want to live here. I have no friends here. I have no one when I am here but you're mother. I can't stand it." "It won't be that way anymore, Betty. She has what she wanted. Surely you two can find a way to get along now. Daddy needs me. I have caused him a lot of worry and grief. This is a way I can make some of it up to him." "I love your daddy, David. He has always tried to be kind to me. He is a fine man but your mother is not someone I can abide. She wants to make me over into her clone. I refuse to be like her. I am me, I don't want to be like her. I do admire her strength and her Intelligence, but she uses it wrong. She judges and runs over others to get what she wants. She wants to cut and kink my hair and dress me like an old lady. Around her, I am not allowed to have an opinion of my own. She bad mouths me and makes fun of me. See we haven't even moved here and we are arguing all ready." "Well, you can't blame this one on Mother," he said laughing. "From now on just tell her no when she tries to bully you. You have learned to stand up for yourself better than you used to. You are not the child I married. You are a grown woman in your own right now. Act like one." Against my better judgment I agreed to move back to Evergreen and try with his family once more.

I took a job at the drapery plant and went to work. I learned to gather a garden and put up canned food. I saw as much of Sandra as I could. Life was all work and no play. David bought me a second hand electric stove that had a short in it. Sometimes, I would set a frying pan on the eye and it would shock the living daylights out of me. At other times, I could lay my hands all over it and nothing would happen. David's parents checked out the stove and the ornery thing behaved fine. "I told you and Alfred she was off in the head," I heard Mrs. Lowery whisper to Granddaddy. "She just wants something to complain about. It's the same reason she claims someone is stealing food out of the house. She thinks it will get Alfred to move her to town."

I worked with a heavy fiberglass material at work so David made me a make shift shower in the outside shed. He punched holes in the bottom of a five gallon bucket, and then hung it from a rafter in the ceiling of the shed. He then ran a water hose from the pump at the well and put it in the bucket. It made a fine shower. I was mad about the remark his mother made over my stove. He went out to the shed to take a shower when he came home. It was coming up a thunder storm. I slipped out to the shed and put a stick through the lock clasp and went back in the house. Lightning popped several times real heavy before I went out and removed the stick from the lock hasp. "Why the hell did you do that," He roared as he ran in the back door. "The crazy woman wants a new stove," I said. He leaned with his hand on the stove and started to say something to me but he never got the words out. The stove chose that moment to do its thing and knocked him about half way across the kitchen. By the time he picked his naked butt up from the floor, he was ready to go buy me a new stove.

Someone was coming in my house and taking my food. I canned twenty two jars of squash. I was so proud of them. I asked David to bring his daddy home for lunch and promised I would fix his favorite dish of stewed squash. The lady who babysat my kids while I worked taught me how to make them real good. When I went to get the squash from the pantry, they were all gone. Not even one jar left. When David and his daddy come in they asked, "Where are the stewed squash?" "Are you willing to admit I had jars of stewed squash in the pantry?" I asked. "Yes, I am the one who set them in there for you. I even counted the pops all night as the jars sealed." "Well they are not there," I said. "They are gone. Now I have been telling you our food was going missing. You need to fix the lock on the back door. Sometimes, I am here at night by myself. Whoever this is may decide to come after more than food one of those times." Granddaddy glared at his son but didn't say anything. He did however take me out into the woods and showed me how to use a shotgun. "Now," he said. "You keep this loaded and hanging on the wall in your bedroom where it is handy. Remember this, don't pick it up unless you are willing to use it." I didn't know if I could or not. When Mrs. Lowery gave me a chicken to kill, it had been a disaster. Bo was visiting at that time. He took the hen from the coop and handed her to me. She settled in my arms and clucked. She seemed so contented and happy there. The sun struck auburn highlights in her feathers. "Oh Bo," I said. "She is so sweet and pretty. She trusts me. I can't kill this chicken!" "Give her to me, I will do it." He wrung her neck and placed her in a foot tub, he handed her to me. I wiped away tears and sniffled as I walked toward the house. Lo and behold, she jumped from the foot tub and ran with her head flopping around on the end of her broken neck. Bo chased her down and wrung her neck again. He put her back in the bucket and said. "Take her on to the house. She is dead for sure this time." When I poured the hot water over her, she squawked. That was enough for me. I carried her, bucket, boiling water, and all and threw her in the woods. I took a store bought chicken from the freezer and fried it. "Mother's old hen fried up real tender," said David as he chewed on a drumstick. I didn't answered him. Granddaddy found the carcass and told on me. I took quite a bit of verbal chastisement from David and his mother over that little escapade. There did come a time when I learned whether I could use a gun or not.

David and his Daddy went coon hunting. With Butch and Connie tucked in for the night, the house was quiet. I placed a tub in front of the living room heater and filled it with warm water to bath in. I had finished and was sitting in a chair with my feet soaking in the warm bath water when I heard a noise on the front porch. I glanced up just in time to see the doorknob slowly turn then ease back. It was locked and my shades were down. I listened as I heard him slip along the length of the porch and off the end into the tall grass that David had not had time to sling blade yet. I could hear the grass as it swished against the intruder's pants legs. Oh my God he was headed for the back door, I thought, and David had not repaired the lock. I left the tub as fast and quietly as I could. I went in the bed room and took the shoot gun off the wall. I cocked the gun and stood in the door between my children's bed room and the kitchen. I could hear him as he moved stealthily through the grass and down the side of the house toward the back door. He paused at the kitchen window. I heard the swishing sound fade away as he changed directions and went toward the woods at the edge of the yard. I stood there a long time and waited but he didn't come back. It was then I realized what had turned him. My shadow with gun in hand was cast against the window shade. That is all that saved that man, for I knew beyond any doubt from the cold hard resolve I felt solidify inside me. Not for the food because I would share freely with someone in need. Not to protect my worldly goods but to protect my children. Yes, I could use the gun. David found me in my chair asleep with his gun across my lap. I told him why. He took his spotlight and went outside. He found the attempted intruder's path through the tall weeds around the house all the way to the back. He put his gun back on the rack and pulled me from my chair and sat us both down on the couch. "I have been looking at houses in town ever sense we had that last big blow up with Mother and Daddy. I think we need to put a little distance between us. I have found us one on Pecan Street, if you want to move. It's a three bed room duplex. The couple next door is about our age. I think you would like them." "I don't know if the town of Evergreen is enough distance or not David," I sighed. "I don't know if the other side of the world is enough distance." "Well, you know you could help from escalating the fights," he said dragging me onto his lap. "Oh and how can I do that?" "You didn't have to call her an old battle ax." I blew on his ear and answered. "No I could have called her worse. After all, she called me hot pants little bitch and said I was going to slide into hell feet first. That's when I called her an old battle ax and informed her, if I didn't see her there I would give up my front row seat and sit on a syrup bucket way back in the back. You know I will get blamed for us moving. She accused me of leading you around by the nose. As if anyone could lead you anywhere you didn't want to go," I exclaimed indignantly. "Well how about leading me to the bed room before this turns into another knock down drag out. I did take the blame for moving to Pecan Street.

"Oh Miss Betty, Miss Betty, wake up." I woke to find my babysitter, Kristine shaking me while she screeched. "Wha, what," I asked trying to get my eyes open. "The trash man, he done took all yo clean laundry. Hurry, git up." She turned me loose and ran for the door. I looked out the front door. I could see the new trash cans sitting on the back of the truck when it stopped for its next pickup. Kristine was waddling down the street waving her arms and shouting. I hiked up my night gown and joined in the chase. When I caught up with the truck I hollered, "You back up and put my clean laundry right back on the back porch where you got it from" "What's laundry doing in trash cans?" He asked. "Never mind that you nincompoop," screeched Kristin. "You put it right back where you got it. You can see with your own eyes them cans is clean and got wet clothes in them. An why you takes cans an all? I ain't no fool." She shook her fist for emphasis. He backed his truck down the street and grumbling all the while he put my belongings back on the porch. "I aught ta make you take em all the way to the clothes line." "You want em at tha clothes line? Whyent ya say so? He picked up both cans and carried them to the line. "See," he grinned. "No harm no foul. Uh, you ain't gonna say nothing to Ma about this is you Aunt Kristine?" "Shoo!" She said as she swatted at him. "Git gone an you pay attention to whose laundry you dragging off next time." I worked the four to twelve night shift now. When I got home from work I always washed the dirty clothes before going to bed. Kristine would take care of the hanging and putting them away for me. Kristine was as a treasure. I liked her a lot. It seemed she would do anything for me she could but Mrs. Lowery complained about her till she got David to fire her. He hired someone his mother sent to us. I didn't like the new person. She was lazy and insubordinate. She gossiped to my mother-in-law about me too. The lady in the other side of the duplex heard and told me what was happening. Mrs. Lowery's work day ended at four pm. As I was going to work, she was getting off. She would come by the house to pick up Sandra on her way home. I fired the new girl myself and hired someone of my choosing. This made Mrs. Lowery mad so she found her own babysitter and stopped bringing Sandra to me during the day. Things seemed to go from bad to worse. David started drinking heavy and staying out late at night. We fought a lot. I called my mother. "I want to come home." I told her. "If I come and get you, will you promise me you will never move back up there again?" "I promise you if you will get me out of here, I will never come back except to see Sandra." "You know David is going to come after you." "He might not, Mother. Things are pretty bad between us right now." "If he does, will you take him back?" "I don't know," I answered. In my heart I did know. I knew I loved him still and always would but I would never live in Evergreen again.

I unpacked and left Butch and Connie with their uncle's as I wandered off to the woods. David was there before dark. "Where is she, Jane? Please let me talk to her." "She is out wandering in those woods somewhere David. You know how she is when she is troubled. Probably down by the river somewhere." "I will find her," he said to mother. "I find that you and she have not been dealing to well with each other. I will tell you this. She had better not come out of those woods with one mark on her. If she does, you won't come out at all. Do we understand each other?" "There is no call for that Jane. I am not here to fight. I am here to beg if that's what it takes. I will do whatever she wants except give her up. I pray she doesn't ask for that." "Just so we understand one another," replied Mother.

I had wandered down to Deer River and sat under a tree. I had done what I had to do but oh it was so hard. My insides felt like a bowl of jelly. I tried to light a cigarette. My hands shook so bad, I broke it. It wasn't only, how am I going to do this? Raise two children alone, although that in itself was a daunting thought. Mostly, it was how I am ever going to break these chains that bind me? No matter what had passed between us, I loved that man with every fiber of my being. It made me physically sick to think of tearing apart everything I had tried to build with him. I wanted to think of all the bad in him so I could harden my heart enough to turn him loose. To free myself from the ties that bound me to him. I couldn't seem to think of anything but the good. I actually sat there and laughed as I wiped away tears thinking of some of the zany things we had done. This was killing me. I knew I was lost when I heard his footsteps on the path and he called my name. He took one look at my face and sunk to his knees beside me. "Aww Honey," he said as he gathered me to him. "I am never going back to Evergreen again," I sobbed as I beat him on the shoulder with my fist. "Never, never! And if you ask me to I swear fore God, I will shoot you dead. If I ever find you with another woman, I will catch you asleep and sew you up in the bed sheets and beat the living hell out of you. I won't be your doormat any more. I wish I never had to lay eyes on your mother again. She will teach Sandra she had to take her because I was a bad mother and I couldn't be trusted to raise my own child." He held and soothed me through my tirade as only my David knew how. He promised never again would I be asked to live around his mother. "I will tell you this," he said. "I know my mother. Someday Sandra will come and ask. When she does, I will tell her the truth. I will make sure she knows where to place blame. It was my fault and I damn well know it. Just don't stop loving me Betty. If you do I will be lost." He kept those promises. Every last one.

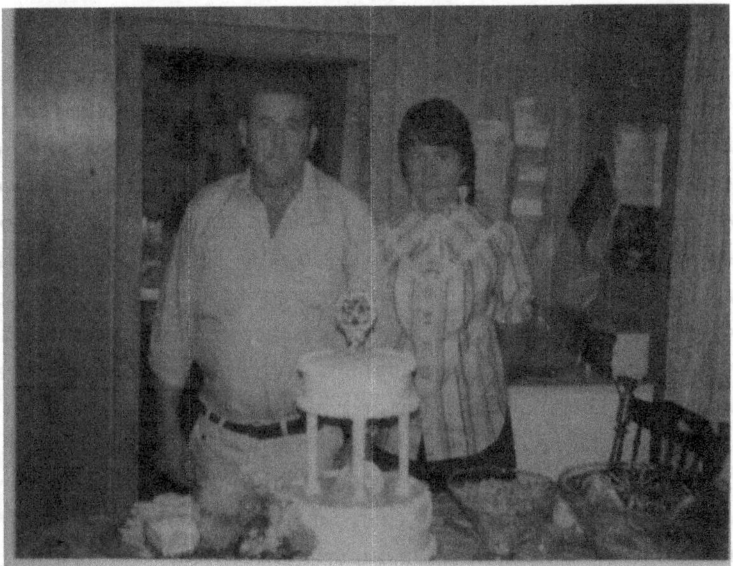

David and Betty Lowery

Chapter 21

TO TAME A LOWERY

"We are not going to make it David." I groaned as I left the front seat and flipped backwards to the back. "Pull over." He pulled the car to the side of the road. "Honey, we are in front of Mrs. Angelo's house, try to hang on. Chester, see if she can spare a blanket and a towel or two. Tell her your sister needs a woman out here." We were on Cedar Point Road. It is now called Dauphine Island Parkway. I was having a baby. By the time Mrs. Angelo got to me with blanket and towels. My Robert was making his presence known loud and clear. His Dad had panicked momentarily. "What do I do? He can't get his breath. There is something over his face." "He was born with a caul over his face. Get it off so he can breathe. Clean out his mouth." Once he began to cry, David handed him to me and tied the cord with my brother's shoe string then cut it with his pocket knife. We thought this was necessary. On our arrival at the hospital we learned different. My doctor was not a happy camper. Well neither was I. The attendants drug me from the car feet first with my night gown over my head and people, mostly men staring at me. The doctor asked, "Who is the father." David pointed at Chester. "Her brother," He answered. "I mean, I am her father. No," he stuttered. "She has no father." "Go to the front desk and sit down son. I think we know who the father is," laughed the doctor. I vowed I would never try to make a trip to the hospital to have a baby again. One would wonder why I didn't vow to never have another baby. Well I can only say when Connie was conceived we were using a prophylactic. It didn't work! Next, I tried a diaphragm and along came Robert. At last, medical science came up with a birth control pill. I was taking it. I had an allergic reaction. The doctor cut my dose and along came Jerry. He was the last. Thank God for a contraceptive called the loop. For the birth of my last child, I searched till I found an older doctor who didn't mind doing things the old fashioned way. Dr. Blake referred me to a midwife named Myrtle Gordon. He took care of my prenatal care and she delivered my last baby at home. I moved within three blocks of her in Creighton. Myrtle came to visit me every month of my pregnancy. She showed me how to set up my bedroom with all we would need to take care of the birthing. On the morning of this event, David took our neighbor Jr. fishing. A heavy wake from a barge capsized their boat. Jr. had only one arm and could not swim out. By the time David helped him from the river; the boat, motor, plus all fish and tackle had sunk to the bottom of the Alabama River. Jr. returned home in shock. His wife gave him a pill to settle his nerves and put him to bed. "How do you feel?" David asked me. "Do you think it will be alright for me to go back to the river and see what I can do about my boat and motor?" "Actually, I feel better today than I have for the last two weeks." I assured him. "I have spent a most miserable two weeks. I even heard the baby cry yesterday. I never knew such a thing was possible. I guess he was as uncomfortable as I was. You go take care of your boat and I think I will hose down the outside of the eves of the house. I feel like I want to do something and that is all I feel capable of doing. At least this little one has got out from under my ribs and I can breathe now. I should have known to keep him there. I had to send Jr. after Myrtle. He was still dopey and backed into a telephone pole but bless him, he came back with the midwife in tow. I sent for her when I felt the first pain and she came to me straight away. Still, she did not have time to don her cap and gown and gloves. She hustled in to the room just in time to take care of my new born babe. Jr. walked the front porch until it was all over and gave David hell for me when he got home. "If I must launch your ship," he declared. "I think it only fair that I should be there at the laying of the keel." Myrtle gave me a shot of blended whiskey with four drops of paregoric to stop afterbirth pains. This had been the easiest birth and recovery I had ever gone through.

Before we moved to this street in Creighton we lived in Prichard homes. All the apartments here looked the same. I recall a night when an elderly gentleman wandered in through my kitchen door. As I stood at the sink washing dishes, he absent mindedly strolled by me and kissed my cheek. "Good evening dear." He mumbled as he wandered on into the living room. David lowered his newspaper and stared at the man without saying a word. He took his hat off and turned to hang it on the wall above the heater. There was nothing there to hang it on. That's when he blinked and looked around. Without a word he turned and left the same way he came in. As he came by me he kissed me on the other cheek and said. "My profound apologies' madam." Then like a thin gray shadow, he slipped out the door.

David and I must have been a fairly colorful couple. While going about my daily chores one day, I heard two children at play. "What do you want to play today," asked a little boy. "Oh, let's play Betty and David," piped a giggly little voice. Now this I have to see, I thought as I eased closer to the window. "Okay honey," said the boy. "I am going to the store. Do you need anything?" "I need to shop," replied the girl. "I am going with you." "Just make a list. I am in a hurry. My football game starts in one hour and I want snacks." "I will hurry." "I ain't got time to fool with you, woman." "Come on," she said. "I will get ready while you get out the car." The little boy grumbled as he set two buckets upside down and laid a board across them. The little girl went inside her house and came back in her mother's high heels and a pocket book over her arm. He pretended to open the passenger door and motioned her to sit on the board. Arms akimbo and her noise in the air, she puckered her lips. "I am driving," she declared. "Oh no, I told you I'm in a hurry." She patted her little foot and looked around and up at the sky. "Then I am not going." "Aww come on honey go ahead and drive." He sat down on the passenger side. She sat on the driver's side and turned her imaginary key. "Grr-rr hic-grr. Oh honey, it won't crank," she cried. The boy threw his hands in the air. "Damn women drivers," he said as he opened his imaginary door and stalked to the other end of the board. "Move over," he snarled. She shuffled to the other side. He sat down and shifted gears and turned his imaginary key. "Vroom buddin, buddin, see how easy that was," he said. "It's just all in how you hold your mouth sweetheart." Argh, I thought as I gritted my teeth and went back to my dusting. I can't even win in a play fight!

It is a sure thing, you can't live with a Lowery and be that meek submissive little woman who was someone's idea of the perfect wife. Probably a man dreamed that up. I tried to live by this way of thinking for a while. I soon became disabused of such a foolish notion. My David liked to brag he wore the pants in the family. Of course he did. I let him. Who wants a panty waist for a husband? He also learned that he who have peace with wife in daytime, have piece at night and good hot meals on the supper table. Oh, and buttons sewed on his favorite shirt. I picked blackberries from beside the road and made him a berry pie. He got downright nasty because I left the seeds in and threw my pie out the door. Without one cross word, I threw the rest of his supper out behind the pie. "Now," I said. "It is fine with me if you want your meals outside, but let me know in advance from now on." He once asked for a button to be sewn on his pants. It was loose. "Okay hon, I will get to it soon" I answered him. "No. Do it right now," he said. "Why, are you going somewhere?" "No but I know you. You will forget. So do it now." I sat and fumed as I sewed the button. How dare he demand! Who did he think he was? My Cat, Fancy laid on the couch beside me. She was a large silver Manx. Reaching up with one curved sharp claw, she plucked a thread in the seat of the pants. "Why Fancy dear, what a smart, err, bad kitty you are!" I tugged on the thread with my needle just the lest little bit. To make sure it was still stable, you understand. Then for good measure Fancy plucked it one more time. Imagine my surprise when David comes home from work the next day wearing his shirt tied around his waist. He shucked the pants and threw them in the trash as he went by. Fancy sniffed, then sat down and washed her face with nary a word. My Fancy would never rat me out.

There was a time the doctor wanted to check all the children for parasites. He admonished me to be sure all the stool samples were fresh. "Mail them to the board of health the same day they are taken and seal the lids to the bottles tight." He explained as he handed me the package of sample bottles. This meant they had to be taken early in the morning before I could go to work. I tried for two mornings with my oldest son Butch. He was so embarrassed by it all, he couldn't or wouldn't go. I called the doctor about the problem. "Well give him castor oil if nothing else works," he said. I informed him I had already tried that, milk of magnesia, and Fletcher's Castoria. "Well for pete's sake," exclaimed the exasperated doctor. "I will phone in a prescription to the drug store and if that don't work, take a stick and beat it out of him." Then he hung up on me. The prescription did work, and worked, and worked. I took the samples and placed them in the brown paper bag to address and send off on our way to work. David and I both worked for the same company in Bayou La Batra at this time. I fixed breakfast, packed lunches, and answered to David for forgetting to prepare grits with his breakfast. "Sorry Dear," I apologized. "I could have sworn I fixed them, maybe not." I taped and addressed the package while he drove and dropped it in the drop box when we went by the post office. When break time came around at work, David brought his coffee cup to my work station and asked for a cup of coffee from my thermos. I opened it and began to pour. Out came his morning grits. All nice, hot, and buttered too! He wandered away. "I wonder if I can find a spoon." he sadly said as he shook his head. I reached for my coworker's thermos as I watched him. "I wonder if this day can get any worse?" I muttered to myself. For sure an all it could and did. When lunch time rolled around David presented himself once more. He pitched his lunch bag on the table. "What am I supposed to do with this?" he asked me. I looked in the bag. So did everyone else that was gathered around the table. My face flamed. Oh Lord I groaned. It's the kids stool samples. Somewhere at the Mobile County Board of Health there is a technician who is scratching his head and wondering what the hell he is supposed to do with one peanut butter and one baloney sandwich. Things went downhill from there. There was a whole lot of shouting going on. Things began to get dicey when the boss ordered me to clean up my language and take our beef outside. He also told David that was no way to talk to a lady and if we came to blows, he would call the law to us. David and I both turned our frustration on the meddling boss man. We might fight among ourselves but against the rest of the world we stood united.

I am now fast forwarding to September twelve, nineteen seventy nine. By this time, David and I worked for Flowerwood Nurseries Inc. I will tell you more about how this occurred later. Some may remember this year and date. Hurricane Fredrick struck Mobile that night. David was working at the Loxley Branch across the bay. I was working my last day at the Mobile Nursery. We had bought our first home in Loxley and I was transferring from the Mobile nursery to the Loxley branch. However, Hurricane Fredrick was closing in fast and I felt it was my duty to stay at work and do whatever I could to help batten down the hatches, so to speak. I worked until four thirty that afternoon. Then went home and loaded the truck. I reached Loxley and got the truck unloaded just before the hurricane hit us. What a miserable night. The wind howled. The walls breathed in and out. Trees crashed all around us. By daylight, we could see part of our roof was gone. I watched in amazement as people took to the tops of their houses and began ripping shingles from their roofs right and left. What in the world are they doing, I wondered. I found exactly what they were about, once the insurance adjuster got there. He prorated my roof and only paid for part of it, as if one could put on half of a roof. Without power for the first two weeks, there was not much I could do to restore order to my new home. We camped there for the duration. David fought with the port-a-potty man. He wanted him to come and pump it out. The man answered. "Mr. Lowery be grateful you even have a port-a-potty. Most folks don't. I have hundreds and hundreds of them scattered and over turned in fields and roads all over Mississippi and Alabama." I made a trip back to Mobile to get my freezer and the two cars I had left behind. The scene was devastation everywhere I looked. Mobile homes were upside down. Trees ripped out by the roots. I saw an elderly lady standing in her yard. She was waving her apron as if she intended to shoo the tree off the roof of her house. I cried for her. The house I moved from was torn up and flooded. Electrical wiring and plumbing had been ripped from the wall. The cars were flattened like pancakes with a tree lying across them.

After things returned to normal, David helped me hang curtains and pictures on the wall. Looking around with his rifle in hand he said. "Honey leave the wall over the head of the bed empty. I think I want to hang my gun there." "Oh no, you shouldn't do that. We don't need it on the wall. Keep it in the closet like you always have. I will hang my doll there. It is light weight." "I want my gun where I can get my hands on it. If an intruder comes in what am I supposed to do? Beat him to death with your doll?" Mr. hard head hung his gun on the wall over our heads. At bedtime, he snuggled in and gave a contented sigh. What say we christen our new home, he whispered. Then he playfully tickled my ribs. I jumped and there was a loud crash. I felt him leave the bed and there was another crash. With a shriek, I rolled to the back of the bed taking the sheet with me. I went between the bed and the wall and covered my head with the sheet. There was the sound of running feet. The bedroom door flew back and the lights flashed on. My two boys were in the door. David was in a fighter's stance in the middle of the floor. "What's going on in here?" my son Robert demanded. Jerry peering over his shoulder giggled. The broken lamp on the floor and the gun lying across the pillows told the story. "Well hell," said David. "I thought I was being attacked." Robert picked up the gun. "I guess the closet is the best place for the gun," he said. Jerry picked up the lamp. "I will put this in the trash. Carry on Dad." He grinned as he switched out the light and closed the door. What David said isn't printable.

After being married to David Lowery for about ten years, I gave up going to the grocery store with him. I would just make a list and send him to shop for the household. He could get really irate when he had to make a trip back to return spoiled meat. He would complain long and loud at what he thought was exorbitant prices. When my man was irate everybody knew it. "Look here honey." He said as he showed me a sale paper. "They got chickens on sale for twenty nine cents a pound. What say we go buy extra for the freezer while they so cheap." On arriving at the store, I grabbed a buggy. (That's what we call a shopping cart down south you all. My Yankee friends are still trying to rehabilitate my English.) Almost running to keep up with him, we headed straight for the meat counter. They were priced as advertised per pound but there was not one chicken in that cooler that weighted less than eight pounds. Moving them around and checking price and pounds, David's face became redder by the minute. "No chicken grows this big. They got em pumped up with something. They are heavy as brick bats. Don't buy any of these damn chickens," he said. "These people are playing Jessie James without the guns." People were beginning to pay attention to him. An elderly gentleman and wife were standing there watching and listening. "Don't buy none of that hamburger either. The last you brought home and cooked, I had to feed to my dogs and it made them sick. They weren't able to hunt for a week." The man took the pack of hamburger meat from his wife and laid it back in the meat cooler. "Umm, umm," he said, "made da dogs sick. That's the way it goes, first your money and then your clothes." I could hear the grumbles coming from David. I knew the explosion was not far behind. The market manager was getting a little red in the face himself by now. I eased my cart from behind David and moved farther down the meat counter. Maybe I could pretend I wasn't with him. That's what he did to me the day I embarrassed him in the egg section of this same store. When I distanced myself from him, another lady pushed her cart beside him and picked up two chickens and put them in her cart. She was reaching for a third when David grabbed the chickens one by one and lobbed them overhand like base balls back into the meat cooler. "I told you not to buy any of them damn chickens!" He roared and grabbing her by her buggy. He began to tug, trying to pull her away from the meat counter. The unfortunate lady held on and dug her heels in. Out in front of David, I was doing a wild dance and waving my arms to get his attention. He saw me and did a double take over his shoulder to see who he was trying to drag off. She was dug in and pulling backwards so hard when he released her, she upended herself and her buggy. He tried to pick her up as he apologized but she slapped his hands away. She wanted none of this mad man. Once alright, she fast trotted herself and her buggy, with nary a chicken to the front of the store. The last I saw of her, she was frantically looking over her shoulder for the lunatic as she hit the door running with one little bag of groceries. On the way home, I gave him the tongue lashing he deserved. He counter attacked. "Well, you get your panty hose in a knot but you have made a few scenes of your own when you get mad. What about the man at the egg cooler? Remember Him?" "I remember you walking away and leaving me to fight my own battle," I snapped. "He insulted my intelligence. I know twelve make a dozen, but I still have to open them to see if any are broke. Be thankful I only called him a bald headed bastard. I should have thrown the eggs at him. He deserved it but the lady you terrorized today was an innocent bystander. Bless her little heart."

When we moved to Staples road, Butch and Connie were in first and second grade. Robert and Jerry were preschoolers. The first day there, they went into the utility shed of an empty house across the street. Finding a bucket of yellow paint, they painted it yellow. Robert also varnished the front of Jerry's head. When the hair grew back it was a darker color. For several years, my youngest son resembled a speckled pup. David was working as a meat cutter. Yep, at the same store where he caused so much grief. It was a pretty house with hard wood floors. I commented that it showed just how shabby my living room suit had become. David decided to surprise me. He took it upon himself to go buy me a new living room suit. Without so much as a by your leave, he didn't even ask what color I preferred. He was so proud of himself when he drove in with an orange couch and chair on the back of his truck. "Look Honey, They gave me the lamps for free." "Ye gads with that living room suit, you didn't need any lamps." He looked like a disappointed little boy. "You don't like it?" he asked me. I almost choked on my answer, but I gathered all the positive energy I could muster and replied. "Well, I think it will look very well, once I buy new curtains and throw rugs and pillows. Maybe olive greens and beige with a touch of white lace will tone it down. We will have to do without curtains in the living room till I can go shopping but first, I have got to get

us unpacked. The kids need to be able to find their school clothes."
"If you will break down your boxes, you can put them and all your
trash in the burning bin. I have set a drum in the back yard for that
purpose. I don't want you to light it. You can't work with unpacking
and keep the boys away from the fire at the same time." I knew he
was referring to the paint job the boys had done. "I will burn it for
you when I come in from work," he offered. So I spent the next day
unpacking and dumping trash in the burn barrel. I did not pay any
attention to what was in the drawers I was dumping. It was just loose
bits and pieces. David set the fire when he got home.

It wasn't long before I heard something that sounded like a
young war out there. I ran to the door to see what was going on. This
had looked like a nice quiet neighborhood when we moved in but
that racket sounded like someone was having a shootout. Someone
was. It was my dear husband. Like a demented witch doctor, he was
jumping around the burn barrel waving his arms and screaming for
a water hose. The gun shots were coming from the barrel! "We don't
have a water hose at the moment." I shouted at him. "I had one,"
he screamed back. "Till that damned brother of yours walked off
with it. What did you put in this barrel? I need water," he cried.
I grabbed my mop bucket and joined the fracas. I ran from the
outside faucet to the barrel many times while he danced, cussed,
and dodged bullets. At last, the fire was out. The last shotgun shell
racked off and all was quiet. He dragged himself into the house and
sat at the table with his head in his hands. "What possessed you to
dump my rifle bullets and shot gun shells in the burning barrel?"
He asked me. Unrepentant, I asked him. "What possessed you to
put loose ammo in the drawers? You should know that's not a safe
practice." "I do now," he answered. "When a man lives with Lucille
Ball, Carole Burnett, and Phyllis Diller all rolled into one little
woman nothing is safe." "Well, we have started our first week in our
new home with a bang. Our neighbors all disappeared indoors real
fast," was all I could say. "They most likely hiding under the bed,"
he snickered. Oh but the fun wasn't over. Not by a long shot. There
was day three. I hung pictures and baked a ham. I left it sitting on
the counter top, turned my radio up so I could listen to my favorite

country song while I took my shower. Before I could even get the soap rinsed off, he was home and there was a terrible racket going on. It sounded like he was tearing the walls out. I could hear my cat yowling and David cussing. I jumped from the tub and grabbed a towel to put around me. I still didn't have my living room curtains up. That was tomorrow's job. I sprinted into the hall and my cat went between my legs, did a u turn and headed back toward the front of the house. David was hot behind her, wildly swinging my broom and hitting the walls. "Stop crazy, before you put a hole in the wall." I grabbed the broom and lost my towel. Holding on to the sweeping end of the broom I followed him as he held the other end and lunged for the living room. I was fast enough to turn loose the broom and snatch the door open. I shooed the cat out while he tried to catch his breath. "Look what she did. She pulled the ham from the counter to the floor. She needed her ass beat." He shouted as he turned the radio down. Before I could say a word, he grinned and pointed at me. "The neighbors are sure getting an eyeful," he snickered. Looking down at myself, I gasped and made a beeline to the bathroom. I got back in the shower to wash the soap off. He went to the kitchen and played musical water faucets. He turned first hot then cold on and off causing my shower to revert from hot to cold back and forth. Sticking his smug face around the bathroom door, he innocently drawled. "Aw, you finished already?" "You will know payback when you see it, buddy." I vowed as I stalked past him. My living room did look really nice, once the new curtains were hung and the fluffy throw rugs down despite the orange living room suit. Before it was time for David to come in, I had the bathroom set up with new towels and his favorite soap and my favorite after shave, old spice. Everything was all ready for his shower, including the bucket of ice water sitting behind the bed room door. "Oh ho." He smirked as picking up the bottle of old spice and winking at me. "Enjoy your shower dear." I said with a sweet smile as I closed the bathroom door without letting the lock catch. When I heard the water running and him singing, I picked up the bucket of ice water and slipped into the bathroom. Ducking around the shower curtain I emptied the bucket on his back. Then I turned and ran for the front door as fast as I could. He was out of the shower and coming behind me as I went out the door. It couldn't have been better. As he left the hall his feet hit a big fluffy throw rug. He looked for all the world like a naked surfer coming across that hardwood floor. His feet flew from beneath him. As he slid toward the door, he grabbed for anything that might save him. All he managed to catch was his guitar that was propped against the couch. I gleefully held the screen open for him as he surfed flat of his back with his precious guitar held aloft onto the front porch. He jumped up and looked around before spinning with his guitar held in front of him and his cute little buns shining like a new moon as he scurried into the house. Looking around myself, I noticed all the lawn mowers and electric hedge trimmers had grown very quiet. I waved my fingers at the man who had dropped his cigar and cut a big gap in his hedge while he stood opened mouthed. I bowed to the one sitting on his lawn mower trying to pick his cap up without getting off, before I jauntily bounced into the house. We had no more incidents of musical faucets.

Finally everything was done and I could have a day of rest. By now I needed it. I mixed a cake and put it in the oven. Spanked both Robert and Jerry for sticking the cat's tail in an open lamp socket and put them to bed for a nap. I had just iced the cake and put on a pot of coffee when I heard a knock on my door. I opened it to find a sweet faced lady there with a cup in her hand. Peeping around the door frame, she whispered. "Is your husband home?" "No," I laughed. "He is at work. Won't you come in?" She timidly stepped into the living. "Oh, how pretty it is in here. It is so cheerful, and something sure smells good. My name is Pauline Doggett, by the way." Pleased with her reaction to all my hard work, I answered her. "I am Betty Lowery. I just finished baking a cake and made fresh coffee. Will you join me?" Holding out her cup, she said with a grin. "I came to borrow a cup of sugar and to be nosy." Liking her honesty, I took her cup and filled it with sugar. Then I poured us a cuppa and sliced both of us piece of cake. "Well, has your nosiness been satisfied?" I asked as I waved my hand around at my sparkling kitchen. "Not quiet," she replied as she sat at my table. "You and your husband have set this neighborhood on its ear. They are all buzzing about you. I don't like gossip so I came to get it straight from the horse's mouth. You know my house sits way back off the road down on the bayou, so I don't get to hear and see all of the excitement that goes on." "What are the neighbors saying? I haven't had time to meet any of them, so I am sure I have not had the chance to offend anyone yet. Oh, except for the brown puppy. I think he belongs to the house at the end of the side street. I did not hurt him on purpose you know. He stays on my back porch and he accidentally got the door slammed on his little tail and broke it. Then he would holler every time he tried to sit down. I felt so sorry for the little feller. I didn't know what else to do." I spread my hands and shrugged my shoulders as I gazed at her across the table. Hoping she wouldn't judge me too harshly. Well what did you do?" she asked me. "Well," I gulped. "The only thing I could do. I took my butcher knife and whacked the tail off at the break. It bobbed off at just the right place to look cute. Then I bandaged it with Iodine and duct tape. When I turned him loose he ran home. I saw him yesterday. The tail looks real nice." My voice dwindled off as I waited for her response to my sorrowful confession. Slapping her hand over her mouth, she rocked back and forth. Finally, she wiped the tears from her eyes and gasped. "What did you do with the tail?" "I buried it under the door step." I confessed as I wiped up the coffee she had spewed from her nosy nose. "Oh my word and garter straps," she hooted. "I bet old lady Macke is growing horse feathers out her ears. She and her bitter half are always finding fault with someone to fuss about. Pay her no attention. Nobody else does. But no Betty, I had not heard that one yet." "What else?" I asked her. I listened wide eyed as she ticked the offences off on her fingers. "Well, your brother is a thief and on your second night here, ya'll had a shootout because he stole your husband's water hose. Then it seems your husband likes to beat you and your cat while you are naked to the tune of loud country music." By that time, I was laughing so hard that I choked on my own coffee. "Last but not least, your husband is a flasher who likes to streak in your front yard while you watch. I have told my husband I feel sure there is a reasonable explanation for this gossip.

I have come to you so you can set the reports straight." "Good lord, where do I begin," I sputtered. By the time I had gave her a full explanation for all the happenings, she was once more beside herself with mirth. "I don't know when I have had so much fun." She said as she wiped her eyes and gathered herself to go home. "I am going to have even more fun telling our neighbors the real truth." Pauline and I remained good friends for a long time.

Chapter 22

THE PROMISE

"I swear David! I have heard I'm coming till my head aches. Can't you learn to pick another song besides Old Black Joe? Listen to the man across the street. He's playing I Still Miss Someone." "Well by all means, let's get that dude over here. Son, run across the street and ask that man if he will come and play with me." The boy ran over and was back shortly. "Daddy, he said do you want him to bring his marbles or his mumble pegs?" "Go tell him if he will bring his guitar and give a lesson or two, there is a cup of coffee and a slice of cake in it for him." Soon, he appeared at our door with his guitar, wife and, two daughters. That is how we met James and Nell Pitts. James taught David how to cord the guitar. We spent many a fun late evening cooking out and having musical gatherings. James' young nephew would come and bring his teenage friends. They all played musical instruments. Some neighbors would send word up the street asking us to turn up the volume. One or two called the law when we did. It didn't matter. We just kept playing. The Law was glad to find the teens somewhere safe with no alcohol.

James hankered to move back to Texas and go back to work for Burns detective agency. David's work in the meat market was causing him some medical problems; a triple hernia, pain in his neck, shoulders, and lower back. He decided he wanted to go to Texas with James and go to work for Burns also. I sold everything I owned except clothes, dishes, and my sewing machine to get us there. We didn't like Texas. I missed my tall oak and pine trees. The trees in Pasadena appeared stunted. There was not much grass, mostly just black dirt and metal prehistoric looking creatures that slowly bobbed their heads up and down. David said they were oil well pumps. If the cold storage and the heavy lifting in the meat market hurt David physically, the patrolman's job with the detective agency hurt his nerves. James explained just how nerve wrecking once when he pulled his gun and started to shoot my wind chimes down. James was a tall man. The chimes brushed his hat and tinkled a merry tune as he walked under them. He had his gun drawn quicker than a cat could wink. He got control of himself before he pulled the trigger and apologized. "Sorry Betty but this job is getting to me and David both, right now. We are patrolling some rough territory these days. The Black panthers and the Hells Angels are on the warpath. Not to mention the drug runners coming out of Mexico. They will shoot for no reason at all." I knew this to be true because David had taken the job of a man who had been shot down for no apparent reason. "Is that why David is having such nightmares?" I asked him. "He wakes up shouting sometimes." "I spec so. We sometimes see some awful rough things going on out there, Betty." Then he chuckled. "Did David tell you about tangling with a drunken chimp last night? That monkey was foaming at the mouth drunk and he kept trying to climb around David's neck to give him sugar." "Where was his owner?" I asked him. "There was a car load of people there. You couldn't see anything but arms and legs waving out the windows. The chimp was lying on top of the car. Every so often he would beat on the top and someone would hand him a beer out the window. That was one stinking drunk monkey. We finally managed to get the chimp in the car and told the people they would have to move on because they were partying in a restricted area. Thankfully, they were cheerful and amiable folk. They left without a fuss so we didn't have to bring in the police." We spent a little less than a year in Pasadena Texas.

I could hear my children laughing in the front yard. The squeals and laughter were joined by a deep melodious voice. I went to the front door to see what or who was making them so happy. It was our mailman. He was a large black man. He carried a leather mail pouch strapped to his back. I could only imagine the weight of that bag plus four laughing children as they clambered all over him. They clung like little leeches to his arms and legs. "Do you have us a letter from home," asked one. "Mama, he's from Mobile, Alabama," cried Butch. "And here I thought it was my sunny personality that was the attraction," smiled the postman as he handed me my letter. "Mama, I do believe the children are homesick." "Aren't we all?" I answered as I received my letter and scolded the kids for climbing all over the man. He knelt down and hugged my children. He took a few moments of his time to talk to them about home before he went on his way. They excitedly told their Daddy all about it when he come home from work. He listened but made no comment.

On Saturday morning, we all gathered at the breakfast table. This morning started out as a typical Saturday but it sure didn't end that way. Everyone was quietly eating their bacon and eggs. There was never disruption allowed at our table. The children were allowed to converse but it was always done in an orderly manner. If not, they were asked to leave the table to be dealt with once the meal was finished. That would be the only reason anyone left the table once seated. David was a strict disciplinarian. He loved his family but he ruled from an authoritarian position instead of showing his love. I, on the other hand, was sometimes too lenient. I think we failed to find a happy medium. David seemed to have a far-away look in his eyes as he slowly raised his coffee cup to his lips and took his first sip. He banged his cup down on the table as he declared in a loud voice. "By God, we are going home." There was total stunned silence for a short span of time. Then complete bedlam ruled as each child jumped from their seats and did a celebratory dance with raised fist shaking in the air and shouts of hoorays for their Daddy. I froze up. Oh no, no. My mind wailed but no sound could pass the constricted muscles in my throat. David reached across the table and took my hand. "Listen to me," he said. "I will go pick up some boxes and bring them back. Then I will go to a man I know who will buy all of our furniture and my lawn mower and freezer. Will you let go of your sewing machine? I will sell my guitar and amp too. With that and my paycheck, we will have enough to go home on. With enough left over to get us by till I am working again. It will be tight,

Honey but we can do it." I swallowed hard and nodded my head yes. I was to numb to cry. "While I am gone, you pack our clothes and dishes. Okay?" He asked me. He left and came back with the boxes. The children brought them into the house. I sat in the living room unable to move or speak. Oh God! What is going to become of us? My precious children, I numbly thought. Butch stood before me. "Mother," he spoke firmly to me as he placed his little hands around my face and lifted my head. He looked me straight in the eyes. His beautiful blue eyes were so much like his Daddy's. "I will take the little ones out in the yard. We will pick up our toys and pack them. I have put you some boxes in the bed room. If you will start there, I will come back and help in the kitchen. Come on Mom, we are going home." He took my hand and led me to the bed room. I went in and closed the door. Everything had turned black as the blackest night. I don't believe I have ever been in such darkness. All my life I had lived with a fear of something, I knew not what. Just that I was going to come to a place and time when something terrible was going to happen and I would still exist but cease to be. It was not a fear of death. I now know what that fear was. It is simply called insecurity. I had finally reached that point that I had so long feared. I was here, but I was not. A wonderful thing happened to me there in the darkness. The room began to glow with a light that was beyond worldly description. I felt arms surround me. I heard these words. "You are my child. I love you. Don't you know I have always loved you? I am going to take care of you and yours. Believe in me. Don't be afraid anymore." I have never felt such love as I felt at that moment, nor have I ever felt that freezing fear again. Do you think this is impossible? Some would say so because I didn't consciously seek God at that time. He came to me. Lifted me from my despair, gave me joy and set me on my feet. {Romans, chapter 10 verse 20. But Esaias was very bold, and said I was found of them that sought me not. I was made manifest of them that asked not after me.} I got off the floor with wings on my feet and a song on my breath. I packed all I would be taking back to Mobile with me. I still did not know what was to become of us but I believed the miracle that had touched me physically and mentally. I knew from whence it had come and I believed. Oooh, but the miracle was not over. Let me tell you the rest! We rode back to Mobile in that old beat up wildcat of ours, pulling a small U-Haul and arrived at our destination without incident around midnight. David stopped at a phone booth. Looking in the phone book, he found mother's phone number and called her. She gave directions to their home. At two o'clock in the morning, we sat at her dining table drinking coffee. The phone rang. It was Uncle Tommy calling. "Jane," he began, I am sorry to wake you at this time of morning, but I woke up and could not go back to sleep. Had you on my mind for some reason, so I felt I needed to call." "We were already up, Tommy. Betty and David came in from Texas a little while ago. We are sitting here drinking coffee and discussing which way they should go to look for jobs. They need to go to work as quickly as possible." Uncle Tommy answered her. "I go to the nursery at five thirty and make coffee. Mr. Meadows comes in at six. I will take him his first morning cup and talk to him before the crowd gets in. You tell Betty and David to be sitting on ready when I call them at seven o'clock." True to his word, he called and said. "Get on over here kids. The boss wants to talk to you." We stood before Mr. Meadows in less than an hour. "Well, well, you have come full circle. I remember you," he said pointing at me. "If I hire you, will you stay with me this time?" "I give you my word. I will stay," I vowed. He stared me in the eye across his desk as I willed my sincerity to show through. "Show up for work tomorrow morning," he said. We thanked him and turned to walk away. We were almost to the door when he called us back and asked David. "Where are you folks staying?" "As of this moment, we are at her mother's house in Creola," answered David. "That's a pretty far distance." Mr. Meadows answered him back. "Now I have a house right close. It's on Bayou road. It's not anything to brag about but it's shelter for your family right away, if you want it. I can promise you better farther on. If you do right by me, I will do right by you." David and I gladly accepted the house. As I stepped out of the office, I looked up through my beloved pine trees to the blue, blue sky. I felt the sun kiss my face. I seemed to hear an echo ride the air. Well done my good and faithful servant. Oh my wonderful God, my heart rejoiced. I was standing on the promise and he was fulfilling it. He had brought me back to the place he wanted me to be, home on Flower wood Nursery.

Mr. Meadows taught me how to root the new cuttings and grow them till they were grown to liner size and ready to go out and plant in gallon size containers. I took care of a lot of green houses where these liners were rooted and grown. I did the best job I could do and enjoyed every minute of my work. One might think I would have gone my way and sinned no more. Not so. There were many times I strayed and did wrong. Not always by accident either but sometimes on purpose, with full knowledge and intent. With the same gentle love he had shown me in the beginning of my personal relationship with him, he brought me back to the fold.

While washing the dirt and debris of the last planting season from the cement planting beds, I let my mind wander back to the time in Texas when I had my personal experience with God. I felt sad for I knew I had lost something very precious. I sensed the presence of someone behind me. Looking over my shoulder I saw Lana. I had a brief moment to wonder why she was there. She worked in the tool room and Plastic house A-1 was a bit out of her territory. I never did get to ask her about that. She smiled and greeted me. "Hi." She said in her soft spoken voice. "You seemed miles away in thought. Do you enjoy what you are doing?" "I do and I guess I was," I answered. "Do you see how pretty and white that old dirty cement comes when I put the water pressure to it? I was just thinking and wishing we could do that to our lives and souls. Wouldn't that be a marvelous thing?" I asked on a wishful sigh. She smiled as she answered. "We can, you know. All we have to do is tell Jesus we are sorry. Then he will make it all go away. He died for us. He paid in full for all our sins. His blood washes them away and leaves us white as snow." Without another word, she turned and walked away. I thought about what Lana had said. It was something I already knew but God had already saved me. How many times could I expect him to pull my bacon out of the fire so to speak? I argued with myself. As many times as it takes was the answer I come up with. I slipped off to myself at lunch time and prayed. From that time forward, I made a conscience effort to not sin. I am sure I slipped up many times along the way but never willfully to do wrong. I think I have done wrong by not telling others of what I believe to be truth. This wrong was done deliberately out of fear of being judged by others. I have done my God a great disservice by being afraid of what others would think of me. I now must correct this disservice regardless of what others think of me. I believe God is love. What is love? It is caring so deeply for others that you can turn loss of greed, selfishness, puffed up pride, and covetousness. It is something inside us that brings us to goodness in spite of our sinful natures. It is God that dwells within each of us. Love does not cause pain nor does it destroy. It does not now nor never has. Jesus came to this earth as a man sent from God his father, our creator. He came not only to pay the supreme price for our sins but to teach us that God is love and wants us to believe this. Read the scriptures of the New Testament, the words of Christ himself, and compare them to the scriptures of old. Jesus came to teach us the way God wanted us to be and what he wanted us to believe and he was crucified to shut him up. From time out of mind, mankind has committed murder and terrible atrocities against each other even to this day, did and does it, saying it is God's will. My God is not a monster and Satan is a liar. I worship my God my creator, soul, mind, and body. I love him because he first loved me. I am too close to my final day on this earth to lie to you about something as important as what I have described in this chapter. It happened just the way I have described it. I am sure only of the mystery of his love and the first part of his plan for our salvation. As for other of his mysteries he will teach me in his own good time. If not on this earth then at that time when I am allowed to see through the glass clearly.

It was after fully surrendering my life to God's love and Christ's teachings that I was able to create the writing of a work I call the greatest gift. I have kept it down through the years. When I meet a place on life's road that is rocky and my faith is shaken I go back and read it. It never fails to uplift and renew my spirit. It is with hope that you will enjoy reading it as much as I do that I share it with you in this chapter. It never seems to grow old to me.

The Greatest Gift

I need not stumble blindly in darkness, chained by the do and do not's of others, nor cry out for the meaning of my existence. The one who created me created a channel of communication between us. I have only to keep the channel clear and open to accept his guidance. This channel is my conscience.

Our God deals with each of us on an individual level. He knows us by name. He even knew and loved our substance before we came to be. What greater gift could he bestow than the gift of life eternal? He leans from his great throne to a small piece of clay, puddled in its own blood to breathe a benediction and say, live. We have only to believe in him and the miracle of his son Jesus Christ who came willingly to teach us what love is all about. Then he made the last and final sacrifice, his life's blood to atone for mankind's sins. He answered the only kind of reasoning man could accept, blood for transgression. He gave his and became the last high priest we will ever need. He asked nothing in return but our faith in God the Father and the practice of the love he tried so very hard to teach us while here on this earth. If we love him, we will serve him by obeying his commandments and living by his word. If we are foolish enough to squander this gift, how can we expect life eternal in the heavens here after? If my words can reach one precious soul, my reason for being here is justified.

I do not seek perfection in the flesh. I know only one who is perfect. I seek to be as close to him in spirit as possible. I would find perfection an extremity to live with. Rather, I seek moderation in everything. It is the key to balance and harmony. To center one's self, dwell on positive can do ideas and positive energy will come. The more positive energy, the more we find we can do. The more we realize we can do, the less I cannot do notions there will be to pull us down. The beauty and magnificence of God's creations are perfection enough for me. He has surrounded us with such bounty! What a shame to destroy and waste it. He wants us to be happy. We are meant to protect and enjoy it. We are the chosen guardians of all we survey.

What a joy to see a baby's funny little cross eyed smile, to hear a child's gurgling laughter. Do you take time to exchange a smile and a cheerful hello with a total stranger? Do you look and see, listen and hear? What joy you may be missing, if you are too busy. There is a parable to be understood by the sight of one small wildflower growing in a crevice, in the corner of a cement parking lot. Bravely she flaunts her colors in the face of her adversity, and her little corner of the world is a brighter place because she is there.

Often I have looked back at a hard day's work and felt the fatigue of by gone hours fall away like tatters of nothingness. In the pleasure of a job well done fatigue cannot overcome. As a child, I lifted my eyes above the squalor of mean streets and looked to the horizon where the glory of a marvelous sunset brought hope to my soul as it pleased my sight. With only a child's faith and comprehension I felt his loving promise breath through my soul. "Reach for it little one. I made it for you." In my heart I knew, man made all things that were ugly. God made all things beautiful. That beauty could be mine, if I choose. I have gazed at the night sky when it lays like folds of cool gray silk studded with exquisite pearls and contemplated on all his wonders. Know they are gifts that cannot be bartered or stole from you by man. They were made by the great artistic hands of he who rides the wind and crowns the sunrise with his glory. He created all and gave it freely. I have dared to pit my strength against impossible odds and felt great satisfaction in my accomplishments and ability to overcome, but remembered to bow my head in thanksgiving to that which my strength came from. There have been times when I miscalculated or for a time did it like I pleased, then asked. "Why, Lord, why?" As I tasted the bitterness of my own betrayal and defeat. Softly he comes. He heals my wounded spirit. He bids me drink deep from the cup of his peace. Then I can pray. Forgive me Father when I stray. Now it's enough to know this night, I have sought and found favor in my Father's sight. Then I feel the angels smile and I know God put things in their place to create for me a harmonious space. I feel blessed, for God has allowed me the rare privilege to look through the windows of his eyes to the depths of my soul. I am humbled for I find no greatness there. I am joyful for I find I am not as despicable as I once believed myself to be. I am worth loving. He proved it to me. Receiving the full measure of God's love and forgiveness, how can I not but reflect that love back to others. To love them as God loves me is to celebrate the life he gave me. To enjoy the gifts of his creations is to say thank you. Why would anyone want to squander the greatest gift when it is so wonderful to live and be happy by the grace of God, our Lord and King?

Chapter 23

NAIL THEM BOOTS
TO THE FLOOR

"Shake them Jack rabbits from your boots and nail em to the floor Mr.! We have found where we belong. I am back among kith and kin and I am where I intend to stay, with or without you." I declared to David. Mr. Meadows took bets with some who knew us that he could make David stay and between the two of us, we did. Oh, David would get mad and whoop and holler and have big cuss fights with the boss and other employees. It got better after his shop foreman, Pat Pierce told him he needed someone to bend him over their knee and give his backside what his mother should have given him years ago. "You are a spoiled brat David Lowery. You need to grow up and act like a man." Pat calmly told him. David admired Pat greatly. He thought about what Pat told him and talked to me about it. "Am I really that bad?" He asked me. "Honey, you are a wonderful and very intelligent man in so many ways but you do not have very good control of yourself when you are in disagreement with someone else. Whether you are right or wrong, there are ways to settle a difference of opinion without acting like the world is ending because you can't have everything the way you want it. Your way cannot always be the only way and you cannot always be in total control of everything. Not on the job anyway. The man who signs your paycheck is the one who has the control. You overkill with very hurtful words which once said, you can't take back." He agreed with

Destiny's Tapestry

me for once and made an effort to change. He succeeded somewhat. Oh well, they didn't call us them damn Lowery's for nothing.

I loved working at Flowerwood Nursery and the people I worked with. There were some amazing people there. They worked hard and played hard. There certainly was never a dull moment. I heard it told and I can picture it in my mind and believe it to be so. A young man came to work on the weekend. He turned the water sprinklers on in the areas which were his responsibility for the weekend watering program. The pumps more often than not picked up trash from the pond and pushing it through the pipes which would stop up the sprinkler heads after your back was turned. Once he had his water going he ambled over to his cart and picked up a fishing pole. Sitting by the pond with his fishing pole in hand, paying no mind to the stopped up sprinklers behind him, he hummed to his self. "The boss thinks I'm working but I ain't." Mr. Meadows stepping from behind some tall five gallon plants and brushing his hands off sang back. "You think I'm goanna pay you but I ain't." I once complained and wondered how on earth the lizards could be so bad at stopping up my sprinkling system. "Are they dead?" Elliot asked me. "Well let me put it this way," I explained. "If I shoved you head first into a three inch pipe and shot a hundred and sixty pounds of pressure in behind you, what do you think would be the last thing that went through your mind?" His eyes bugged but he didn't answer. He had swallowed his tobacco.

Mr. Meadows had a fun sense of humor but he could get riled real quick if he saw someone neglect his plants or take advantage of the nursery in any form or fashion. I got my Sunday school lesson preached more than once while learning the proper way to care for the little rooting cuttings. Lessons like, "Don't let me find you anywhere but in this plastic house at midday. If you are going to parboil my plants by damn I want to see you parboiled with them. Cool this damn place down, it's a hundred and ten degrees in here. I expected to see you with horns and a pitchfork when I came in. Parboiled." He shouted as he went out the door shaking his finger at the sky. I collapsed holding my sides. The propagator, Drew Hanson who had stood behind me the whole time I was taking my scolding

287

said, "Betty, I was so scared you were going to do that before he walked out. I was all set to strangle the life out of you." "Ha! Do I look like a fool to you? I would choke myself before I would laugh when that man is that angry." I also knew better than to tell him Mr. Smith was the one who came in before lunch and told me to leave the doors and vents closed. I knew better than to do what Mr. Smith told me to do too, but after all he was the owner.

Mr. Meadows drove a white station wagon. When the supervisors would see him moving around the nursery they would use their radios to contact each other with this warning. "Heads up, that white tornado is heading your way!" That message made Jesse Campbell so nervous when he heard it, he turned to his crew and shouted. "Hey ya'll stop you horsing around and work. That white man is coming!"

When I think of Tim Gawltney who was another propagator for Flowerwood, I remember the day he put me in his truck and took the time to show me something very special. He drove to the canal where he stopped and pointed at a large log. Two big birds were perched there. "I saw those Tim," I exclaimed. "I wondered what they were. They look like small sized Pterodactyl. What are they?" "They are Ivory Billed woodpeckers," He replied. "They mate for life and they are a protected species. They are almost extinct because people kill them for their Ivory. Look, he is trying to get her to accept the home he has made in the log." We laughed when upon entering her new home the female flew out and scolded her mate soundly and refused to reenter till he went to work and remodeled whatever it was that did not suit her. He furiously pecked away while the wood chips flew until she finally accepted her new home and settled in. "Well time to get back to work," Tim said. "I just thought you might enjoy seeing that." I did enjoy it and will always appreciate Tim's thoughtfulness in sharing it with me.

In the summer months, college students taking horticulture and agriculture classes would work on the nursery. One such student, Beth Summerlin from Auburn University worked with us. Beth was an outgoing delightful young lady. Her hobby was sky diving. Mr. Meadow's hobby was bird shooting. He raised his birds himself.

He and his fellow sportsmen would release the birds over a large open field then shoot them down as they flew over. They did prepare and eat what they shot. Beth the sky diver flew out with a group of her comrades to dive one day. Approaching a large field, their pilot informed them they must jump now or never. It would seem that he did not fill his fuel tank with enough to take them to their normal jumping place and make the return trip. So they all bailed out. You guessed it. Right on top of Mr. Meadow's bird shooting field. He had just released his birds and the men were sighting their guns on the targets when people began falling from the sky. With a rueful sigh, she plopped herself down beside where I sat eating my lunch and groused. "My Mom did tell me the only thing that fell out of the sky was fools and bird poop." Beth is the same young lady who brought me a poem her baby sister wrote. The six line words of this poem were so entrancing that I placed my own interpretation on the extraordinary thought process of this teenage girl and finished the poem. I named it, Summerlin's Melody. I have lost touch with Beth over the years. I am still currently searching for her. I could not stand to leave the Melody moldering and forgotten in a file cabinet. If Beth or her sister, whose name I cannot remember read this and will reach me on Facebook, I will do whatever is required to make this right.

In the late fall, the plastic houses would be covered with new plastic for the coming winter months. Sometimes, I would be called to help with this job. After spreading the large plastic sheets, part of the crew would follow up with batten strips and nail them around the sides to secure the plastic to the framework of the house. I was so worn out from swinging that hammer I had lost the strength in my arms. The hammer would hit the nail and bounce. I became a wee bit aggravated with the nail and myself. I drew the hammer back like a Louisville Slugger. With a loud curse and a mighty swing, I drove that nail home. I glanced behind me when I heard hoots of laughter. Sure enough that white station wagon was on the road behind me. Mr. Meadows had slid down in his seat with his hands over his face. He had the wagon loaded with customers he was giving a grand tour. They all seemed to be enjoying themselves immensely. Giving them a dour look and a small salute, I turned back to my work. Uncle Tommy bought me a coke for lunch. Handing it to me, he said with a grin. "Mr. Meadows sends this with his compliments. He bet each man in the wagon ten bucks, A-4 plastic house would be finished by lunch time. He had me and Ralph watching and by damn he won it all. You drove the last nail in the last batten as the dinner horn blew."

We do not get much snow in Mobile, Alabama. Believe you me, the natives go a little bonkers when it does. It is a big event as welcome as Christmas or Mardi Gras. In mid-1970 give or take a year, there was a good snow fall. I was as delighted as everyone else. Upon my arrival at work, I crouched behind the white station wagon with a snowball in hand packed and ready. When the man walked out the door of his office and around the vehicle to the driver's side, I let fly the snowball across the top. "Good one!" I gleefully shouted. It knocked his hat off. Oh my Lord above. It was not Mr. Meadows. I had clobbered Mr. Smith. The owner of Flowerwood Nurseries Inc. He began to run around the back end of the wagon. I, on hands and knees scrambled around the front and around the corner of the building where I took to my heels and in a dead heat went around the next corner. I made it, I thought. Then I heard him shout. "I know who you are. You will know payback when you see it." I kept running. I heard not a word for a few days and I began to breathe easy and forgot about the snowball caper.

I was in the stripping shed. This is a building where new cuttings are brought in and prepared for planting in the plastic or glass houses. I heard the sound of an engine pulling a heavy load. Miss Beaola looked out the door and exclaimed. "What is this?" Stepping out the door, I was confounded by a sight to see. There was a huge flatbed truck with four palm trees loaded on it. It had entered at the front gate and was laboring its way around the corner of the green house. The palms were at least 70 to 80 feet long. The burlap wrapped root systems were nestled firmly against the cab of the truck and the trees were roped down. The tops of the trees hung way over the end of the flat bed. Four men, one female person, and a large mixed breed junkyard dog that looked like he had been whipped with an ugly stick walked on each side and behind the truck. They all had long straight black hair. They were all dressed in black from their floppy felt hats, muscle shirts, and vest right on down to black jeans and boots. They each carried a big stick in their hand. The truck tag said they come out of Florida. They appeared travel weary. I wondered if they had walked all the way. They stopped long enough to ask where they might find the owner of this outfit. I directed them to the office then stepped back inside. That dog had a nasty disposition. It was not long before I heard the voice of Mr. Smith ring loud and clear over the P.A. speaker. "Betty Lowery, go to C-4 and unload palm trees." Everyone in the stripping shed knew I had been waiting for the ax to fall over the snowball shenanigan. They snickered at the incredulous look on my face. I crawled on my old golf cart and headed for C-4. What the devil, I thought. Did the man not look at those palms before he bought them? Of course to hell he did, I snorted to myself. Did I know payback when I saw it? Yes indeed I did. Well, we would just see what could be done about this! Wheeling into C-4 and on my humble little golf cart, I sat and stared in consternation at the big truck load of big trees and silently cursed the ill-fated snowball. One of the fellows dressed in black squatted beneath a pine tree. He raised his head and peered at me from beneath his hat brim. He chewed his pine straw as he silently took my measure. "You be the Betty Lowery that's goanna unload these trees," he drawled. "Yep, that be me," I answered. All Five foot three, one hundred and forty pounds of you've been had. A slow grin spread across his face as that tall drink of water eased to a standing position and leaned against the pine tree. "I'll watch," he said. "I just bet you will oh thou man of few words," I muttered. Putting my cart in reverse, I smiled and said. "Ya'll rest a spell, why don't cha? I got me a bee in my bonnet. I'll be back in a short-short." Thank goodness, the dog was shut up in the truck cab. I went straight to the dirt mixing area, hoping to find Henry Douglas. He was always a very accommodating fellow but I was still running short on luck. I found Blow instead. He was a little harder to deal with. "Hi Blow. You keeping it busy today?" I greeted him. "Oh, so-so I guess and what's Miss Betty up to today? As if I don't know." He said with a grin. I laughed. "You saw the truck come in," I replied ruefully. "You got anything here that will work to move those palms?" He leaned against the front end loader and crossed his massive arms akimbo. "Got this," he answered pointing his thumb over his shoulder. Beaming a hearty smile, I said. "Yea, we can do it with that, I betcha. Will you bring it out to C-4?" I remembered to ask very politely. Straightening upright like he had been stung by a bee, he slapped his big hands emphatically against his chest. "We. Now hold on a minute here! What's with this we business? I know I heard the man say, Betty Lowery, unload palm trees. He dint day nuthin bout no Blow Jones." "Aww come on Blow, give a girl a break. It won't take you no time," I wheedled. "I got a slice of homemade caramel pecan cake here to make it worth your while." "Betty Lowery, you ain't nuthin but a humbug." Smiling, he held out his hand and waggled his fingers in a gimmie gesture. With a sad sigh, I handed over my last slice of homemade caramel pecan cake. Blow munched happily as he and his front end loader jostled along behind my cart. I went back by C-4 later in the afternoon to see how my palm trees were fairing. I found Mr. Meadows, hands on hips and Mr. Smith, hat in hand scratching his bald head while they gazed at my handiwork. Four giant palm trees all laid out in a neat row on the edge of the area. "Debt paid." I chortled as I drove away.

I had so many kin folk working on the nursery I had to explain to new comers. "No we don't own the place, there are just a lot of us working here." One of those kin folk was my Uncle Doyle and his wife Big Judy. We had two Judies in the family so one had to have a nick name to keep the two sorted out and keep down confusion. Aunt Judy carried her weight well for she was a very tall woman as well as big otherwise. She, for the most part wore loose flowing clothing, especially her lounging or sleeping apparel. She was a sweet and caring as well as fun loving kind of person. I said she missed her calling. She should have been a standup comedian. We had one television in our house and it quit working. For Friday night entertainment, David and I would load up the kids and go down the street to Uncle Doyle's and Aunt Judy's to play cards. It took something like a month to save enough to purchase a new TV. After a hard week's work, we were ready for Friday night and our new TV. With our bag of Kristal burgers and fries in hand, we flopped on the couch. David with the remote in his other hand was flipping through the channels. "What do you want to watch?" He asked me. "Oh I don't know, whatever," I answered. He tried to smother a sheepish grin as he said to me. "I rather watch Doyle and Judy." "Me too," I giggled. "Eat your burger and come on," he laughed.

"Aunt Judy, you and Uncle Doyle amaze me with the way you quarrel. You say the funniest things to each other. But you never seem to be mad when you do." "You're Uncle Doyle and I learned a long time ago not to take ourselves and each other to seriously when we disagree, and we are forever disagreeing about something," she said. "It was the last big fight we had that made us realize, we should not get angry enough to let our tempers get out of hand. I sensed a story here so I encouraged her to keep talking. We were going at it hot and loud when he cursed me and I threw the frying pan at his head," she continued. "He sprang from the couch roaring like a bull elephant. I ran in the bed room and locked the door. He was kicking the door down and yelling at the top of his lungs. I raised the window and looked down. Our apartment was on the second floor. I hated it but there was no place to go but down. As the door crashed in, I took a preachers seat out the window. I figured it was best to land on where I had the most padding, on my rump. I had on my purple P.J.'s and robe. I landed in a heap in front of two old winos that were leaning against the alley wall enjoying their late evening libation. 'Did you see that,' squeaked one of the men. 'No I ain't seen nuthin. What did it look like?' 'Hit were either a very fat angel or a purple cow what just landed there. Don't you see it?' "No I don't and you don't either. You're hallucinating,' cried the other wino. Right then your Uncle let fly a blistering string of cussing and my battery operated radio out the window. Willie Nelson warbled Angel Flying to Close to the Ground all the way to the pavement before it shattered. 'I guess you didn't see that either?' Mumbled the old man around the mouth of the wine bottle he was chugging. 'No but I heard enough to know it's time to get the hell out of Dodge. And throw that damn bottle down. They don't call it Sneaky Peat for nuthin. It'll get you ever time.' I gathered myself up and hobbled down the alley," Aunt Judy said. "I could hear their quarrelsome voices echoing of the alley walls as they hot footed it in the opposite direction. 'I know what I seen.' 'You ain't seen nuthin. Cheap wine. Hallucinating.' 'Purple cow or fat angel, I tell ya. Willie saw it too!'"

My cousin Judy Gail had a lovely church wedding. Everything went off without a hitch except the very beginning of the ceremony. Her father, my Uncle Tommy had very poor eyesight and the wind was blowing really hard that day. The proud father was all set to walk his pretty daughter down the aisle and give her away when the wind decided otherwise. As Uncle Tommy opened the heavy church door, the wind took it from his hand and blew it shut on them, catching the pocket of Uncks tuxedo with the doorknob. He paused and struggled with the pocket and doorknob. Judy Gail with her arm latched in his kept walking. He, doing his best to release himself from the door and hold on to his daughter at the same time, lost his cool when he heard his tux rip. His frantic protest waffled throughout the church. "Hells bells Judy Gail, slow down. We got him hemmed in. It ain't likely he's gonna git away!"

There were so many people with varied and colorful personalities I knew and worked with at Flowerwood, I think I could write a whole book about just them. There is no way I can cover them all here. There was Pat Duck, a warm and wonderful man. He was the propagator for the Loxley branch and I worked for him for a few years. Pat got to feeling poorly and went to the doctor. He came back to work and told me. "Doctor Lucky says I am suffering from Bettybugites. There is no medication for this disease. You must stop finding bugs on my plants." I think what really floored Dr. Lucky was Pat asking him for a script for birth control. Someone had told Pat, if he mixed one tablet to a gallon of water the plants would multiply faster.

I did miss a lot of my co-workers at Loxley when I transferred back to Mobile. Those in Mobile thought they missed me while I was gone till I returned. I called Wayne D'Arcy to one of my areas. I had a leaking water valve and it was practically buried. Wayne dug it out for me then took it apart to replace a washer. I thought to keep up with my watering program and not to waste time I would open another line and go on with my watering. Never thinking that to do so, the main line would also require opening. I opened it! Wayne, bent low over the valve he was working on, had it about half screwed in when the pressure hit. It shot straight up, putting a knot on his head and his face full of muddy water. Trying to mop his face with a muddy do rag he moaned, "Betty Lowery, I was so happy when I heard you were coming back. Now I wonder why." Wayne had the heart of a gypsy. Fun loving and outgoing, he made the hours pass fast at work. Then there was Miss Beaola Hester, a tall statuesque woman, of sterling character. This lady worked on Flowerwood and as a single parent sent her children to college. "You know," she said to me one day. "That boy of mine come in from school yesterday and told me a man had walked on the moon. I tore his tail up for talking such nonsense. These children will believe any kind of tales they hear. And then want to argue with me about it like I don't know anything. I tore his behind up I did." "But Miss Beaola," I began to protest, and then shut my mouth. She looked as if she might tear mine up too.

The elections were over and George Wallace had been voted in as governor of Alabama. The Crepe Myrtle trees had lost all their leaves and gone dormant for the winter. The planters took cuttings from the trees all day. When I come home that afternoon I found a pile of silverware lying on my doorsteps. The cutters found them under the trees where my kids left them after they played in the dirt with them. No wonder I had to go out and buy new forks and spoons so regular. Thank God for the dollar store! Bags full of Crepe Myrtle cuttings were brought in and waiting to be prepared for planting. This was the first time they had ever been taken for planting in their dormant stage. As she sat and snipped her cuttings to the proper length Miss California suddenly spoke. "Um-um," she said. "George Wallace ain't even in the office yet and the man's done started planting dead sticks. You knows we gonna eat crap for the next two years." Pursing her lips Lottie Mae spoke. "Recon I spent some bad years in Tin Pan Alley. Hope it don't get that bad again." I dropped my clippers. "Lottie, what and where is Tin Pan Alley?"

"It be the black quarters in Birmingham," she answered. "I was there in the thirties when it was soup kitchens and standing in long lines with a tin cup hoping and praying the pot didn't git empty or I didn't faint from hunger before I got to the front of the line. If you did you jist got shoved aside and passed over." "I lived in Birmingham in the early forties," I explained. "When I misbehaved my Mother used to threaten to send me back to Tin Pan Alley if I didn't straighten up and fly right! I always wondered where and what it was. Did you ever eat stone soup Lottie?" "Sure did," she replied. "It come from the Hobo camps. Called Hobo Jungles, they was. What you know of stone soup, little white girl?" "Mama, my Grandmother Dovie Walden, told me about it. She lived in a Hobo Jungle for a time." Then I told them the story of The Woodsman's Daughter, of Mama's lonely exile on the mountain. "When she felt it was safe to return to civilization once more she went into Gadsden, Alabama," I explained. "There she took a job working as a house keeper for her room and board. The man of the house would not keep his hands to himself. As he grew more aggressive in his pursuit of her, Mama became afraid of him. She complained to the woman of the house, who immediately dismissed her. Out in the cold without a feather to fly with, there was no place to go but to the Hobo Jungle." There is where my dear Mama learned about stone soup." "Build a fire," she said. "Put water in your pot and place a stone in it. Set it on the fire. As those unfortunates who have no pot, come in from foraging they will place whatever they have found in your pot. Be it a carrot, an onion or potato, or hopefully a piece of meat and you don't want to look too closely or ask what kind. You just keep the fire burning and water in your pot till all is done. Then everyone eats." "What ever became of your Mama," asked Lottie. "Why didn't she stay with her children or friends?" "She was still hiding from the sheriff," I answered. "Her friends, the Collins, lived in his jurisdiction as did her children that weren't scattered. All of her grown unmarried children did finally get together and took Mama with them to Birmingham. There they all worked at the Avondale Cotton Mill and lived together in a place called Noah's Ark." Lottie's eyes glowed. "I remember that place," she chuckled. "I used to ride by there on the rag pickers wagon." "Dear lord Lottie," I screeched. There was a young black girl with little pigtails all over her head that jumped off and on that wagon to take the rags that were brought out." "Ain't it a small world," she grinned. They paid me a nickel a day to sing, rag-g-g pick-errs-s-s. Bring out yer rags. I sang it real loud. Then jump down and git the rags folks was throwing away. You know them people got rich off them rags. They say when that woman died the old man gave her the finest funeral money could buy. Then he bought him a new wagon en painted it bright red. Then he up and bought a fancy hat for his old horse." There was laughter around the table as the women went back to their previous discussion. I sat there and listened to their political views and my heart went out to this hard working honest group of women who were struggling for a better way of life. I prayed for their success though I spoke not a word. These were good people and they deserved better than they had been served.

It was with many fond memories that I took an early retirement from Flowerwood Nursery. After the death of Mr. Meadows, it seemed to me the heart went out of my beloved nursery. My children had all flown from the nest. I thought I could enjoy staying home and just be a housewife. We all know by now what comes of my best laid plans.

Chapter 24

HOUSE WORK MAKES YOU UGLY

I did get to enjoy being a housewife for a year before circumstances drove me to pat and turner. Pat the pavement and turn the corner in search of gainful employment. David's health forced him to an early retirement and medical disability. This left us both without hospital insurance. I was fifty five years old and had never learned to drive. I approached David with these problems. "You know I need to go back to work," I said. "To do this, I have to be able to transport myself. What will become of us when you get to the point when you are too sick to even go to the grocery store? There is no way we can survive without transportation and I need to go back to work to help supplement your income." I was very much surprised when he agreed with me. He hired a driving teacher to teach me and within four weeks, I had my license. During those four weeks, I thought about what type of work I might best be suited for.

I remembered in my younger working days, what a struggle it was to keep my house clean. No way did I earn enough to hire help very often. I could muck it out on the weekend and keep it in some order till Wednesday. Then everything seemed to pile up on me and the house would go to hell in a hand basket. Most weekends I worked. I remembered hiring Leah, a teenage girl to come in one Saturday to help me clean. She opened the door to my boy's room, screamed and stepping back with her hand over her heart, she slammed the door shut. "How on earth did they do that?" Easing the door open, I peeked inside. It was total chaos. I looked up toward the ceiling fan where two pair of under shorts was slowly circling. Stepping around me Leah marched into the room. With hands on hips, she surveyed the wreckage. "Oh I see how they did it," she said while picking up a hurricane tracking chart from the bed. I was so glad she had a good sense of humor. I was also glad I had her help that day. I was finishing up the floor mopping when in through the front door marched my youngest son. Behind him in a line were fifteen, I counted them, fifteen little boys. They marched like troopers across my wet living room, dining room, and kitchen floor, then out the back door. With a smile, remembering those good old days I asked myself, why can't I do house work?

I began to call around and put out the word. It did not take long for the calls to get answered. Most of my clients were women and men who worked on Flowerwood, my ex bosses or their wives. Soon, I had a house to clean every day of the week Monday through Friday. I undercut the prices of the expensive maid services and furnished my own cleaning supplies. I did a thorough job and even did laundry for some of my clients. Most days, the chores and hours flowed through my hands smooth as silk threads. However, there were days when nothing went right. One of my clients and friend Janis Sullivan coined the phrase, [I have been bettasized] I wondered if she knew some days I bettasized my own self after working all day.

Such as the day I was headed home, in a hurry to be sure but keeping within the speed limit. A woman driver, who I assumed wanted me to move along a little faster kept running up behind me real fast and slamming on her breaks. Finally, she pulled around me. Cutting me short, she wheeled in front of me, forcing me almost into the ditch. Then she flipped me off before she took off like a bat out of hell! I floor boarded my car and made a race for home. I forgot about the intersection coming up ahead. Oh luck, I muttered. At least the light was green. Then it turned red. I braked hard, slid through the intersection and hit the edge of the black top on the other side. I was sitting there shaking and congratulating myself on my excellent handling of a bad situation when I heard a siren. I peeped in my mirror and watched the nice policeman step from his vehicle. The expression on his face did not indicate he thought I had done well at all. He stepped up to my window and asked. "Do you have a license?" I began to bounce around the car seat like a crazy ball as I frantically searched for my purse. I found it in the floor board and banged my head on the dash as I retrieved it. "Calm down," he said. "Did you not know the intersection was there?" I cleared my throat and answered him. "Yes sir, I come this way every day. Officer, may I crank my car and pull it up and over a little farther?" He frowned then asked, "Why would you want to do that?" "Because," I said. "You are standing in the traffic lane and these fools will run over you!" Then slapping my hand over my mouth, I bounced some more and squeaked. "Oh, I can't believe I said that after what I just did." He reached his hand through the window and patted my back and said. "Calm down. Now tell me this, If you come this way every day why did you not slow down for the intersection?" I tried to explain about the woman who ran me off the road. "She scared me, and two, I have a very sick husband at home and I had getting off the road and home to him on my mind and I was not thinking clear. Officer, I have a perfect driving record. I have never had a ticket before." I did not think to include that I had only been driving three months. "Did you have your seat belt on?" He asked me. "No sir." His face turned red and he began to pace back and forth beside my car. "Speeding, no seat belt, reckless driving, out of control of your vehicle, running a red light." His voice rose louder and his face grew redder as he shouted and counted of each of my infractions on his fingers. He leaned his head in the car window once more. "Do you know what grace is?" He snarled. "Yes Sir. I live by grace every day." "Well today you are living by my grace. If I ever catch you doing a trick like this again I swear I will, well I don't know what I will do, but I promise you won't like it. How far do you live from here?" "About a mile past the next intersection," I answered. "Do you think you can make it through the next intersection," he growled. "Yes Sir," I answered. "Then you crank this car up and get on home at a normal rate of speed, and stop letting these other drivers intimidate you." I cranked up and crept along at twenty miles an hour thanking my good Lord all the way.

One afternoon on leaving Janis's house, I reached into the refrigerator and grabbed what I took to be a coke to drink on the way home. I paid no attention to what I had in my hand. I just put it in the can holder while I took the time to load my cleaning supplies and unload her cat Lilly from my back seat. Once on the main road, I popped the top on my can and turned it up. In my surprise I shot gunned it. It went up my nose and sprayed my wind shield, and ran all down the front of me. It was a Budweiser! When my eyes stopped running water, I looked in front of me and there was one of Mobiles finest, one behind me, and one just pulling into the lane beside me. He was the one who gave me the speeding ticket the week before. It was not the first one he had given me, but it might be the last. If he stopped me now he would surely lock me away for drunk driving. I slapped the beer between my thighs to hide it. We were almost to the city limits. Oh please, I prayed, I hope they did not see what I had in my hand. I would never make them believe I thought I had a coke and I stank like a Budweiser Clydesdale. Sure enough at the city limits, they peeled off and went back the way they came. My nerves were shot so I pulled into the Winn Dixie parking lot and calmed myself with the rest of the beer. Hey, in for a penny in for a pound! If I got stopped between there and home I would go to jail anyway. So you see my clients were not the only ones who got bettasized on my bad days.

There was my friend Nancy Chaney. She had more teapots then the law allowed. I was real careful. I do not remember breaking any of them; well maybe one, but her ex-husband's Indian statue did not fare to well. Old Hunk-a-Papa three feathers soon became Hunk-a-Papa one feather. I swear I think that statue was possessed. Each time it saw me coming with a dust cloth, it jumped from its resting place to the floor. Nancy would follow me to my car every time I worked for her with the excuse she was saying bye, when in reality she was snooping to make sure I fastened my seat belt. She was wonderful to carry me to places I needed to go where I was afraid to drive. Like down town to pay my speeding tickets. She is to this day trying to teach me what she calls proper English. (Lean close and I will whisper this.) She is one of them Connecticut Yankees ya'll and one of the best friends a southern gal could wish for.

It was not unusual to get a phone call after four PM asking questions like, "Betty, do you remember where you put my cord to my electric skillet? Tom says he hasn't had a piece of fried chicken since the last day you worked." Crossing my fingers for luck, I asked. "Sally, did you find the frying pan?" "Oh Yes, I have it right here. It was in the pantry." With a sigh of relief I chuckled. "I think I put the cord with the pan. Look under the lid." "Well there it is. You know that is a smart place to keep it." "Save me a piece of chicken Sally. See ya next Friday." I was lucky that time. Sometimes, I was not. Like the afternoon the phone rang and I answered to, "I protest. I been bettasized. Again. Well maybe not me but Chuckles has." I heard Chuck's deep voice rumbling in the background and Janis burst into peals of laughter. "What have you done to Chuckles that you intend to blame on me Janis Sullivan," I demanded. "Oh you did it alright. I just got in from work and Chuck made us a pot of coffee. He reached up into the cabinet to get us a clean cup and you know what? There was a cup full of coffee up there. He grabbed it and poured it all in his face. Now he is cleaning the floor and cabinet facing and the counter top. He is all wet." She sounded like she was thoroughly enjoying herself. "You know," I said. "I wondered where that cup of coffee got off to. I thought I drank it and just didn't remember doing it." I hung up the phone with her laughter still ringing in my ears.

Then there was Clyde Sanderfer. He was so neat and easy going. Things seldom ever went wrong in his house unless I come in a day early and unexpected. His kitchen counter was n shaped beginning with the stove on my left and going all the way around the kitchen. As I stepped in the door, my eyes followed the path of destruction. From the over turned grease can on the stove all the way down and around the counter top. Canisters and all other kitchen implements were over turned and scattered helter skelter. As my eyes settled at the other end of the counter, I burst into laughter over the mental picture I was receiving. There on top of the trash can was a large pine bug with all eight legs pointing heavenward. A big left footed shoe lay beside the unfortunate insect. Still chuckling, I carried the shoe to his closet to put with its mate. Frowning I searched in vain for the mate to no avail. That's when I began to count. There were nine left footed shoes in there. To me, an unmated shoe is as worthless as a nun without her rosary. I left him a note telling him so and threw away the shoes. "But Betty," he later explained. "The right one wore out before the left one. Someday a left legged man may come along who might need a left shoe." Such a lovely thoughtful man, is my Clyde.

Tim Gwaltney might complain that he was bettasized on a weekly basis. He was another very neat man, except for his mail and magazines. I do believe he has the first National Geographic ever printed and all subsequent issues thereafter. If one was mislaid, he knew it and went searching. I worked for Jerry Pittman, who was an extra-large man in size when compared to Tim. Tim was very health conscious and kept a close eye on his waist line. He joined a diet group that was having good results with weight problems as long as one was very careful to follow their instructions. If not, the consequences could be drastic, even fatale. I cautioned him heavily about this. I worked for Jerry one day and Tim the next. I always furnished my own cleaning clothes. I found worn out tee shirts good for dust clothes. While searching in my bag for such an item, I found a whole, almost new tee shirt. "Well my goodness," I exclaimed. "How did that get in here?" Without noticing the name Jerry Pittman wrote inside the neck line, I removed, folded it and placed it in Tim's underwear drawer.

Tim had been on his diet a week, when he came home from work, showered and put on his clean tee shirt. It wrapped around him about three times. He screamed and ran for the scales. How relieved he must have been when removing the offending garment, he found Jerry's name on it.

I will explain one horrendous day while working in Janis's house, so you will understand the note I left behind. Her laundry room was situated out the back door and to one side of her patio. She had a cat named Lilly and a large dog named Chaney. Chaney was scared to death of lightning and thunder. So was I. Mama always told me during this kind of weather I was to sit still and let the Lord do his work. The last load of laundry was finishing up in the dryer when the storm rolled in. As I gathered my courage to make a dash out the back door, the phone rang. I answered it quickly. A lady was babbling at me about Mardi Gras balls and something she had lost. "I will let Janis know, I screamed as I slammed the receiver down and ran out the back door. Coming back in with an arm load of laundry, I was not able to fight Chaney from the door. He made a wild foray between my legs dumping me end over teakettle. I am as bowlegged as a west Texas cowboy to begin with. As I gathered myself up, lightning was flashing and popping steadily. I spotted Lilly jumping from Chaney's back and climbing the window curtain. Chaney headed for the back bed room. I folded the towels as fast as possible and ran to put them in the bath room. The light blew with another lightning flash. I replaced the bulb but when I made the attempt to put the globe back in place I cross threaded the screw. Reasoning to myself that it might be dangerous to leave it like that, I removed the globe and laid it and the stripped screw in the sink. I had actually had one fall on my head once when practicing my bible verse for the day. I had walked into Tim's bathroom quoting out loud, "All things work together for good for those who love the Lord." Right then, the light fixture fell on my head. I was thankful it was plastic. This one was glass. It could hurt. So after laying it in the bathroom sink, I proceeded to the kitchen to leave Janis a note of explanation. In a nervous haste, this is what I wrote. "Dear Janis, Some lady called. Here is her number. She said something about Mardi Gras and she has lost her balls. Chaney is under bed. Can't get him out so must leave in. Lilly is on top of the window. A blub flew in your bathroom and you have a loose screw. Sorry but can't help. Is lightning like crazy and I am out of here." That hard hearted Janis took my note to Flowerwood and tacked it on the bulletin board. Now I ask you. Who got bettasized in this deal? Oh, the phone call; The lady had lost her ticket to the Mardi Gras ball.

This next incident, I refer to as one good tern deserves another. Business had prospered enough by then that I needed extra help. My first cousin Virginia became my partner in crime. We were to clean house for an elderly gentleman, Mr. Jackson. His home was on the Codean belt line right on the bay. Thus it was built on high stilts. The front of his home was solid windows all the way around, giving a great view of the bay. The last time we had worked for Mr. Jackson, we had taken him to the hospital. We found him having a heart attack when we arrived at his house. They did emergency by-pass surgery. He swore he would never ride in the car with us again. This was our first trip back to his home since that day. We pulled into his driveway and the first thing to meet my eyes was a deep hole, a pile of dirt, and a big shovel. "Would you look at that? That rascal has been out here digging a hole and he is not even well from his surgery. I bet, I put a flea in his ear when I get up those stairs. One he won't forget for a while." I grumbled and fussed all the way up the stairs, then lit into him hot and heavy as I went in the door. "Oh stop your fuss woman. Come and look out the window. Something is in trouble out here." Gin went to the window. I kept fussing as I set my cleaning kit down. "Come see, Betty," Gin said as she peered out the window. "It's a big bird." For the moment, I shushed about the digging and went to the window. I watched as the large bird rolled to one side raising one wing high in the air then rolled back, only to roll once more seeming to beacon with that one wing. Trouble calls just so, does it not? "Well are you going to just stand there and watch?" Mr. Jackson snapped. "Go help it." Gin and I raced back down the stairs. Beneath the house was stored all manner of nautical gear. Gin had presence of mind enough to grab a long handled dipper net as we went past and down the drive. We ran down the road alongside the bay, trying to get ahead of the distressed bird. We reached a wharf ahead of the creature. Another young lady saw us running and followed us out on to the wharf. "What's wrong," she gasped. I noticed she had long legs and a longer reach then me, so I handed her the net. "Catch that bird as he comes by. Let's see what we can do for him." She caught him in the net and brought him to the road side for us. He was such a pitiful sight, I wanted to cry. He had one wing and his head bound to his side with fishing line. Lord have mercy, he had swallowed the hook. I pulled his beak open and could see the hook but there was no way I could remove it without causing irreparable damage. Gin brought me scissors and I cut away the fishing line to release his head and wing. That was my first mistake. I massaged his neck till he could straighten it. I think that was my second mistake. "What should we do with the poor critter, Gin?" I asked. "Well if he is on the endangered list, I think the EPA will take care of him," She answered. "I don't even know what he is." I asked the long legged girl in the sizzle suit if she would call the EPA, give a description of the bird and find out if they would help us. She agreed and come back with good news and bad news. "I told them what it looked like," she said. "They say it is a tern and is on the endangered species list. They will take care of the bird, but you have to bring it to them. They don't have the transport to come and get it." "Horse feathers," I muttered. I turned with the intentions of asking her if she would consider taking the bird in for us. All I saw was thin air. From the corner of my eye, I caught a mere glimpse of one long leg and the flounce of the sizzle suit as it went around the corner of the house across the street. Wow that girl was fast! I felt Gin's warm presence as she stepped up behind me. Strong and loyal was this woman. She always had my back when I needed her. "Betty what do you want to do? We have got to clean this house but it shouldn't take long. It is not in too much need because Mr. Jackson has been in the hospital. It won't take us long I don't think, but I have to take Mother to the doctor this afternoon." I knelt over the bird and thought. I felt something rise up my backbone that felt like cold steel. I straighten my shoulders and answered her. "This creature is in this condition because of a thoughtless don't give a damn human. We can't abandon him." She thought a moment then replied. "Linda is sitting with Mother. After we get the house clean, I can drive you that far and let Linda drive you on to the EPA." I picked him up and carried him to the car. He settled quietly into the front floorboard. There he stayed as calm as could be while we finished cleaning Mr. Jackson's house. The trouble started when we pulled off the belt line on to Highway 188. That bird decided he wanted the car all to himself. He began to peck his way up my denim clad legs. As he came up onto the seat, I left it. My butt was parked on the back of the front seat while my head was jammed into the headliner.

"Whadaya want me to do," screamed Gin. "I don't know," I screamed back, but whatever you do don't hit a pot hole and hold to your side of the road till I figure it out." Another vehicle was coming toward us. The driver's eyes were stretched wide. He passed and did a U-turn, came back and passed us again. "What is that lookie lou doing," hollered Gin. "I guess he didn't believe what he saw the first time. The stupid man want's a second peep see." I screamed when the bird took a wicked swipe at my crotch. "Whadaya want me to do Gin yelled again." "I don't know, but do it quick. I got an appointment with my GYN in a few days. How will I ever explain a third orifice put there by a twelve inch pecker?" The lookie lou was coming back for a third look. The bird was coming back for a third attack. I went from the back of the front seat to the back seat. The bird then went after Gin. She did not ask what to do then. She pulled the car to the side of the road and bailed on me, slamming the car door and leaving me shut in with the bird from hell. I tumbled around amongst the mops, brooms and cleaners for a bit then rose up with a bucket on my head. Twoc! Thwack! He gave me two good raps on the bucket. I had been told when upset I should quote the first ten lines of Hiawatha. No one can stay upset and quote Hiawatha. In a shaky voice, I whispered. "By the shores of gitchie gommie." Thwack! "Damn," I said and threw off the bucket as I vacated the car in a hurry. Once he had the car to himself, he settled on the front seat as pretty as you please. I found Gin sprawled across the hood kicking her feet. "Ooh, I gotta pee. Ooh, I gotta pee," she moaned. "Well the sooner we get home, the sooner you can. Let's get this stuff loaded into the trunk then see if we can encourage our feathered friend to ride in the back seat." How are you going to get him there?" She asked as we transferred the cleaning stuff to the trunk. "We will do it very carefully," I answered. "What we, you got a mouse in your pocket? I only see you and me here. And I know you ain't talking to me." Where did that strong little woman go who stuck by me through thick and thin. Seemed when things got thick, she thinned out. "Okay, I will move him while you open and close the doors for me." "Cover his face with a towel," she advised. By George, it worked. He stayed peaceable through the seat and driver switching. Upon arriving at the EPA, I opened the rear car door. My bird did not want to come along peaceable, so I slammed it shut and left him with Linda standing guard while I went in search of assistance. There were several people in the office. One man with a lot of military looking hash on his shirt sat behind a desk nursing a cup of coffee. He appeared to be someone of authority, so I approached him first. "Hello," I said. "I have a wounded bird, I have brought in for you. The one that swallowed the fish hook?" He smiled quiet charmingly and answered. "Oh yes. You work at the Dauphin Island Aquariums." "No, I don't," and I began to explain my credentials and how I come to have the bird in my possession. As I spoke, his smile dimmed till finally it was nonexistent and he cut me off short. All his geniality seemed to have vanished by the wayside. "Well bring it in," he snapped. I decided his attitude was not much better than the birds. The bird I would excuse, him I would not! Stepping closer to his desk, I snapped right back. "He is in the blue Grand am with my driver right outside." I lifted my nose in a haughty fashion. "I brought him here, you may bring him in. I have had enough of that bird." With a deep put upon sigh, he swiveled his chair to face a man dressed in denim and rubber boots. "Go bring the tern in." He quietly went back to sipping his coffee while I waited beside his desk. The secretary reached for the filing cabinet drawer with one hand while balancing a stack of papers with the other just as the door burst open. The man who was sent to retrieve my bird skidded into the office, minus the expected bird. "Loony bird, It's a loon," he panted. "I beg your pardon," I said with an injured tone. The boss man choked on his coffee, and slammed his cup down so hard it splattered as he shoved his rolling chair hard against the filing cabinet behind him. The secretary's papers went airborne to drift down in various sections of the office. For a second, we all seemed to be in a frozen time frame. Then Bedlam took its way as everyone ran to and fro shouting orders and grabbing nets while the secretary chased her papers. I had not a clue till the captain turned to me. "You told me you had a tern," he said accusingly. "No, you told me I had a tern." He paid no mind to my objection. "A loon is the most dangerous bird on the water. I have an employee in the hospital because a loon put its beak through her wrist. How did you get it here anyway?" "With respect and kindness," I said as I walked out the door. It took six men and a big net to remove the ornery Loon from my car. I have always wondered if he survived. I hope he made it.

I brought my mother home to live with me and worked another two years after David died. Then I lost Mother and my ability to work about the same time. Spondylolisthesis robbed me of the ability to stay on my feet for very long, at the time. There was no one left for me to take care of, so I decided to rest from it all and that's when I began to write Destiny's Tapestry. I managed on my own for a while but eventually my daughter, Sandra, packed me up and moved me back to Sand Mountain. She did not realize this was the place of her Mama's birth when she chose to buy her home here. She only knew it was a place she liked. We were thrilled when we found the old barn, where I was born still standing. My eldest son laughed and said, "Mom, you should have named your book {a biography of someone you never knew}." I laughed and agreed with him. Then I thought, no, you do know me. I am one of the many people you pass on the street or stand in line with at your neighborhood grocery, any given day. I am a survivor. I have made my mark on my tapestry. There are many such as mine. We are here. Do not forget us.

Amanda kelley / BD 1850

Chapter 25

SECRETS OF THE MOUNTAIN

"Well would you look at this," I exclaimed as I unfolded a hundred dollar bill. I was visiting Mama today, on a search mission for the names of her parents and any other information I might manage to wheedle from her about her ancestry. Two weeks prior, I had made a fruitless search of her family bible records for names. There was nothing there but records of her marriage and children's birth and two one hundred dollar bills. Now I was back again, determined to ask her right out about them. Before I had a chance to ask questions, she asked me to change the light bulb in her floor lamp. I swapped new bulbs three times to no avail before I leaned the lamp down and squinted into the receptacle. Spotting what appeared to be a piece of green paper, I fished it out to find to my surprise a hundred dollar bill. "Well I remember putting it there now," she laughed. "I had forgot about it." "Mama," I scolded. "You have got to stop doing this. There is no telling how much you have poked in hidey holes around this place. God forbid what if the house burned down? You should get Uncle Tommy to take you to his bank and let you set up a bank account." "Ach! Betty June, what do I need with a bank? I don't have enough money to be worrying with banking. Now go get us a glass of iced tea and sit down." We sat and gossiped about this and that while I worked up my nerve to ask the questions I wanted answers to. During a comfortable lull in the conversation, I asked her, "Mama, what were your parent's name?" She seemed a little surprised by my question and after a brief hesitation answered. "My mother's name was Minerva Kelly." Thinking about this, I felt perplexed. "That was your maiden name," I stated as I tried to get things straight in my mind. "Yes it was. Kelly was my Daddy's name. My mother was a Smith before she married." "Where did your mothers' people come from originally?" "She was Welch," Mama answered. "I see. Then where did our Cherokee blood come from?" She seemed a bit slow to answer me, "From my daddy's people." "Kelly is an Irish name, Mama. How can he be Indian and Irish too?" Raising her head and looking me in the eye, she gave me the same old lie my mother had told me. "An Irishman named Kelly met and married a Cherokee woman of the wolf clan during the time of the trail of tears. I am Wahya," she proudly declared. "Do you know this Irishman's first name?" I questioned her. Something here was not adding up. "The ancestral name comes down through the male blood line. Nor do the dates of your birthday match with the date of the Indian removal. It is missing a whole generation. I just cannot wrap my mind around this and get it clear, but I will before I stop searching. I can promise the world that," I vowed. "Let dead dogs lay, Pat. Why is it so important to you?" "Because Mama, He was your father, my great grandfather and it's like he is lost to us. It should not be allowed to stand this way. I care and so should you." She looked down at her apron and began to pleat it with slow deliberation. "My mother's people were well of," she said. "I married down when I married John Walden, but it was necessary, else I would have been put on a reservation when I applied for government assistance all those years ago. I did love John to begin with." Then she began her tuneless little shu-shu-shu whistle as she pleated that old apron with a vengeance. I knew I would get no more answers from her. I did not want to upset her, so I carried the tea glasses back to the kitchen and quietly slipped out the door. She did not even give me his first name, I sadly thought. Oh well, I was not beat yet. There was Uncle Tommy, I could go to. He was the oldest of Mamas children. Surely, he would remember his maternal grandfather.

Mama's old house did burn down. She had bought the place with the money she received from the federal government, as her share of one of the settlements' given to the Indians as payment for the land, taken from them at the time of the Indian removal. She was found listed in a tribe she had never belonged to. Her name was placed by government officials in that tribe at the time she applied for government aid in the early 1900s. Many years later, the tribe had grown so small in numbers they were incorporated into other tribes and all records have sense been lost.

When the old house burned down, Mama grabbed a box of trash from behind the stove and ran out the door with it in one hand and her bible in the other. All else was lost. Mama and Aunt Lilly bought another house and had it moved to the property. They dwelled there together till first Mama and then Aunt Lilly moved on to the Happy Hunting Ground as Mama referred to heaven. After Aunt Lilly's death, Mother and Aunt Burma were cleaning out the old house. Aunt Burma found a box of trash stuffed away in a closet. "Well my land Jane! Look it this. This is tha old box of trash Mama saved when tha ole house burnt down. Take it out by tha road and put it with tha rest ah tha trash." I was not a bit surprised to see Mother out by the road, taking time to search through the box. I am so glad she did. She found some money there. A few hundred dollars, but what was more important was a piece of film she fished out of there. Holding it up to the light, she called to me. "I do believe this is Mama and Daddy." I urged her to take it to a photo shop and have it developed. It is now one of my most precious earthly possessions. It was a picture of Mama and Grandpa Walden. Aunt Merty was a baby sitting on Mama's lap. Uncle Tommy was a boy, approximately three or four years old, standing propped against his daddy's knee. According to Uncle Tommy's age at the time of finding the piece of film, it would have been seventy eight or seventy nine years old. Talk about leaving your memories to Kodak, I would say it was a right on slogan!

I let my inquiries and curiosity rest till Mama died. Then I renewed my quest once more. I went to see my Uncle Tommy. He poured me a little shine in a cup and we settled back for his favorite thing to be doing. It was story time. Aunt Ethel sat and monitored all he said just to keep him straight. She would listen and nod her head from time to time. She had known the moonshiner Marshal Baldwin, my great Aunt Mandy, and their thirteen daughters personally, as did Uncle Tommy. "But Unck!" I exclaimed as I tried to dispute his words. "The census say," he disputed my word with, "naa no. Now I don't care what they say. You can pay that no never mind. You hear what I say. If them olden folks was ta home an somebody was approaching, they knew it well before they got there and ever body melted away like shadows into the woods or corn cribs or where ever. The woman of the house answered the questions in the way her man told her to. Whether it be a revenue man or a census taker or even sometimes a law man. Real clannish and close mouthed them Moonshiners were."

"Did you know my Daddy, Thomas?" I asked him. Stretching back and clasping his hands behind his head he drawled. "Yea, I knew Thomas fairly well. Used to run around with him some while I was single. You take after him some. Your size and a lot of your mannerisms and facial expressions and tha vigorous temper of yours sometime puts me in tha mind of your daddy. He was a small man in size but boy howdy, it didn't pay for a body to get on his bad side. I watched that little man whip six sailor boys one night before you could say scat cat your tails on fire. One of em wanted to beat his time with his girlfriend, who so happened to be your mother. Thomas knocked him over the porch rail right off Frank Collins front porch. His buddy's thought they wanted to take up the fight. He soon changed their mind. I did try to warn Jane about Thomas. I liked him but he weren't husband material. He didn't stay in one place long. He was a rambler. Hell, his nick name was Takeoff! She wouldn't listen. She insisted they loved each other and he would change once they were married. Nobody could tell her any different. She was eighteen and old enough to sign for herself. So Daddy let her have her way. I guess he had already learned his lesson about meddling in his girl's love affairs when Merty slipped off and married Lewis Smith. Daddy got so riled up, he said more en he should have. He threw one of them stomp down Walden fits and disowned her. He almost lost his oldest daughter over it. Merty didn't speak to Daddy for quite a spell. Daddy finally broke down and went to her house and apologized." "Why did he get so outraged over it?" I asked him. "Didn't he like Uncle Lewis?" "Liking or not didn't have nothing to do with it. Daddy thought Merty was too young. She weren't but sixteen years old. Daddy had divorced Mama and was tied to Kate and they had given up the farm and was moving to a new place in Alabama City. Daddy was trying to wrestle his old wood stove off the wagon to get it set up in the house when Lewis just passing by, first laid eyes on Merty. She had her dress tail caught up in her hands and full of wood chips, she was gathering. One look at them legs and he was caught. He stopped and offered to help his new neighbors move in and set up housekeeping. Lewis was as handsome and sweet talking as old scratch. Merty was a pretty girl and one of the sweetest natured females you could want to know. Lewis came to be a regular fixture around the place. I think Merty had about as much of Kate as she was willing to endure, so she wasn't that hard for Lewis to convince to become his wife. He and Merty slipped off to the court house with Uncle Jack, Daddy's brother. Uncle Jack signed the license as J. Walden, giving permission for Lewis and Merty to marry. They met at the dance in town the next night. Went in the front door and straight out the back and over to the church where the preacher man tied the knot for them. John Walden never knew Jack Walden had signed for Merty and Lewis. Jack was a real rounder, he was. He laughed over the trick he pulled on his brother, but he had sense enough to lay low and out of Daddy's sight till things cooled off.

"Uncle Tommy, did you know you're Grandfather? Mama's daddy, I am asking about." "Yes I knew Bed," he answered. "Bed wasn't his real name was it?" "No, he was called Bed Kelly cause he never slept in a bed." "Why not?" I asked him. "Well," drawled Uncle Tommy. "fer one reason, he was too big to fit in a bed. Never saw one made long enough his feet wouldn't hang over the end. An nuther reason, he lived in the woods most of his life. Hunting and trapping, sometimes working on farms for other people. Planting and gathering. That sort of thing. When he come to visit us he made camp in the edge of the woods and that's where he stayed. Oh, he would come and sit on the porch with Daddy and Mama late in the evening. Mama would bring him out a cup of coffee. He loved his coffee with sugar and cream in it. He said sugar was hard to come by amongst the Indians. He would tell us kids stories about his hunting and trapping trips. He would stay gone, sometimes a year or better at the time, before he would show back up. He tried living at home like a white man while he was married to Grandma but that didn't last long. He was too used to moving around with the Indians. When he hit the trail, the last time after Aunt Rilla was born Grandma and him split for good. She got a divorce and married a man named Whorley. Most of the Indians Bed had rambled with, were dead and gone by then or had been caught and sent to the rez or prison. You know that sheriff in Birmingham was good at sending prisoners to the coal mines. Most of em died there." "Do you think it possible Bed ended up like that?" I asked him. "No, Bed was a free man and never ran afoul of the law to my knowing." "Do you know his real name?" "No, never heard him called anything but Bed. You should have asked Mama all this while she was still on this earth. She probably could have answered your questions better than me." "I did ask her, Uncle Tommy. She wouldn't tell me anything. It's like she felt she had something she had to hide." "Well maybe she thought she did, Betty. You know how them old folks thought. Things most people don't pay no attention to now-a-days they looked down on, and if they thought they had skeletons in the closet, they kept a close lock and key on them. All I know about grandfather Bed Kelly is, he was a half breed Cherokee who hunted and trapped the mountains from Sand Mountain to up past the Carolinas' and even into North and West Virginia." "Do you know how and when he died and where he is buried?" I asked him. "No young'un, I don't. You know what they say about old Indians. They never die, they just fade away."

I left Uncle Tommy that day, wondering what more I could do. I let it alone for a few more years, hoping more information would show. Eventually, my daughter Sandra bought a new home and moved to Etowah County Alabama. When she called and told me this, I asked her. "What possessed you to move way off up there? That's on Sand Mountain." "Yes it is," she answered. "When Tracy brought me here to show me the place, I felt at home right away. For some reason I fell in love with this mountain." "I can understand that," I replied. "You do know I was born there?" "Well no, I didn't. I thought you had always lived in Mobile." "No honey, I was born on that mountain in a barn, at a little place called Snead Cross Roads." I could hear the excitement in her voice as she exclaimed. "Oh Mama, I am only about three miles from there." It was then I told her some about my beginnings and of the search for Bed Kelly, my great grandfather. "I want to write a book, Sandra. I want to write it for my family so they will know about all of us. First, I want to know about my grandfather Bed. I don't want to write the book without knowledge of him. I want to know his name. I want to know where he was laid to rest. I want to visit his grave and make sure he is remembered, but I don't know which way to go to find what I need to know. I have tried searching the census. I find his wife and three daughters. Minerva Kelly was his wife. The three daughters were Dovey Kelly, Mandy Kelly, and Rilla Kelly. They were living in a boarding house in Guntersville, but no mention of their father. I don't know how to go any further with my search, Sandra." "You start writing Mama. Do it for me. I will put an ad in the paper. Bed is an unusual name, surely someone around these parts will have heard something of him." So I began my story and Sandra picked up my search.

It was about two weeks later, my phone rang. I answered to hear a woman's voice asked. "Who wants to know about Bed Kelly?" I felt my heart take a leap in my chest. "I am Betty Lowery," I answered her. "My daughter Sandra placed the request for information in the paper for me. I want any information about Bed Kelly, I can get. Will you tell me anything you may know about him?" "I am Dianna Patterson. Kelly was my maiden name," she answered. "Why do you want this information?" I took a deep breath, and explained. "Bed Kelly was my great grandfather. I am writing a book about my past life and putting in stories of my ancestors. All I know about him is, he was half Cherokee and Irish. Bed was not his real name. I would at least like to know what it was. I think he lived with the Indians a lot. According to family stories, he was a hunter and a trapper and he worked as a laborer on farms. That's all I know about him." "Well," the lady replied. "His name was Bedford Kelly. He

Betty June Gilliland

was a distant cousin to me. He was a carpenter, but there was no Indian blood there. He was French." Oh dear, I thought, another dead end. I thanked Dianna for calling me and tried not to let my disappointment show. "Don't give up," she encouraged. "You keep digging. I will go through what papers I have. We are bound to find something about him. If he lived on this mountain and he was a Kelly, there is bound to be a trace of him left somewhere. I felt better after I talked to this delightful lady. We exchanged email addresses and I promised her I would stay in touch to let her know how my search was going. I felt I had made a friend and that was worth a lot to me.

It was soon after hurricane Katrina I lost David, my dear husband. Two years later, my mother died. It was then I told Sandra about my wish to write the book and she placed the ad for me and I began writing.

I was searching for the registration paper I needed on David's boat. I went to my son's house and asked. "Butch, do you remember which way the registration on your Daddy's boat went?" His wife began to search. Presently, she returned to the living room. "I didn't find the papers you need," Ruby said. "But look what I did find. When Grandmother stayed here during hurricane Ivan, she left this behind when she went home." She handed me my Grandmother Dovey's family Bible. I was so thrilled I forgot all about the boat registration papers. I could hardly wait to get home with it. I sat at the dining table and began to turn pages to look up favorite scripture Mama had made note of. It seemed to me I felt her presence there, so close I could smell the essence of her. I could feel the warmth of the love she held for me. A lot of questions I had wondered about, were answered there in those scriptures. Then I came to the family marriage and birth records. Everyone was there except Great Grandfather Bed, and Great Grandmother Menerva Kelly. I noticed that one page felt different from the rest of the pages in the bible. A bit thicker it seemed. It had a piece of tape around the edge of it. Taking it between my thumb and finger, I began to rub gently back and forth. I was startled to feel the paper slid just a bit in one spot. I patiently worked with it and flicked the edge of the

318

page with my fingernail. At last, I was able to peel the pages apart. It was a fold over page that had been stuck together. The scotch tape had been used to keep the fold from breaking away from the main page. Over the years, the fold over page had stuck to the main page around the edges, or maybe Mama had sealed them, hiding the secret they protected. There was recorded the name and burial place of my Great Grandparents. Oh, I breathed, thank you Mama. For I felt this was truly her gift to me. Her bible and the names I sought. Right away I sat down at the computer and wrote Dianna an email, telling her of my discovery." His name is Cicero Kelly and he is buried at a cemetery called Mt. Olive. Great Grandmother Menerva is buried at Beulah. No birth or death dates, except the month of March 6, on Grandfathers page, their names and burial place." In a few minutes, an email from Dianna was sent back to me. "Oh my, Cicero, I know about this person! I had forgotten. Call me now." I felt the blood rush to my head and my face flame. With shaking hands and bated breath, I dialed her number. This is the story Dianna told to me as told to her by her father.

"Betty, I am going to tell you what my Daddy told me when I was just a young girl about Cicero Kelly, and why he was called Bed. Daddy said, "I am going to tell you a true story about a man named Cicero Kelly. It is important that you remember and never forget this name for he was one of ours. I had a second cousin. Her name was Amanda Kelly. She was the daughter of Octavia and Daniel Kelly. He was a farmer before he fought in the civil war on the Confederate side. He died as a prisoner of war on 8-16-1863. He is buried in Camp Chase Confederate Cemetery in Columbus, Ohio. While out in the woods behind their home gathering nuts, his daughter, Amanda was found by an Indian renegade. This was after the Indian removal, but you know some of the Indians had managed to escape removal to hide here on this mountain. It was a vast and very unpopulated forest at that time." Daddy being mindful, he was talking to a young female did not use the word rape. I believe the term he used was, (had his way with her.) Anyway, rape was claimed when it became known she was pregnant." I wanted to protest but I swallowed my words. I remained silent as Dianna related the rest of the sad story to me. "'Amanda gave birth to a half breed baby boy and named him Cicero Kelly. He loved his mother and she loved him very much but eventually, Amanda married a man named Andrew Jackson Mosley on October 23, 1872. Jack was a well thought of man by everyone who knew him. He was considered hard working and honest. Jack would not allow the child to stay in the house,'" Dianna said. "'He put him out to live on his own. Cicero lived in the woods. He slept where ever he could. He slept in old barns or sometimes in the woods. He would come to the farm and visit his mother, only during the times when Jack was away for the day, fishing, or hunting, or maybe making a trip to town for supplies. Cicero never had a bed to sleep in. Thus he was called Bed Kelly for the rest of his days." It was hard to reconcile myself to what I was hearing. I could only believe he went to his father's people. I did not believe the story of the rape. The child could not have survived in the wilderness on his own without adult supervision from some source. Someone taught him survival skills, the lore of the forest, how to live off the land. I did not believe it was a white man. I believed his mother knew his father and sent him to live with his Indian family, who taught him their ways. Cicero lived like a shadow between the two worlds, belonging to neither. When I shared these thoughts with Dianna, she agreed with me. "Dianna, I don't understand a woman agreeing to let a man do this to her child," I protested. "I don't believe she did," Dianna answered. "I think once she was married, she was overruled by her husband and maybe other family members for a time."

Then Dianna went back to telling the rest of the story. "'Jack eventually loaded up Amanda and their children in a covered wagon and went to Haiti, Missouri, which is a very small town near Caruthers Missouri. Bed was not allowed to ride in the wagon with the rest of the family. During the day, he scouted ahead of the wagon. Before nightfall, he would stop and set up camp, build a campfire, and have supper started. He slept rolled in a blanket under the wagon. He did this all the way to Missouri.

Jack Mosley returned to Guntersville, Alabama in the year of 1888 with his and Amanda's children. He told the family Amanda had died in childbirth in Haiti and was buried there. Betty, she was never heard from again. I proved Jack Mosley a liar on that. My husband and I went there and I searched for her. She was not buried where Jack said she was. I went to the court house to look for any information on her. Amanda Kelly Mosley divorced Andrew Jack Mosley in 1888. She remarried a man named William Davidson in 1889. I could find no trace of her after that. She completely vanished. We have a memorial set in her memory at Mt. Olive, where so many Kellies are buried, but she has no grave there." "Do you suppose this William Davidson was Bed's Indian father?" I asked. I know its way out there but could he have followed Amanda; then married and took her west or to the Indian reservation in Oklahoma?" "I don't know," she mused. "I suppose anything is possible." "Well, we do know that Cicero is buried at Mt Olive as stated in Mama's bible, which tells us he did eventually return to Guntersville, Alabama." "Oh, I know he did," she replied. "I have a copy of a marriage bond between Cicero Kelly and Minerva E. Smith dated July 9, 1898. And an arrest warrant on him for assault and breaking jaw of someone named Price, April 26th 1893." I stood gaping like a fish out of water. Well shoot the moon and call me Hawk Eye, I thought. What an extraordinary lady this is. I have struck gold! "You do know this makes us long lost cousins of some kind. Don't you," she giggled. "Second or third at least," I smiled. "As close as we can get it, anyway." She promised to send me copies of everything she had. I hung up the phone with my head in the clouds. I felt like the Maxwell house coffee pot. I was happily percolating. I knew there would be no sleep for me that night. There is where our luck ended. There is no farther records of Bed Kelly nor any way to connect him to Amanda Kelly, except through the handed down story told by Dianna's father.

Eventually, I lost my ability to walk as much as I would need to in order to take care of myself and my home. Sandra came and packed me up bag and baggage. She moved me back to my mountain to live with her. I got to meet my new found family at a Kelly family reunion. They all are very nice people. Some accept the story of Bed Kelly. Some do not but I believe it. Dianna had a distant cousin who was very old. He called her to his bedside before he died. I believe at that time, Dianna was researching and working on her family tree. "I have something that is important I wish to tell you," he said to her. "I want you to remember it. It is about a man named Cicero Kelly. We cast him out, but he was one of ours. I want you to remember him, Dianna." "My Daddy has told me the same story about this man," she assured him. "I promise, I will not forget him." Her story of Bed was told to her by two family members. I believe this Bed Kelly to be one and the same as my great Grandfather.

Allen Funderburk, is one of my Wilmer Hall siblings. He is in truth, my brother of the soul. Al designed the cover for Destiny's Tapestry for me. We talked about my book and the search for Cicero Kelly. He told me, he did background research and had all the programs to help in my search for records on Cicero Kelly. He picked up the search for me. What he found outraged him. "Betty this can't be. Why this means the child was put out to fend for himself when he was six years old. There are laws against that, even back then." "But Al," I tried to explain. He cut me off practically sputtering. "They would have put those people in jail." When he finally quieted down somewhat, I gave him my thoughts about Bed's mother giving her child to his Indian family to raise. Sounding a bit out of sorts he said, "I bet she gave him to another member of her family to raise." With a sigh, I answered him. "If she did, there would be a census record of him in one of their households. Sandra and I have searched diligently because I want one document to prove his parentage. It is not out there. It is like he never existed. Well he did. I, my Grandmother, and her sisters are living proof of this." "I will keep searching," said Al. "I bet you, I find your Bed Kelly living in the household of another of Amanda's family." He never found it. There are no records of Bed Kelly as a child anywhere. There is only Mama's bible, the arrest warrant and the marriage license. According to Mama's bible, he rest with other Kelly family members in the Mount Olive Cemetery. Dianna carried me to the cemetery to search for his grave. This cemetery is so old there are no records there. Tornados have struck it twice. Some of the head stones have broken away from the graves and scattered. I found two head stones with the name Cicero Kelly on them. It is my intentions to go back to Mount Olive and take someone with me who will be strong enough to find where those head stones belong and restore the one belonging to the grave of Grandfather Bed Kelly.

I saw the memorial to Amanda Kelly. It is as Dianna told me. There is no grave for the lost Amanda at Mount Olive Cemetery. I could never finished this part of my search and the mountain would never have gave up her secrets, if not for Mama, Dovey Kelly Walden's bible, and my beloved cousin, Dianna Kelly Patterson.

The mountain is beautiful in the spring. There is a lot of rainfall to contend with as the warm air tries to settle in, but old man winter does not want to let go. Eventually, Sister Spring softly steals her way in to breathe a kiss upon the frozen brow of Mother Earth. "Awake Mother," I can hear her silver toned voice shimmer in the pure crisp streams that flow from the artesian springs which abound in the layers of earth and rock strata. It echoes over the mountain crest and into the valleys. The mountain stirs and life once more blooms. She puts on her new garb of green, decorated with the flowers of nature in multi-faceted colors. Though, my mountain is settled and tamed, there are still a few places unspoiled by the habitation of man. Wooded areas reminiscent of the wild splendor that once was.

As lovely as I find spring on my mountain, I must say it is autumn that truly stirs the spirit. Though, I know it heralds the return of winter once more and icy winds are painful for old bones, I still rejoice in the breathtaking sight. The green becomes every hue of orange and yellow with touches of blazing reds. The leaves cling till with a sigh they give way and drift earthward. Mischievous breezes laugh as they skirl and toss them about like playful children.

It is then, one can go down the bluff and look out to enjoy the magnificent works of nature or look down, down, like looking into forever. I can relax there as I soak in the ambiance while I let my fanciful thoughts ponder the imponderables. In my musings, I wonder. Did Grandfather Bed walk here? Did he leave his footprints on this path? What would we say to each other, if we could meet face to face? It seems to me, my heart has heard him call to me many times. In my search for him, I have endeavored to answer that call. I have found not only Grandfather Bed, as I searched for records of him, I found a history of a rich heritage left by those ancient ones from whence we came. His people. My people. The Cherokee Indian. I have learned of the strength of these people, who withstood the treachery of the white man when in their greed, they took everything the Cherokee worked to build. The heart break when they looked back and saw their homes being looted and burned before they were marched out of sight. As they struggled along the miles of what is now known as the Trail of Tears, many of them died. There were some who refused the government orders to remove themselves from this, their land given to them by the Great Spirit. They escaped into the vast wilderness of the mountains, where they hid from the soldiers. Some eventually turned themselves in. Some lived and died running and hiding, but in their minds they were free. I have learned from the courage, the stamina, and the will to overcome all hardships and rebuild stronger to survive. This is what Great Grandfather Bed wished me to find. Now he can rest in peace and I am content.

MARSHALL COUNTY. ☙ PROBATE COURT.

TO ANY OF THE STATE JUDGES, OR TO ANY LICENSED MINISTER OF THE GOSPEL, OR TO ANY
JUSTICE OF THE PEACE OF THE SAID COUNTY, OR TO ANY PERSON QUALIFIED
BY LAW TO SOLEMNIZE MARRIAGE:

*Know Ye, that you are hereby authorized and licensed
to join together in*

The Bonds of Matrimony,

Cicero Kelly

AND

Manervia E. Smith

Given under my hand, this the 9 *day
of* July *A. D. 189 8*

J. A. Street
JUDGE OF PROBATE.

FIFTY DOLLARS FINE FOR FAILING TO RETURN THIS LICENSE.

THE STATE OF ALABAMA, MARSHALL COUNTY.

I hereby certify that on the 9 th *day
of* July *A. D. 189 8 I solemnized the Rites of
Matrimony between* Cicero Kelly
and Manervia E. Smith
at Mr. Smith's *, in said County.*

Witness this 9 th *day of* July *A. D. 189 8*

J. C. Dunkapiler

To J. A. Street
JUDGE OF PROBATE OF SAID COUNTY.

THE STATE OF ALABAMA, | CAPIAS.
MARSHALL COUNTY.

TO ANY SHERIFF OF THE STATE OF ALABAMA GREETING:

An Indictment having been found at the _Spring_ Term, 189_3_, of the Circuit Court of Marshall County against _Cicero Kelly_

for the offence of _Assaulting and beating Saml. Price._

you are therefore commanded forthwith to arrest the said _Cicero Kelly_

_____ and commit _him_ to jail unless _he_

gives bail to answer such Indictment; and that you return this writ according to law.

Witness _Geo. C. Hall_, Clerk of said Circuit Court of Marshall County, this the _24th_ day of _April_, 189_3_

Geo. C. Hall, Clerk.

SHERIFF'S RETURN.

Executed by arresting the within named defendant and taking bond, this May 26th 1893

by _James Campbell Dpty_   _C. C. Campbell_
                                                    Sheriff.

BOND.

The State of Ala. }
Marshall Co. } Circuit Court

We Cicero Kelly agrees to pay the State of Alabama Four Hundred _____ unless the said Cicero Kelly appear at the next term of the Circuit Court of said County Marshall and from term to term thereafter until discharged by law to answer a criminal prosecution for the offence of Assaulting and beating Saml. Price. And to secure the payment of which we waive the right to all exemptions under the Constitution and laws of the State of Alabama.

Cicero Kelly L. S.
John W. Brashier L. S.
J. T. Kelly, L. S.
L. S. Harrel

Approved this 26th day of May A.D. 1893. C. C. Campbell Sheriff.
by James Campbell Deputy.

The State Of Alabama / CAPIAS

Marshall County

To any Sheriff of the State of Alabama, Greetings:

An indictment having been found at the____Spring____.

Term 1893, Of the Circuit Court of Marshall County

Against____Cicero Kelly_____

For the offence of Assaulting and breaking Jaw. Price._____

You are therefore commanded forthwith to arrest said____Cicero Kelly___

And commit him to jail unless he gives lean to answer such indictment; and

then you return this writ according to law.

Witness Geo. C hall Clerk of said Circuit Court of Marshall County.

This the 24th day of April 1893.

Geo. C Hall Clerk.

Sherriff's Return

Complied by arresting the within named defendant and making Bond This

may 26th 1893

By James Campbull Deputy   Bond   T.C. Campbull Sherrif

In State of Alabama

Marshall Co. Municipal court

Mr. Cicero Kelly agrees to pay the State of Alabama Three hundred dollars

unless the said Cicero Kelly Agrees at the next term of the Circuit Court of said

county Marshall and pays term to term thereafter Until finish paying by law

to answer a criminal fine. Incurred for the offence of assaulting and breaking

Jaw Price Albert to secure the payments of which ever answers the right to all

restitution under the Constitution. Recorded here of the State of Alabama.

Document 2 -B

Cicero Kelly. L.S.

John L.Brashrie. L.S.

J.F. Kelly. L.S.